Tolstoy as Teacher

TOLSTOY AS TEACHER

Leo Tolstoy's
Writings on Education

Edited by Bob Blaisdell

Translated by Christopher Edgar

Teachers & Writers Collaborative
New York

Library of Congress Cataloguing-in-Publication Data

Tolstoy, Leo, graf, 1828–1910.
   [Selections. English. 2000]
    Tolstoy as teacher : Leo Tolstoy's writings on education / edited
by Bob Blaisdell : translated by Christopher Edgar.
    p.   cm.
   Includes bibliographical references (p.)
   ISBN 0-915924-96-X (pbk. : alk. paper)
   1. Tolstoy, Leo, graf, 1828–1910. 2. Education--Philosophy.
I. Title.
LB675.T62T65 2000
370' .1--dc21

Teachers & Writers Collaborative
5 Union Square West
New York, NY 10003-3306

Cover and page design: Christopher Edgar
Cover photos: Leo Tolstoy in 1868; Tolstoy leading a group
of young students to the river to swim, June 1901.

Printed by Philmark Lithographics, New York, N.Y.

Acknowledgments

Many thanks to Mary McDonnell, Jessica Sager, Daniel Kane, Masha Friedman, Amy Gelber, and Jordan Davis for their help with this book.

. . . . .

Teachers & Writers Collaborative receives funds from the New York State Council on the Arts, the National Endowment for the Arts, and the New York City Department of Cultural Affairs.

T&W programs are also made possible by funding from Bell Atlantic Foundation, Bertelsmann USA, Bronx Borough President and City Council, The Bydale Foundation, The Louis Calder Foundation, The Cerimon Fund, The Chase Manhattan Foundation, Con Edison, E.H.A. Foundation, Lannan Foundation, Morgan Stanley Dean Witter Foundation, NBC, New York Times Company Foundation, Henry Nias Foundation, Open Society Institute, Overbrook Foundation, Queens Borough President and City Council, Joshua Ringel Memorial Fund, Maurice R. Robinson Fund, Helena Rubinstein Foundation, The Scherman Foundation, Lila Wallace-Reader's Digest Fund, Alison Wyegala (in memory of Sergio Guerrero), anonymous donors, and T&W's many individual members.

Table of Contents

৯০

Translator's Note

One interesting challenge this book presented was the contrasts in the authors' styles. The obvious contrast is that between the academic style Tolstoy most often uses in his articles—with its long strings of clauses and frequent use of passive voice—and the peasant dialect of the boys' stories. (The latter is by no means simple, especially for the non-native speaker!) But there are also contrasts within Tolstoy's writing, contrasts that are less apparent. Just when you start to feel Tolstoy is becoming a little too much like the pedagogues he rails against and something less than a great master of prose, he jumps from the weighty and prolix to the lyrical or casual. Tolstoy also eschewed polishing things too much, and he deliberately left a few rough edges in these essays.

Russian words in this book follow a fairly standard, if old-fashioned, transliteration system. We use *y* in proper names (e.g., Vassily, Shklovsky, Seryozha), and female surnames use Russian endings (e.g., Tolstaya).

We have provided footnotes for most of the distinctly Russian terms that may be new to many English-speaking readers—particularly those relating to peasant life, Russian history, and so forth. We have been less thorough in regard to providing commentary for the many references Tolstoy makes to educational theorists and practices of his day. For better or worse, we thought it best to spare readers some of this detail.

I worked from two Russian texts, both published during the Soviet era: *Pedagogicheskie Sochineniya* (*Pedagogical Writings*), published by the Educational Publishing House of the Ministry of Enlightenment (Moscow, 1953, second edition); and Volume 8 of Tolstoy's *Polnoe Sobranie Sochinenii* (*Complete Collected Works*) edited by V. G. Chertkov, published by the State Publishing House ("Gosizdat") in 1936. (Interestingly but not surprisingly, both editions omitted passages on the Yasnaya Polyana school's classes in Bible study.)

—Christopher Edgar

Leo Tolstoy in 1861

Introduction

by Bob Blaisdell

Every artistic word, whether it belongs to Goethe or to Fedka, differs from the inartistic in that it evokes an endless mass of thoughts, images, and explanations.
—Leo Tolstoy, in "Are the Peasant Children to Learn to Write from Us, or Are We to Learn from the Peasant Children?"*

IN 1859, the thirty-one-year-old Count Leo Tolstoy—already a famous author, a veteran of two army campaigns, a university dropout, a gambler, the father of a boy by a married peasant woman—opened a free, noncompulsory school in one of the buildings on his estate. Written over the doors of his school at Yasnaya Polyana were the words "Come and Go Freely." The disciplines ranged from literature to music to biology, with the students' interests directing the daily course of study. By the time Tolstoy began work on his magazine, *Yasnaya Polyana*, in 1861—which he published to inform and attract other educators—he had formulated his own dynamic, clearly drawn ideas, rejecting as twaddle or harmful most of the pedagogies he had read about or observed:

> The best teacher is the one who can instantly recognize what is bothering a particular student. This ability in turn gives the teacher a knowledge of the greatest possible number of methods; the ability to invent new methods; and above all—rather than the blind adherence to one method—the conviction that all methods are one-sided, that the best possible method is the one that answers best all the possible difficulties incurred by the student. This is not a method, but an art and talent.[1]

Tolstoy saw teaching as an "art," and like any of the arts, it only works when it works. He knew from experience that what was successful in the classroom one day did not necessarily succeed the next. To Tolstoy, theories weren't to be bowed to. Pedagogical theory was something for teachers to use or not use; it was simply one of many resources available.

---

* I would like to thank my friend Ross Robins for introducing me, many years ago, to Tolstoy's articles on education.—*Editor*

At the same time there were rules of thumb he and his teachers observed. The chaos and clamor of everyday classroom activity was not to be squashed by teacherly authority; the "chaos" was natural, even necessary, and Tolstoy discovered that the children themselves justly regulated its duration and limits.[2]

The Yasnaya Polyana school was a paradise for Tolstoy.[3] In early August 1861, he wrote to a friend, Countess Alexandrine Andreevna Tolstaya, that he had "a charming and poetic occupation which I can't tear myself away from, and that's the school":

> When I break away from my office . . . I go to the school; but as it's undergoing alterations the classes are held alongside, in the garden under the apple trees, and it's so overgrown that you can only get there by stooping down. The teacher sits there with the schoolchildren all round him, nibbling blades of grass and making the lime and maple leaves crackle. The teacher teaches according to my advice, but even so, not too well, and the children feel it. They are fonder of me. And we begin to chat for three or four hours, and nobody is bored. It's impossible to describe these children—they have to be seen. I've never seen the like among children of our own dear class. Just imagine that in two years, in the complete absence of discipline, not a single boy or girl has been punished.[4] There's never any laziness, coarseness, stupid jokes, or unseemly language. The schoolhouse is now almost completed. The school occupies three large rooms: one pink, and two blue. One room, moreover, is a museum. On the shelves round the wall, stones, butterflies, skeletons, grasses, flowers, physics instruments, etc., are laid out. On Sundays the museum is open to everyone, and a German from Jena [a teacher named Keller] (who's turned out to be an excellent young fellow) does experiments. Once a week there's a botany class, and we all go off to the woods to look for flowers, grasses and mushrooms. Four singing classes a week, and six of drawing (the German again), and it's all going very well. . . . Excluding myself there are three teachers in all. . . . The classes are supposed to be from 8 to 12 and from 3 to 6, but they always go on till 2 o'clock because it's impossible to get the children to leave the school—they ask for more. In the evening it often happens that more than half of them stay and spend the night in the garden, in a hut. At lunch and supper and after supper we—the teachers—confer together. On Saturdays we read our notes to each other and prepare for the following week.[5]

Two of Tolstoy's *Yasnaya Polyana* essays in particular—"Are the Peasant Children to Learn to Write from Us, or Are We to Learn from the Peasant Children?" and "The School at Yasnaya Polyana"—are more exciting and important than Tolstoy's theories about teaching, for a simple reason: they give accounts of his interactions with the peasant boys and girls ("more important," because these two articles show more about successful teaching than even any of Tolstoy's brilliant formulations can). When Tolstoy was with his students, his eyes were wide open; he was amazed and appreciative, and the sparkling conversations and classroom scenes he describes reveal a joy found nowhere else in his life or work. Some narrative passages are as beautiful and evocative as his fiction:

> Fedka kept looking up at me from his notebook, and smiled, winked, and repeated, "Write, write, or I'll give it to you!" He was evidently quite amused to see a grown-up write a theme.
>
> Having finished his own composition worse and faster than usual, Fedka climbed on the back of my chair and began to read over my shoulder. I could not go on; others came up to us, and I read them what I had written.
>
> They did not like it, and nobody praised it. I felt ashamed, and to soothe my literary ambitions I began to tell them of my plan for what was to follow. The further I got in the story, the more enthusiastic I became; I corrected myself, and they kept helping me out. One student said that the old man should turn out to be a magician; another remarked: "No, that won't do, he should just be a soldier.... The best thing would be if he steals from him.... No, that wouldn't go with the proverb," and so on.
>
> All were exceedingly interested. It was obviously a new and exciting sensation for the students to be present at the process of creation, and to take part in it. The decisions they made were for the most part all the same, and were true to the plot as well as in the details and characterizations. Almost all of them took part in the composing process, but from the start Semka and Fedka especially distinguished themselves: Semka, by his perceptive, artistic descriptions, and Fedka, by the acuity of his poetic gifts, and especially by the glow and rapidity of his imagination.[6]

When *Yasnaya Polyana* first appeared, its articles were overlooked and ignored by almost everyone in Russia but the tsarist secret police. The Minister of the Interior, however, was onto Tolstoy when hardly anyone else had raised an eyebrow:

> The careful reading of the educational review *Yasnaya Polyana*, edited by Count Tolstoy, leads to the conclusion that this review, in preaching new methods of tuition and principles of popular schools, frequently spreads ideas which, besides being incorrect, are injurious in their teaching. Without entering into a full examination of the doctrines of the review, and without pointing out any particular articles or expressions—which, however, could be easily done—I consider it necessary to draw the attention of your Excellency to the general tendency and spirit of the review, which very often attacks the fundamental rules of religion and morality. The continuation of the review in the same spirit must, in my opinion, be considered more dangerous as its

editor is a man of remarkable and one may say even a fascinating talent, who cannot be suspected to be a criminal or an unprincipled man. The evil lies in the sophistry and eccentricity of his convictions which, being expounded with extraordinary eloquence, may carry away inexperienced teachers in this direction, and thus give a wrong turn to popular education. I have the honor to inform you of this hoping you may consider it useful to draw the special attention of the censor to this publication.[7]

All nineteenth-century Russian writers were at the mercy of government censors. (For instance, in January 1862, the first issue of *Yasnaya Polyana* had to await "release" by the censor.) The Minister of the Interior had little to fear, though, because Tolstoy's influence on educational practice through *Yasnaya Polyana* was limited and local enough. Later in life, of course, Tolstoy could offer his opinions and pronouncements on (among other topics) religion and civil disobedience to a worldwide and receptive audience even when the censors blocked publication in Russia.

Although Tolstoy was very fond of titles in question form—"What Then Must We Do?"; "What Is Art?"; "How Much Land Does a Man Need?"—the answers to these questions were never in doubt. He answers the question "Are the Peasant Children to Learn to Write from Us, or Are We to Learn from the Peasant Children?" with a resounding "We have to learn from them!"

> It's impossible and absurd to teach and educate a child for the simple reason that the child stands closer than I do—and than any grown-up does—to that ideal of harmony, truth, beauty, and goodness to which I, in my pride, wish to raise him. The consciousness of this ideal lies more powerfully in him than in me. All he needs of me is the necessary material to fulfill himself, harmoniously and multifariously. The moment I gave Fedka complete freedom and stopped teaching him, he wrote a poetic work, one that is unique in Russian literature. And thus it is my conviction that we cannot teach children in general, and peasant children in particular, to write and to compose—particularly artistic works. All that we need teach them is how to set about writing.[8]

No commentator in Tolstoy's time—or our own—has admitted the full truth of this assertion about children's writing, but we hope this anthology will show it is true and that Tolstoy's writings on education were also "a poetic work, one that is unique in Russian [or any] literature." He reminds us to recognize and value our students' artistry, an artistry he feels we have lost and should strive to rediscover.

While Tolstoy's opinions in the pedagogical essays are compelling and persuasive, their greatest value is, just as he suggests, in their descriptiveness. "In presenting a description of the Yasnaya Polyana school," he writes, "I do not mean to offer a model of what's needed and what is good for a school, but simply to furnish a true description of the school. I assume that such descriptions have their use."[9] These are not the descriptions of a theorist or of a naive observer; they are the masterful narratives of an extraordinary teacher and an unsurpassed novelist. The critic John Bayley has pointed out Tolstoy's ability to make completely remote or peculiar settings seem universal and familiar.[10] The peasant school was located on Tolstoy's country estate from 1859 to 1862, 130 miles southwest of Moscow, yet through Tolstoy's descriptions I feel almost more familiar with the daily life of his catch-as-catch-can school than I do with the schools in which I was taught and have taught.

* * * *

Leo Nikolaevich Tolstoy was born on September 9, 1828, at Yasnaya Polyana ("Clear Glade"), the family estate. Tolstoy and his three older brothers and younger sister were orphans from the time Leo was eight. His mother died before he turned two. (It is touching to note, in the education articles, his belief that the most important education any child receives is at his mother's knee.)

His first tutor, Karl Ivanovich Rössel, the Russian-born German on whom the tutor Karl Ivanovich in Tolstoy's fictional *Childhood* is based, was a good, simple man, responsive and kind to the children, although somewhat limited, Tolstoy's guardians thought, by his ignorance. From him Tolstoy learned reading, writing, mathematics, and German. When Prosper Saint-Thomas, a Frenchman, replaced Rössel when Tolstoy was eight, the boy began his lifelong battle with educational authority. Saint-Thomas had rules; he knew what had to be taught and what had to be learned. He was confident, disciplined, and demanding; the relationship he established with his charges required that they be obedient, that they answer what he wanted them to answer, and that they think about what he wanted them to think about. He expected them to bow to his authority as if he were a priest and they initiates in the faith of education. Tolstoy felt Saint-Thomas was fairly typical of boys' teachers in aristocratic Russian families of the time.

Tolstoy did not attend a conventional school until he was sixteen, but by then—with the help of several specialized tutors—he had become fluent in a handful of languages (German, French, and English, as well as Russian), and also well-versed in Arabic, Tartar, and Turkish. (His aunts and other relatives, meanwhile, "educated" him in the manners and attitudes that encouraged the moral laxity and class divisions that he later came to mock and reject.)

Tolstoy's years at Kazan University (1844–1847), where he first studied Oriental languages and then law, left him with a lifelong disdain for higher education. This was the only formal education he ever had, and to Tolstoy, "formal" almost always meant something to fight against:

> I was little interested in the lectures of our teachers in Kazan. To begin with, for about a year I studied Oriental languages, but made very little progress. I plunged eagerly into everything, I read a countless number of books but always in one or another particular direction. When I became interested in some problem, I did not swerve away from it to the left or to the right, and tried to read everything that could shed a light on this one problem. It was like that with me in Kazan too. There were two reasons for my leaving the university: one was that my brother had completed his studies and was going away, and the other, strange as it may sound, was my work on [Catherine the Great's] *Instructions* and [Montesquieu's] *Esprit des lois* (I have a copy now), which opened up for me a new field of independent mental endeavor, whereas the university with its demands, far from helping me in it, hindered me.[11]

As Tolstoy's wife noted years later, "He was a poor student and always had difficulty in learning what others said he must. Whatever he learned in life he learned of his own accord, and did it spontaneously, quickly, with intense application."[12] (For instance, at the age of forty-three Tolstoy taught himself Greek, which, besides giving him a new appreciation of Homer, enabled him to teach Greek to his older sons and to translate, "correct," and revise a version of the gospels. He also taught himself Hebrew, and then, as an old man, Danish (in a matter of weeks). This is not to mention how he apprenticed himself to skilled workers to learn to farm, to repair wagon wheels, and to make shoes and clothes.)

When Tolstoy was nineteen, he and his brothers decided it was time to divide their family inheritance. As was customary in the Russian aristocracy, the youngest son, Leo, received the family estate. Atypically, the brothers portioned out an equal share to their sister.

At age twenty-one, Tolstoy passed two examinations in Criminal Law at St. Petersburg University (he bragged that he had spent only a week studying for them). Before completing the next two examinations that would have given him a degree, he moved home to reform his estate in the interests, he hoped, of the serfs. With his servant Foka, he opened a school for peasant children, a short-lived endeavor that Tolstoy never wrote about and hardly mentioned again, except to say that it was an illegal operation, as all self-governed schools in Russia were. (Even so, to start a school for serf children was not an unusual undertaking for estate owners.) In retrospect, this first effort at educational and social reform seems largely a whim.

In 1851 he followed his brother Nikolai to the Caucasus, where Nikolai was serving as an officer. The Cossacks (Russian peasants who had long lived in this mountain region where they could avoid serfdom) and the native Tartars immediately caught Tolstoy's imagination and later bore fruit in his fiction. While serving as a volunteer in the army, Tolstoy wrote the novel titled *Childhood*. He gambled and lost money, eventually squandering the family house and portions of the Yasnaya Polyana land. He drank too much and chased women. He saw and participated in battles as a noncommissioned officer. *Childhood*, its sequels, and *The Sevastopol Sketches* (descriptive accounts of the battles in the Crimea between Russia and England in 1854–55) led to his being hailed as a new voice in Russian literature. He retired from the army in 1856.

Tolstoy then became disillusioned with the rewards of his aristocratic, artistic circle, and longed for a new, fulfilling purpose. Before that purpose came to him, he fled Yasnaya Polyana and broke off a marriage engagement with a neighboring landowner's daughter. His "grand tour" of Western Europe in 1857 was spent visiting sites and museums. In Paris he became acquainted with Ivan Turgenev, with whom he began a long-lived but difficult friendship. While in Europe, Tolstoy noted in his journal that he wanted to return to project that would become a consuming passion: a school for peasant children. The twentieth-century critic Viktor Shklovsky suggests, however, that Tolstoy's ideas for the Yasnaya Polyana school were inspired by what he had seen among the Cossacks:

> Tolstoy thought that the Cossack community could serve as a model for the whole of Russia—peasantry without the nobility. That is how he felt when he was finishing *The Cossacks*, and when he taught at the Yasnaya Polyana school. [The Yasnaya Polyana school was like] Cossack schools, so to speak, a devel-

opment of Cossack ideas in pedagogy. [Cossack schools'] purpose was to discover and rear gifted children; there was no definite program and pupils were free to come and go as they liked. The gang of children without superiors was the realization of Tolstoy's dream about "Cossackdom."[13]

Tolstoy's second effort as an educator, the Yasnaya Polyana school of 1859–62, was as vast, involving, and important an undertaking to him as the writing of his later novels *War and Peace*, *Anna Karenina*, or *Resurrection*. Fellow authors (including Turgenev) saw Tolstoy's expedition into pedagogy as a diversion from his true calling; his daughter and biographer Alexandra wrote, "He threw his whole being into his schoolwork; thoughts of living in the village, of marrying a village girl passed through his mind. He was so absorbed in his surroundings that all other classes of society vanished, as it were, from his life. . . ."[14] In a letter of 1861 Tolstoy wrote to a friend: "What has this school done for me since I opened it? It has been my whole life, it has been my monastery, my church into which I escaped, finding refuge from all the anxieties, doubts, and temptations of life."[15]

Nearly fifty years after the Yasnaya Polyana school closed, Vassily Morozov (Fedka) recalled its first days:

In three months' time we were deep in our studies. By that time we could read with facility and the number of scholars had grown from twenty-two to seventy.

All seventy of us would swoop down on Tolstoy, one with a question, another with a lesson book to show.

"Lev Nikolaevich, is this right?"

He would look at the book.

"Yes, it's right, only you've left something out here. Otherwise it's fine. Don't hurry so."

"What about mine—how do I write?" and another copy-book would be thrust under his nose, and then another, until the whole group was clamoring for his attention.

He would examine the books seriously and say a few kind words of approval sprinkled with remarks like:

"You'll have to rewrite that. You've left out too much."[16]

In the beginning Tolstoy and an Orthodox priest, who taught theology, were able to manage the teaching load. Within the next three years, in his capacity as a government arbiter Tolstoy hired about a dozen more teachers for the Yasnaya Polyana school and other schools he set up nearby. Most of the young teachers were former university students who had been expelled for political agitation. He liked to point out that these would-be revolutionaries, on encountering the needs and interests of the children, immediately gave up "their Herzen"[17] and learned to teach Bible stories.

Petr Morozov, one of those teachers, published some reminiscences. He remarked that on first entering the school, "What struck me was the inconceivable din the children were making."[18] He grew used to this occasional "din." Morozov remembered: "We would work all day. . . . Some would leave, others would come, and so it went on from early morning until late in the evening."[19] Even with the rigors of the work and simple living conditions, said Morozov, "The school did not weary me, thanks to the lack of official discipline." Tolstoy had ideas about how to let teachers be most effective, and these included allowing them to teach as they had been most effectively taught, even if those methods ran counter to Tolstoy's own.

Fedka remembered one of their ventures into writing:

> We happened to be reading a certain book along with Lev Nikolaevich, I cannot remember the title of the book, but it was very good. Pausing at the full stops I would often put this question to Lev Nikolaevich: "But, Lev Nikolaevich, can you make things up like that yourself?" "I don't know." After reading the book, Lev Nikolaevich said to us, to the whole class: "If you like we'll write something ourselves, we'll invent it."[20]

One such "invention" is the story by "Fedka" and "Semka" based on Snegirev's proverb, "He Feeds with the Spoon, then Pokes the Eye with the Handle" (which you can find in this volume).

In 1860, the fatal illness of Tolstoy's brother Nikolai in France pulled Tolstoy away from his school. This was the last time Tolstoy went abroad, and he used the trip to pursue his abiding interest: he examined the educational methods in the most famous school systems in Europe. Tolstoy hated the thought that there might be better ways to educate students than the ones he himself was discovering, by trial and error, at his school.

In Germany he met Berthold Auerbach, the educator and novelist whose fictional *A New Life* Tolstoy greatly admired: "It was owing to [*A New Life*] that I started a school for my peasants and became interested in popular education."[21] Auerbach said: "You yourself are the best teacher. With the help of the children you create your own method and all will go well. Any abstract method is an absurdity. The best that a teacher can do in a school will depend on him personally, on his own capacities."[22] However, most of what Tolstoy saw in the schools of Germany, France, and England left him disappointed. "Modern" progressive systems such as those of Friedrich Froebel (1782–1852), the German inventor and popularizer of kindergarten, and Jean Heinrich Pestalozzi (1746–1827), the Swiss educator, had become dogmatic, trusting more in the method than in the dynamics of the classroom or the individuality of the students. There was also the old-fashioned approach of intimidation, punishment, and rote-learning. Even the better schools assumed the right to compel the minds and spirits of the students.

In Marseilles, Tolstoy had a revelation:

> The very boy who told me that Henry IV had been killed by Julius Caesar knew very well the history of the *Three Musketeers* and of *Monte Cristo*. I found twenty-eight illustrated editions of these in Marseilles, costing from five to ten centimes. To a population of 250,000 they sell 30,000 of them—consequently, if we suppose that ten people read or listen to one copy, we find that everyone knows their history. In addition there are the museum, the public libraries, the theaters. Then there are the cafés—two large *cafés chantants*, where each may enter for fifty centimes' worth of food or drink, and where there are daily as many as 25,000 people—and this is not counting the smaller cafés, which hold as many more—in each of these cafés they produce little comedies and skits, and recite verses. Taking the lowest calculation, we get one-fifth of the population—one-fifth who get their daily oral instruction just as the Greeks and Romans were instructed in their amphitheaters.
>
> Whether this education is good or bad is another matter; but here it is, this unconscious education that is so much more powerful than the one by compulsion. Here is the unconscious school that has undermined the compulsory school and has made the latter's substance dwindle down to almost nothing. The only thing left is a despotic form, one almost without content. I say "almost without content" because I exclude the mere mechanical ability of putting letters together and writing down words—the only knowledge that can be taken away after five or six years' study. Here it must be remarked that even the mere mechanical art of reading and writing is frequently acquired outside of school in a much shorter period, and that frequently the students do not take this ability with them when they leave the school—or it is lost, finding no application in life. Where school attendance is made compulsory by law, there is no need to teach a second generation to read, write, and figure, because the parents, we should think, would be able to do that at home, and the children would learn much more easily that way than in school.
>
> What I saw in Marseilles takes place in all the other countries: everywhere the greater part of one's education is acquired not at school but in life. Where life is instructive—in London, Paris, and generally in all large cities—

the masses are educated; where life is not instructive, in the country, the people are uneducated, in spite of the fact that the schools are the same in both. The knowledge acquired in the country is lost. The direction and spirit of the popular education, both in the cities and in the villages, is absolutely independent from, and generally contrary to, the spirit that it is intended to instill in the schools. Education goes on quite independently of the schools.[23]

Tolstoy's observations about culture made him modest about his own educational project. He was revolutionary but deliberately nondogmatic. He did not attack the popular cultural education of the day (later, for instance, he raised his own children on the novels of Alexandre Dumas, Charles Dickens, and Jules Verne, and in the 1880s moved his family to Moscow for a period of years for his children's schooling), but instead bowed to it and supplemented it with complementary material. At the same time, he eagerly offered children as much education as they desired. Tolstoy firmly believed that teachers should choose subjects that aligned with their own interests and enthusiasms: "If you wish to educate the student by science, love your science and know it, and the students will love both you and the science, and you will educate them; but if you yourself do not love it, the science will have no educational influence, no matter how much you may compel them to learn it."[24]

Tolstoy saw the use of force as causing the most harm in education:

> How is this? The need of education lies in every man; the people love and seek education, as they love and seek the air for breathing; the government and society burn with the desire to educate the masses, and yet, notwithstanding all the force of cunning and the persistence of governments and societies, the masses constantly manifest their dissatisfaction with the education which is offered to them, and step by step submit only to force.[25]

After Tolstoy returned from Europe in April 1861, he applied for governmental permission to publish an educational magazine. Originally to be titled *The Country Schoolmaster*, it became known as *Yasnaya Polyana*. He secured subscriptions, less than 400, and budgeted 3,000 rubles for its production (which because of gambling debts he could hardly afford).

Tolstoy anticipated that his magazine would ruffle feathers. In the introduction to the first issue, he wrote:

> Entering on a new work, I am under some fear, both for myself and for those thoughts which have been for years developing in me, and which I regard as true. I am certain beforehand that many of these thoughts will turn out to be mistaken. However carefully I have endeavored to study the subject, and

have involuntarily looked upon it from one side, I hope that my thoughts will call forth the expression of a contrary opinion. I shall be glad to afford room for all opinions in my magazine. Of one thing only am I afraid—that these opinions may be expressed with acridity, and that the discussion of a subject so dear and important to all as that of national education may degenerate into sarcasms, personalities, and journalistic polemics; and I will not say that sarcasms and personalities could not affect me, or that I hope to be above them. On the contrary, I confess that I fear as much for myself as for the cause itself; I fear being carried away by personal polemics instead of quietly and persistently working at my subject.

I therefore beg all future opponents of my views to express their thoughts so that I may explain myself, and substantiate my statements in those cases in which our disagreement is caused by our not understanding one another, and might agree with my opponents when the error of my view is proved.[26]

Tolstoy's view, his theory—or "anti-theory," as Reginald D. Archambault would have it[27]—was based not on idealistic notions but on what happens in the classroom and how things work and evolve. Tolstoy, better than most teachers, understood what worked and why; this was partly because he was even more critical of himself than he was of other educators. He was able to take into account and to dramatize many dynamics of the classroom better than anyone before or since; he saw situations not through pedagogical goggles but with his own two eyes. His theories, then, have a substantiality often missing in pedagogy. The one factor he failed to account for in his anti-theoretical theories of teaching was his own unique personality and charisma.

When Tolstoy the teacher is discussed by critics or biographers, he is sometimes caricatured as being a romantic protégé of his idol, Jean-Jacques Rousseau, whose pedagogical writings contain much that is beautiful to imagine but even more that is just plain silly.[28] In any case, Rousseau's recommended practices are not based on observed experiences, as Tolstoy's rigorously are.

Try as Tolstoy might to find a unifying pedagogical idea that others could follow, the best he could do in this line was to attack and ridicule compulsion and recommend a few teaching methods and tactics. Since he believed teaching was an "art and talent"—though the highest praise he gave himself was that he had "a certain pedagogical tact"—could these writings become the basis of a Tolstoyan pedagogy? No, because according to Tolstoy himself, art—and therefore the art of teaching—can't be taught:

> The feeling of infection by the art of music, which seems so simple and so easily obtained, is a thing we receive only when the performer finds those infinitely minute degrees which are necessary to perfection in music. It is the same in all arts: a wee bit lighter, a wee bit darker, a wee bit higher, lower, to the right or the left—in painting; a wee bit weaker or stronger in intonation, a wee bit sooner or later—in dramatic art; a wee bit omitted, overemphasized, or exaggerated—in poetry, and there is no contagion. Infection is only obtained when an artist finds those infinitely minute degrees of which a work of art consists, and only to the extent to which he finds them. And it is quite impossible to teach people by external means to find these minute degrees: they can only be found when a man yields to his feeling. No instruction can make a dancer catch just the time of the music, or a singer or a fiddler take exactly the infinitely minute center of his note, or a sketcher draw of all possible lines the only right one, or a poet find the only right arrangement of the only suitable words. All that is found only by feeling. And therefore schools may teach what is necessary in order to produce something resembling art, but not art itself.
>
> The teaching of the schools stops where the wee bit begins—consequently where art begins.[29]

Tolstoy's school was like all "experimental" schools that have cultivated "student-directed" programs, and yet there is no evidence that Tolstoy's writings on education have influenced or inspired any school but the dozen or so he set up in the Tula district while he held the position of public arbiter in 1861–62. The leading Russian thinker on education in Tolstoy's time was Konstantin Ushinsky, a school inspector and author of very popular elementary school texts. Ushinsky worked within the government, while Tolstoy—though happy to set up governmentally *funded* schools—whenever possible tried to shake off any official influence in the classroom. Even so, Ushinsky and Tolstoy shared some beliefs, including the fundamental one of goodwill toward the peasants.

In the twentieth century, John Dewey, though an admirer of Tolstoy and sympathetic to his ideas, did not concern himself as Tolstoy did with individual students or individual schoolrooms.[30] On the other hand, the most important wisdom Tolstoy gained from teaching—his belief and delight in students' writing—has been shared by individual teachers everywhere.[31]

Tolstoy expected to challenge and influence his contemporaries' attitudes about education, but instead—when they bothered to respond—they dismissed the ideas and opinions of *Yasnaya Polyana* as unimportant or impractical. In 1874, Tolstoy, recalling his disappointment over *Yasnaya Polyana* not having been taken seriously, wrote:

> The question of what [the criteria were] as to what to teach and how to teach received an even greater meaning for me; only by solving it could I be convinced that what I taught was neither injurious nor useless. This question both then and now has appeared to me as a cornerstone of the whole pedagogy, and to the solution of this question I devoted the publication of the pedagogical periodical *Yasnaya Polyana*. In several articles (I do not renounce anything I then said) I tried to put the question in all its significance and to solve it as much as I could. At that time I found no sympathy in all the pedagogical literature, not even any contradiction, but the most complete indifference to the question which I put. There were some attacks on certain details and trifles, but the question itself evidently did not interest anyone. I was young then, and that indifference grieved me. I did not understand that with my question, "How do you know what to teach and how to teach?" I was like a man who, let us say, in a gathering of Turkish pashas discussing the question in what manner they may collect the greatest revenue from the people, should propose to them the following: "Gentlemen, in order to know how much revenue to collect from each, we must first analyze the question on what your right to exact that revenue is based." Obviously all the pashas would continue their discussion of the measures of extortion, and would reply only with silence to his irrelevant question.[32]

"[*Yasnaya Polyana*] has become a bibliographical rarity," wrote Pavel Biryukov in 1905. "True, Tolstoy's own principal articles have been included in the fourth volume of the full edition of his works, but, besides those articles, there appeared in the magazine many different short notices, descriptions and reports of great interest for teachers in a theoretical as well as in a practical sense." That is, "each number contained one or two theoretical articles, then reports of the progress of the school under the management of Tolstoy, bibliography, description of school libraries, accounts of donations, and a supplement in the shape of a book for reading. The motto of the magazine was the saying: *Glaubst zu schieben und wirst geschoben*, that is to say, 'You mean to push, but in reality it is you who are pushed.'"[33]

Tolstoy devoted himself to the school for three years. Then, in the spring of 1862, exhausted by his work at the school and as public arbiter, he left to recover on a vacation on the Russian steppes. While he was gone, Tsarist secret police raided and searched his estate, hoping to turn up evidence of revolutionary activity by Tolstoy or his teachers. In an angry letter to Alexandrine Tolstaya, his friend, he explained:

> They write to me from Yasnaya that on July 6 three troikas full of police drove up, ordered no one, including Auntie no doubt, to leave the premises, and began to ransack the place. What they were searching for we still do not know. One of your friends, a filthy colonel [Alexandrine Tolstaya was a member of the court, and so is being scolded for her association with the government], read through all my letters and journals, which I had intended before my death to turn over to the friend who would be closest to me at the time; he read two sets of correspondence which I would have given anything in the world to keep secret—and then he drove off after asserting that he had found nothing of a *suspicious* character. It was my good fortune and also that of my friend that I was not there—I should have killed him. How lovely! How endearing! This is how the government wins friends for itself. If you recall what my political interests are you know that I have always been, and especially since I have been wrapped up in my school, completely indifferent to the government, and even more indifferent to the present-day liberals whom I despise with all my heart. Now I can no longer say this of myself. I am full of anger, revulsion, almost hatred for that sweet government which undertakes a police search of my home for lithographic and typographic presses for printing proclamations by Herzen, whom I scorn, and which bore me so I have not even the patience to read them through. . . . And suddenly I and my student teachers are subjected to a police search! . . .[34]

Nothing was found, but when Tolstoy got word of the raid he was outraged and protested to the Tsar. Though the episode grieved him, Tolstoy never cited it as a cause for the school's demise. It was his unquenchable passion for literature and his desire for marriage and family that led him to give up teaching in the fall of 1862. The student Vassily Morozov remarked:

> That year our school did not reopen, something in our attitude to it had disintegrated and grown confused. The field work had come to an end, the fields were cleared and the school could have begun, but it was as if a sort of silent strike had been declared; instead of the former seventy pupils only fifteen turned up. Practically nobody came from the distant villages and nearby districts. Many of our Yasnaya Polyana children held off because of their parents. . . . Lev Nikolaevich was annoyed and regretted this, saying they shouldn't have given up, they should have gone on studying, but Lev Nikolaevich too seemed to have something else in mind.[35]

After his marriage in September of 1862 to Sonya Behrs, the daughter of one of the royal physicians, Morozov continues, "Lev Nikolaevich rarely visited us, and the school began to flag."[36]

Although scholars such as Shklovsky have argued that Sonya was jealous of his involvement in the school, Tolstoy himself never hinted that she had spoiled or deterred his experiment in educating the peasants. What nagged at him was his impulse, his compulsion, to write. All his life he would periodically renounce the value of his own writing, but he always returned to it. His new great project at this time was researching background for a novel about "the Decembrists" of 1825.[37] Tolstoy's writing and research on the Decembrists led him further into the past, to Napoleon's campaign of 1812 and the response of Russia's military and of her people—and thus, the great project of *War and Peace*.

After Tolstoy completed *War and Peace* in 1869, he returned to a challenge he himself had set forth in *Yasnaya Polyana*: "To print good books for the masses! How simple and easy it looks, just like all great ideas. There is just one difficulty: there are no good books for the people, not only in our country, but even not in Europe. In order to print such books they must be written first, but not one of the benefactors will think of undertaking this task."[38] So Tolstoy became the "benefactor" who undertook this task. His *ABC Book* and the four levels of *Readers* (graded primers) that followed were his primary literary work between *War and Peace* and *Anna Karenina*, and in them he distilled, revised, and adapted world literature for the purpose of teaching and promoting reading. Simultaneously, he took up the question of his own children's education. By 1869, he and Sonya had four children (they eventually had thirteen, the last of whom was born when Tolstoy was sixty).

Both detractors and devotees of Tolstoy cannot help but notice that Tolstoy did not always follow his stated beliefs. Tolstoy's own children received a far more conventional and orderly education than the peasant children had. (In spite of his hard-earned views on education, he felt he should defer to his wife's wishes about their children's upbringing.) Tutors did the bulk of the teaching, with Tolstoy and Sonya also taking teaching duties (Tolstoy's primary topic was mathematics). His oldest children listened to and helped him correct the stories he wrote for his *ABC Book* and *Readers*, and themselves served as teachers in a new, short-lived school he set up for peasant children in 1872. Tolstoy did not publish work on this new school, though his daughter Tatyana described the daily routine in her memoirs:

> Having completed the *Readers* and the *ABC*, Papa decided he really ought to try them out for himself, so he resumed teaching the peasant children.
>
> Seryozha and I could already read and write quite passably. Ilya, then about six, could only just read and was very bad at writing; nevertheless he announced that he was going to teach the youngest class. Papa agreed, and the lessons began.
>
> They lasted for slightly over two hours every day, beginning after our dinner, which was served between five and six, and continuing till it was time for us to go to bed. Papa took the boys' class in his study. The girls were Mama's responsibility, and she taught them in another room. We three children taught the absolute beginners their alphabet. Our classroom was the hall, and fat Ilya, a big pointer clutched in one hand, would try to teach the alphabet to rows of stolid little children much the same size as himself. . . .[39]

This teaching project did not involve Tolstoy's full attention or energy. "When summer came," continues Tatyana Tolstaya, "the school was closed, and the next year it didn't reopen."[40]

Soon after, in 1874, he was named to the county council and served on the Education Committee. At something of a standstill with the early writing of *Anna Karenina*, he relished his new role as a school inspector. He wrote to a friend: "I have now jumped out of abstract pedagogy into the practical on one side and the abstract on the other—the work of the schools in our district. And I straightway began to love these thousands of children with whom I'm concerned, as I did fourteen years ago."[41] After much lobbying of the government he got the go-ahead in 1876 to open a teachers college, a "university in bast shoes,"[42] in which he would train young, bright peasants to teach other peasants. He had to give up this treasured plan when there were too few applicants to continue, and he never again deeply involved himself in public education.[43]

One of the themes of the second half of *Anna Karenina* is the spiritual crisis of the Tolstoy-like Konstantin Levin. Even before the completion of the novel in 1877, Tolstoy found himself in despair over the meaning of life; he was on the verge of suicide. This crisis was resolved by a deep and idiosyncratic acceptance of Christianity (so idiosyncratic that the Orthodox Church eventually excommunicated him for heresy). Afterward, Tolstoy saw and judged the world in a new way, and his artistic output, though impressive for almost anyone else, dropped off.

Over the last thirty years of his life his greatest endeavor in educating the people had nothing to do with schools. In 1884, Tolstoy, Pavel Biryukov, and Vladimir Chertkov, who would become his longtime associate and secretary, took over a St. Petersburg publishing house, christened it The Intermediary (*Posrednik*), and began printing and distributing millions of copies of inexpensive booklets of classic and contemporary moral literature, including many stories by Tolstoy himself. This non-profit venture was wonderfully successful, as had been his *ABC Book* and graded *Readers*. But as *Yasnaya Polyana* had done, The Intermediary occasionally ran afoul of government censors. The publishers' implied criticisms of the government eventually resulted in the deportation of Biryukov.

Tolstoy's religious writings, his essays on social and moral issues, and his efforts to solve social problems occupied him much of the rest of his life. He became an advocate for the Dukhobors and Molokans, two persecuted religious groups whose emigration he helped fund. During a terrible drought and famine in western Russia during the early 1890s, he raised money and set up soup kitchens with his friends and children. Too famous for the government to silence, Tolstoy publicly challenged capital punishment and conscription, and he ceaselessly promoted tolerance, peace, and civil disobedience to a larger and larger international audience. He also fought continually with his wife and sons over property and his sons' excesses. (In many ways, his sons' lives mirrored his own vice-ridden youth.)

Meanwhile, Tolstoy also wrote the novel *Resurrection* (1898) and several famous novellas, including *The Death of Ivan Ilych* (1886), *The Kreutzer Sonata* (1889), and *Master and Man* (1895). Great as they are, these works are often relentlessly didactic and, compared to his earlier fiction, reductive. It was his social and religious consciousness and activism—and copyright disputes between his wife and Chertkov—that made it harder for Tolstoy to justify to himself his works of the imagination. One of the results of his internal conflicts about writing more fiction, however, was the sometimes wonderful, occasionally delightful, often narrow-minded *What Is Art?* (1898), in which Tolstoy rigorously (and perversely) excludes from the realms of art the classical music he continued to love and the great literature he still guiltily composed (most notably the sensational *Hadji Murad*, an admiring, exciting, fictional portrait of a real-life Tartar warrior). Tolstoy also momentarily reflects on his teaching experiences at the Yasnaya Polyana school in *What Is Art?*, but he is much less generous about art in this work than he was in the education articles, where he clearly outlined or even discovered some of the artistic aspirations for his own novels and stories.

As for the fates of the Yasnaya Polyana students, Fedka's life in particular was not a happy or lucky one. After the dissolution of the school, he and Ignat Makarov (that is, Semka) worked as hands on Tolstoy's farm, but were fired when they lied about having allowed some horses to get loose. Fedka and Semka then worked as carriage drivers in Tula, but Fedka failed to keep this job and was down and out for some time. As a middle-aged family man, he renewed his friendship with Tolstoy and, with the famous author's help, even published a new story. When Thomas Edison sent Tolstoy a phonograph, Tolstoy recorded his own and Fedka's voice.

In 1889, meanwhile, Ignat Makarov (Semka) returned to Yasnaya Polyana as a discharged soldier, and Tolstoy, after chatting with his former pupil, put him in charge of his estate at Samara. In 1910, the year of Tolstoy's death, Prokofy Vlasov, another former student, was arrested by one of the guards Sonya Tolstoy had hired to patrol the grounds. The impoverished Vlasov had chopped down a tree, he said, to prop up the side of his shack. (Tolstoy released Vlasov and asked Sonya to fire the guard, but she refused.)

When Tolstoy died his body was returned to the site of the imaginary buried "green stick"—upon which, his brother Nikolai as a child had said, was written the secret of mankind's happiness. At the site was one of Tolstoy's first students, Taraska Fokanov. Fokanov helped dig the grave and thereafter tended it.

* * * *

There have been three major translations into English of Tolstoy's "Collected Works." All three date from around the turn of the twentieth century. The only one that does not bypass most of the articles on education is the twenty-four volume 1904 edition (*The Complete Works of Count Tolstoy*) by Leo Wiener, a Harvard professor of Slavic Languages. Wiener has been the only translator to tackle the fine "On Popular Education" of 1874, and the only one who attempted to find an audience for Tolstoy's pedagogical ideas. (He compiled a long section of "Notes on

Education and Instruction" from Tolstoy's diaries and letters.) Wiener also translated many of the children's stories from the *Readers*.

Nathan Haskell Dole's 1898 edition of *The Complete Works of Lyof N. Tolstoi* contains "The School at Yasnaya Polyana," "Are the Peasant Children to Learn to Write from Us . . .?," and many of the stories from the *Readers*, in a volume entitled *The Long Exile and Other Stories*. Aylmer Maude, who lauds the education articles in his good, comprehensive biography, translated only a measly eight-page excerpt from "The School at Yasnaya Polyana" in the twenty-one-volume *Centenary Edition* (1928–1937). In 1982 Alan Pinch translated five articles, reminiscences by a student and a teacher, and two student stories, in *Tolstoy on Education*.

For this volume, Christopher Edgar has translated two of Tolstoy's *Yasnaya Polyana* articles: the vital and relevant "Are the Peasant Children to Learn to Write from Us, or Are We to Learn from the Peasant Children?" and the comprehensive "The School at Yasnaya Polyana." In addition, we include a new translation of lengthy excerpts from the remaining *Yasnaya Polyana* articles—"On Popular Education," "On Methods of Teaching the Rudiments," "A Project of a General Plan for the Establishment of Popular Schools," "Education and Culture," and "Progress and the Definition of Education"—as well as passages from the article of 1874 titled "On Public Education" and Goldenweiser's *Talks with Tolstoy*. We have also included two stories by Tolstoy's students, "They Feed with the Spoon, Then Poke the Eye with the Handle" and "The Life of a Soldier's Wife."

There are numerous and excellent modern translations of Tolstoy's more famous works, as well as biographies and studies. Please see the annotated bibliography on p. 237.

Notes

1. Leo Tolstoy, in "On Methods of Teaching the Rudiments." See p. 186 of the current volume. For the entire article, see *Tolstoy on Education* translated by Leo Wiener (University of Chicago Press, 1967).

2. "We think that the disorder is growing greater and greater and that it has no limits—it seems we have no other means of stopping it except the use of force—whereas we only need to wait a little, and the disorder (or animation) calms down naturally, by itself, growing into an order much better and more solid than what we might have come up with." Leo Tolstoy in "The School at Yasnaya Polyana." See p. 81 of the current volume.

3. I have chosen to ignore Tolstoy's later repudiation of his teaching efforts as expressed in *A Confession* (1882): "It amuses me now when I remember how I shuffled in trying to satisfy my desire to teach, while in the depth of my soul I knew very well that I could not teach anything needful for I did not know what was needful." In *The Portable Tolstoy* (Penguin, 1978), p. 675. Much later, in 1904, Tolstoy remembered the Yasnaya Polyana school years as "the brightest period of my life." See Ernest Simmons, *Leo Tolstoy* (Vintage Books, 1960), Volume I , p. 237.

4. But as will be noted by his own children, Tolstoy sometimes had a short fuse and could behave with impatience to dimwittedness. Aylmer Maude tells us of an incident that occurred at the school sometime within a year of his glowing letter (in *The Life of Tolstoy* [Oxford, 1929] Volume 1, p. 255.):

> N. V. Uspensky, the writer, narrates that he visited Yasnaya Polyana in 1862, and Tolstoy, having to leave Uspensky alone for a while, asked him to glance at some of the compositions the boys had written in school. Taking up one of these, Uspensky read: "One day Lev Nikolaevich [Tolstoy] called Savoskin up to the blackboard and told him to solve a problem in arithmetic. 'If I give you five rolls and you eat one of them, how many rolls will you have left?' . . . Savoskin could nohow solve this problem, and the Count pulled his hair for it. . . ." When Tolstoy returned Uspensky pointed out to him this essay, and Tolstoy, sighing heavily, crossed his hands before him and merely said: "Life in this world is a hard task."

5. Tolstoy's *Letters*. Volume 1, pp. 149–150.

6. Tolstoy, in "Are the Peasant Children to Write from Us, or Are We to Learn to Write from the Peasant Children?" See pp. 26–27 of the current volume.

7. Pavel Birukoff [Biryukov]. *Leo Tolstoy: His Life and Work* (Charles Scribner's Sons, 1906), pp. 358–359. (Letter of October 3, 1862, from the Minister of the Interior to the Minister of Public Instruction.) Birukoff also provides the follow-up to the Minister of the Interior's letter: "On October 24th of the same year, [the Minister of Instruction] informed the Minister of the Interior that . . . he saw nothing dangerous or contrary to religion in the review *Yasnaya Polyana*. One only came at times across extreme views upon the subject of education, which might very well be criticized in scientific educational reviews, but not forbidden by the censor. 'On the whole,' continued the Minister of Public Instruction, 'I must say that Count Tolstoy's work as an educationist deserves full respect, and the Minister of Public Instruction is bound to help him and give encouragement, even though not sharing all his views, which, after maturer consideration, he will probably give up himself.'" Unfortunately, how true this last prediction was!

8. Tolstoy, in "Are the Peasant Children to Write from Us, or Are We to Learn to Write from the Peasant Children?" See p. 48 of the current volume.

9. In "The School at Yasnaya Polyana." See p. 80 of the current volume.

10. See John Bayley's *Tolstoy and the Novel* (Viking, 1967).

11. Viktor Shklovsky, *Lev Tolstoy* (Progress Publishers, 1978), p. 88.

12. Sonia Tolstaya, in *Reminiscences of Tolstoy by His Contemporaries* (Foreign Languages Publishing House, no date), p. 38.

13. Shklovsky, op cit., p. 137. It should be noted that neither Tolstoy nor any other biographers took up—or shed light upon—Shklovsky's speculation.

14. Alexandra Tolstaya, *Tolstoy: A Life of My Father* (Harper, 1953), p. 138.

15. Ibid.

16. V. S. Morozov, in "Recollections of a Pupil of the Yasnaya Polyana School." See *Reminiscences of Lev Tolstoi by His Contemporaries*, p. 146.

17. A reference to Aleksandr Herzen (1812–70), the revolutionary leader and writer.

18. Alan Pinch, *Tolstoy on Education* (Farleigh Dickinson University Press, 1982), p. 185.

19. Ibid., p. 186.

20. Ibid., p. 246.

21. As quoted by Eugene Schuyler in his essay "Count Tolstoy Twenty Years Ago." See Schuyler's *Collected Essays* (Scribner's Sons, 1901), p. 274.

22. Alexandra Tolstaya, op cit., p. 125.

23. Tolstoy, in "On Popular Education." See pp. 178–180 of the current volume, or Wiener's *Tolstoy on Education* for the complete essay. As far as I know, Tolstoy never again expressed belief in the benefits of urban culture.

24. Tolstoy, in "Education and Culture." See Wiener, op cit., p. 149.

25. Tolstoy, in "On Popular Education." See Wiener, op cit., p. 5.

26. Quoted in Birukoff [Biryukov], op cit., pp. 329–330.

27. Reginald D. Archambault, in his Preface to Wiener, *Tolstoy on Education*, p. xv.

28. "In thus relieving children from all obligations, I free them from their greatest source of misery, namely books. Reading is the scourge of childhood, yet it is usually the only occupation that is given. At twelve years of age Emile will hardly know what a book is. But you will say, 'Surely he ought at least to learn to read.' Yes, he shall learn to read when reading will be of any use to him; till then, it only serves to disgust him." Jean-Jacques Rousseau in *Emile, Julie, and Other Writings* (Barron's Educational Series, 1964), p. 119.

29. Tolstoy, in *What Is Art?* See Aylmer Maude's *What Is Art? and Essays on Art* (Oxford, 1930), pp. 200–201.

30. I could not find evidence from Dewey's writings that he even knew of Tolstoy's *Yasnaya Polyana* articles. Daniel Murphy's *Tolstoy and Education* (Irish Academic Press, 1992) usefully compares and contrasts Tolstoy's methods and philosophies to Dewey's, Martin Buber's, and the Ukrainian Sukhomklinsky's. See pp. 251–260.

31. Kenneth Koch's *Wishes, Lies, and Dreams* (New York: HarperPerennial, 1970) and *I Never Told Anybody* (New York: Teachers & Writers Collaborative, 1997), for instance, vividly illustrate his diverse students' "unexpected" talent for writing.

32. Tolstoy, in "On Popular Education," which appeared in the popular Russian magazine *Notes of the Fatherland* (September, 1874).

33. Birukoff [Biryukov], op cit., p. 330.

34. As quoted in Aleksandra Tolstaya, op cit., pp. 144–145.

35. Pinch, op cit., pp. 217–218.

36. Ibid., p. 218.

37. The Decembrists: the name for those involved in the aborted rebellion of December, 1825. The Decembrists were composed of disaffected, generally politically liberal members of the officer corps and the educated classes.

38. Tolstoy, in "On Methods of Teaching the Rudiments." See Wiener, op cit., p. 33.

39. Tatyana Tolstaya in *Tolstoy Remembered* (McGraw-Hill, 1977), pp. 108–109. See also Ilya Tolstoy's *Tolstoy, My Father* (Cowles Book Company, 1971) and Sergei ("Seryozha") Tolstoy's memoirs in *Reminiscences of Tolstoy by His Contemporaries*.

40. Ibid., p. 111.

41. Simmons, *Leo Tolstoy*, Volume 1, p. 351.

42. Ibid., p. 352. *Bast shoes*: a reference to the crude wooden shoes typically worn by the Russian peasants (the Yasnaya Polyana students in the photo on the next page are wearing them).

43. In the spring of 1860, after his daughters Tanya and Masha set up their own short-lived school for peasant children, Tolstoy helped with the teaching. In 1907, Tolstoy taught the Bible and "moral lessons" to informal classes of a dozen children. See Simmons, *Leo Tolstoy*, Volume 2, pp. 136, 297–299.

The Yasnaya Polyana students, 1861

Are the Peasant Children to Learn to Write from Us, or Are We to Learn from the Peasant Children?

by Leo Tolstoy

IN THE FOURTH ISSUE of *Yasnaya Polyana*, in the section with children's compositions, the editors mistakenly printed "A Story of How a Boy Was Frightened in Tula." This story was composed not by a boy, but by the teacher to whom the boy's dream was related. Some of the readers of *Yasnaya Polyana* expressed doubts about the authorship of the story. I hasten to beg the readers' indulgence for this oversight, and to say that in such cases falsification is impossible. The story was found out not because it was better, but because it was worse, far worse, than any child's composition. All the other stories are the children's own. Two of them, "They Feed with the Spoon, Then Poke the Eye with the Handle," and "The Life of a Soldier's Wife," were composed in the following manner.

The chief art of the teacher in the study of language, and the chief goal in having children write compositions, consists not just in giving them themes, but in presenting them with a large choice, in pointing out the scope of the composition, and in indicating the initial steps. At first many clever and talented students of mine wrote nonsense, such as, "Fire started to burn, they began to drag out things, and I went out into the street," and nothing came of it in spite of the fact that the theme had been rich, and the description had made a deep impression on the children. They did not understand the main thing, which was why they should write and what good there was in writing. As I wrote in the second issue of *Yasnaya Polyana*, I tried many different ways of giving the students themes to write on. I gave them, according to their inclinations, specific, artistic, touching, funny, or epic ones—and all for naught. Here is how I unexpectedly came up with the right method.

Reading Snegirev's collected proverbs has long been one of my favorite occupations—or rather, enjoyments. For each proverb I imagine faces in the crowd and individual conflicts to fit the context. Along with a number of unrealizable fantasies, I always imagine a series of pictures, or stories, written to fit the proverbs. Once, last winter, after dinner I lost myself in Snegirev's book, and came to school with it the next day. The class was studying Russian.

"Well, write something on a proverb!" I said.

The best students—Fedka, Semka, and a few others—pricked up their ears.

"What do you mean by 'on a proverb'? What's that? Tell us!" they asked.

I happened to open the book to "He feeds with the spoon, then pokes the eye with the handle."

"Now picture this," I said. "A peasant takes a beggar into his home, and then the peasant begins to rebuke the beggar for the good he has done him, and you will get 'he feeds with the spoon, then pokes the eye with the handle.'"

"But how are you going to write that?" said Fedka, and the rest of them pricked up their ears. Then they suddenly retreated, having convinced themselves that this was beyond their powers, and went back to what they had been working on previously.

"Write it yourself," one said to me.

The students were all busy with their work. I took my pen and inkstand and began to write.

"Well," I said, "who will write it best? My guess is that you will."

I myself began the story published in the fourth issue of *Yasnaya Polyana*, writing the first page. Any unbiased person with common sense and an artistic sensibility will, after reading the first page, written by me, and then what follows, written by the students, note the differences as he would distinguish a fly from the milk: this first page is so false, so artificial, and written in such poor language. I should note too that in the first draft it was even more monstrous, since much was corrected thanks to the students' directions.

Fedka kept looking up at me from his notebook, and smiled, winked, and repeated, "Write, write, or I'll write it for you!" He was evidently quite amused to see a grown-up write a theme.

Having finished his own composition worse and faster than usual, Fedka climbed on the back of my chair and began to read over my shoulder. I could not go on; others came up to us, and I read them what I had written.

They did not like it, and nobody praised it. I felt ashamed, and to soothe my literary ambitions I began to tell them of my plan for what was to follow. The further I got in the story, the more enthusiastic I became; I corrected myself, and they kept helping me out. One student said that the old man should turn out to be a magician; another remarked: "No, that won't do, he should just be a soldier. . . . The best thing would be if he steals from him. . . . No, that wouldn't go with the proverb," and so on.

All were exceedingly interested. It was obviously a new and exciting sensation for the students to be present at the process of creation and to take part in it. The decisions they made were for the most part all the same, and were true to the plot as well as in the details and characterizations. Almost all of them took part in the composing process, but from the start Semka and Fedka especially distinguished themselves: Semka, by his perceptive, artistic descriptions, and Fedka, by the acuity of his poetic gifts, and especially by the glow and rapidity of his imagination.

The students' queries had so little of the accidental in them and were so assured that more than once I started to argue with the students only to abandon my argument posthaste. I was wholly focused on the requirements of a regular structure and of an exact correspondence between the idea of the proverb and the story; the students, on the other hand, were concerned only with the demands of artistic truth. For example, I wanted the peasant who had taken the beggar in to regret his good deed, whereas the students considered this impossible, and created a cross old wife for the peasant instead.

"The peasant was sorry for the old man at first, and later he was sorry to give away the bread," I said.

Fedka replied that this would be problematic: "He [the peasant] did not obey the old woman in the beginning, so he wouldn't later on."

"What kind of man do you think he is?" I asked.

"He is like Uncle Timofei," Fedka said, smiling. "He has a scraggly beard and keeps bees."

"Is he good, but stubborn?" I asked.

"Yes," said Fedka, "he will not obey the old woman."

After the point that the old man was brought into the hut, the work became animated. The students felt, evidently for the first time, the delight of clothing artistic details in words. Semka distinguished himself more than the rest in this: the truest details poured out one after the other. The only reproach that might be made to him was that his details rendered only the present moment, with no connection to the general mood of the story. I could hardly write everything down fast enough, and had to ask them to wait and not to forget what they had told me.

Semka seemingly saw and described exactly what was in his mind's eye: the stiff, frozen bast shoes*, the mud and dirty water that oozed out of them as they thawed, and the toast into which the shoes changed when the old woman threw them in the oven.

Fedka, on the other hand, saw only those details that evoked in him the particular feelings he had for given characters. Fedka saw the snow drifting behind the beggar's cloth puttees* and felt the compassion with which the peasant said: "Lord, how it snows!" (Fedka's face even expressed how the peasant would have said it—he shook his head, swaying his hands.) Fedka saw, from the mass of rags and patches, an overcoat and a torn shirt, behind which the haggard body of the old man was visible, still wet from the thawing snow. Fedka created the old woman, who grumbled when her husband ordered her to take off the beggar's bast shoes, and the old man's pathetic groan as he muttered through his teeth: "Gently, mamakins, I have sores there."

Semka for the most part needed concrete images—the bast shoes, the overcoat, the old man, the woman—with almost no connection between them; Fedka evoked the feelings of pity that permeated him. Fedka forged ahead, telling how he would feed the old man, how he would fall in the night, and how later he would teach the boy in the field to read. I was obliged to ask Fedka not to be in such a hurry, and not to forget the things he had said. His eyes sparkled almost tearfully; his dark, thin little hands

---

* *Bast shoes*: crude wooden shoes worn by the Russian peasantry.

† *Cloth puttees*: cloth wrappings covering the legs up to the knee; worn with bast shoes. Sometimes called "leg rags," these puttees were similar to those worn by soldiers in World War I.

convulsed; he got angry with me, and kept urging me on. "Did you write that? Did you write that?" he kept asking.

Fedka treated his classmates despotically. He wanted to talk all the time—not as a story is told, but as it is written—that is, to clothe sensory images in words, like an artist. Thus, for example, he would not allow words to be transposed: if he said, "I have sores on my feet," he would not permit me to say, "On my feet I have sores." His soul, softened and provoked by sentiments of pity—that is, of love—dressed every image in an artistic form, and denied everything that did not correspond to an ideal of eternal beauty and harmony.

When Semka got carried away expressing innumerable details about the lambs in the entryway and so forth, Fedka grew angry and said, "What a lot of hogwash!" I needed only to suggest what the peasant might be doing while his wife went off to the neighbor, when in Fedka's imagination there would immediately arise a picture of lambs bleating in the doorway, the sigh of the old man and the delirium of the boy Seryozhka. If I were to suggest an artificial or a false image, Fedka would remark angrily that that image was extraneous. For example, I suggested a physical description of the peasant, which Fedka agreed to. But I had proposed to describe what the peasant was thinking when his wife had run off to the neighbor. Fedka was suddenly struck by the thought: "If you got in the way of Savoska the corpse, he'd tear all your hair out." Fedka said this in such a tired, calmly serious, and characteristically good-natured voice, head in hand, that the other children rolled with laughter.

The chief quality in every art, the feeling of measure, had developed in Fedka to an extraordinary degree. If one of the other boys suggested adding something superfluous, it sickened Fedka. Fedka ruled over the plot of the story so despotically, and with so much authority in his despotism, that the other boys soon went home, and only he and Semka, who would not give in to him when the two were at cross-purposes, were left.

We worked from seven to eleven o'clock; they felt neither hunger nor fatigue, and got angry at me whenever I stopped writing. They tried to relieve me in the task of writing, but soon gave up that idea as it did not work out. Fedka asked me my name, for the first time. We laughed at the fact that he had not known.

---

* *Sic.*

"I know what we call you," he said. "But what do they call you in the manor house? We have names like Fokanychev, Ziabrev, Ermilin."

I told him.

"Are we going to print it?" he asked.

"Yes."

"Then we will have to print: Composed by Makarov, Morozov, and Tolstoy."*

Fedka was agitated for a long time and could not fall asleep. I cannot express the feeling of agitation, joy, fear, and near-regret that I myself experienced that evening. I felt that a new world of pleasure and suffering had opened up to Fedka: the world of art. I thought that I had gleaned an insight into what no one has the right to see: the germination of the secret flower of poetry.

I felt both dread and joy, like the treasure hunter who suddenly recognizes the amazing green color of ferns in the forest. I was glad, because suddenly and unexpectedly the philosophers' stone was revealed to me, what I had been vainly trying to find for two years: the art of teaching the expression of thought. Likewise, I felt dread because this art created new demands, a whole new world of desires that had no relation to the students' environment, or so it seemed to me then. There was no mistaking it. It was no accident, but a conscious creation.

I ask the reader to read the first chapter of the story and to note the rich evidence of true creative talent scattered through it: for example, the instance in which the old woman angrily complains about her husband to the neighbor, and—although the author clearly dislikes her—how she weeps when the neighbor reminds her of the ruin of her house. To the story's author, who takes cues from both reason and memory, the cross old woman represents the antithesis of the peasant—she makes her invitation to the neighbor for no other reason than to annoy her husband. Still, Fedka's artistic feelings reached out to the woman—note how she, too, weeps, fears, and suffers. To Fedka's mind, she is not guilty. From that follows the scene in which the neighbor puts on a woman's fur coat. I remember how struck I was by this, and how I asked, "Why a woman's fur coat?" None of us had given Fedka the idea that the neighbor should put on a fur coat.

Fedka said, "It is more like him."

---

* That is, Semka, Fedka, and Leo.—*Ed.*

When I asked Fedka if it might be more apt to say the neighbor put on a man's fur coat, he said: "No, a woman's fur coat is better."

Indeed, the detail works extraordinarily well. At first it does not occur to one why it should be a woman's fur coat, and yet you feel that the detail is excellent and cannot be otherwise.

Every artistic word, whether it belongs to Goethe or to Fedka, differs from the inartistic in that it evokes an endless stream of thoughts, images, and explanations.

The neighbor in the woman's fur coat naturally presents us with a sickly, narrow-chested peasant, just as he should be. The addition of the woman's fur coat, carelessly thrown on the bench, then falling into his hands, presents us with the typical evening scene in the life of a peasant. The fur coat prompts you to imagine the late evening scene, the peasant sitting half-undressed by a lit torch, and the women coming and attending to the cattle—all the external disorder of peasant life, in which no one has his own proper clothes and nothing has a definite place. With one phrase, "He put on a woman's fur coat," the whole nature of the context in which the action takes place is clearly outlined. And this phrase is not accidental, but quite deliberate.

I still remember vividly how the peasant's words arose in Fedka's imagination, the words the peasant used when he found the paper he could not read: "If my Seryozha knew how to read and write, he'd jump up, tear this book out of my hands, read it from start to finish, and tell me exactly who this old man is."

One can almost see the relation of this working man to the book he is holding in his sunburnt hands. The kind man, the pious patriarch, stands before you in full. You sense the author has taken a deep liking to the peasant and therefore understands him, so that soon after the author lets him digress about how times are such nowadays that before one knows it, one's soul has perished.

I suggested the idea of the dream, but it was Fedka's idea to give the goat sores on its legs, and this peculiarity gave him much pleasure. The peasant, in a moment of reflection as his back itches—the whole scene with its nocturnal quiet—all is far from accidental, and the cumulative power of these details makes us feel the conscious power of the artist!

I also remember how when the peasant was supposed to be asleep, I proposed having him reflect on his son's future and the future of the relationship between the son and the old beggar—to let the old beggar teach Seryozhka to read, and so on.

Fedka frowned and said: "Yes, yes, that's good," but it was obvious that he did not like my suggestion, and twice he forgot about it.

The feeling for artistic measure was stronger in him than in any authors I know—that sense of measure that only a few artists acquire after immense labor and study—lived with its primeval force in Fedka's uncorrupted, child's soul.

I stopped the lesson because I had become much too agitated.

"What's wrong with you? You're so pale. . . . Are you ill?" my companion asked me. Indeed, only two or three times in my life have I experienced as strong a sensation as I did on that evening, and for a long time I was unable to account for what I was experiencing. I dimly felt as if I were surreptitiously watching a beehive behind glass, in which the work of the bees was concealed from mortal eyes. It seemed to me that I had corrupted the pure, primitive soul of a peasant boy. I dimly felt something like remorse for an act of sacrilege I had committed. I thought of those children, before whom idle and debauched old men cavort and to whom they show lewd pictures in order to titillate their weary and worn-out imaginations, but at the same time I was ecstatic, happy as a man who has seen something no one has seen before.

For a long time I was unable to account for this impression, though I felt that it was one that teaches a mature person something, leading him to a new stage of life, making him renounce the old and devote himself to the new. Even the next day I could not make myself believe my experience. It seemed strange to me that a half-literate peasant boy should suddenly arrive at such conscious artistic powers—powers that Goethe, for all his immeasurable achievements, was unable to equal. It seemed strange and offensive to me that I, the author of *Childhood*, who had garnered some success and earned recognition for artistic talent from a cultivated Russian public—that I, in the matter of art, should be unable to teach anything to eleven-year-old Semka or Fedka, or to help them in any way, but that only with difficulty and in a happy moment of excitement should I be able to follow them or understand them. All that seemed so strange to me that I could not believe what had happened to me the previous day.

The next evening we sat down to continue the story. When I asked Fedka whether he had thought about how it should continue, he merely waved his hands about and said, "I know, I know! Who will write?" We set to work, and the children displayed the same enthusiasm and the same feelings for artistic truth and measure.

In the middle of the lesson I was obliged to leave them. They continued to write without me, and finished two pages that were just as good, just as well-felt, and just as true as the first page. The only thing about the two new pages was that the details were paler and less apt, and that there were two or three repetitions. All that was obviously due to the fact that the mechanics of writing had hampered them.

The same thing happened the third day. During the writing sessions other boys frequently joined us, and these boys often helped us out by adding their own fresh details. Semka came and went. Only Fedka saw the story through to its conclusion and considered all the proposed changes.

There could no longer be any doubt that our success was no accident: we had apparently found a method that was more natural and more conducive than anything tried before. But it was all so unusual that I could not believe my eyes. It seemed some remarkable event was necessary to eradicate all my doubts. I was forced to leave [Yasnaya Polyana] for a few days, and the story remained unfinished. The manuscript, three large sheets covered with writing, was left in the room of a teacher to whom I had shown it.

Even before my departure, while I was busy composing, a new student demonstrated to our boys the art of making paper crackers and, as often happens, the whole school began a period of paper crackers—which followed a period of snowballs, and before it a period of whittling sticks. The period of paper crackers took place during my absence.

Semka and Fedka were among the singers who came to this teacher's room for rehearsals, and remained there whole evenings and even nights. Between and during the singing, it goes without saying that the paper crackers were the first order of business, and any form of paper that fell into the students' hands was transformed into a paper cracker.

The teacher went out for supper, having forgotten to mention that the papers on the table were important, and thus the manuscript of Makarov, Morozov, and Tolstoy was soon turned into paper crackers. The next day, before class, the cracking sounds of the paper crackers were so annoying that the students themselves agreed to ban paper crackers: the latter were confiscated with shouts and screams, and solemnly stuck into the fiery oven.

The period of paper crackers came to an end, but with it perished our manuscript. Never had any loss been so hard for me to bear as the loss of those three sheets of writing. I was in total despair. I wanted to give it all up and begin a new story, but I could not forget the loss, and every other minute I couldn't help reproaching the teacher and the makers of the paper crackers.

(I should remark here that it was actually due to the external disorder and the complete freedom the students enjoy—which Mr. Markov so charmingly takes to task in *Russian Messenger*, as does Mr. Glyebov in the fourth number of *Education*—that I was able to learn, without the least effort, threats, or cunning, the whole complicated story in full detail of the transformation of the manuscript into paper crackers, and of the manuscript's consignment to the flames.)

Although they did not immediately understand the cause, Semka and Fedka saw I was distressed and sympathized with me. Finally Fedka timidly proposed to me that we begin another story.

"The two of you?" I asked. "I shall not help you now."

"Semka and I will stay here overnight," said Fedka.

And so they did. At nine o'clock, when the lessons were over, they came to the house and locked themselves in my office—which pleased me greatly—laughed awhile, and then grew quiet. Until midnight I could still hear them; every time I came to the door, they were talking to each other in low tones and scratching away with their pens. Only once did they debate about what should come first and what should come later—whether the old man looked for the wallet before the old woman went to the neighbor, or after—and they called upon me to judge. I told them it made no difference.

At midnight I knocked and asked to be let in. Fedka, in a new white fur coat with black trim, was sitting deep in the armchair with his legs crossed, leaning his shaggy little head on one hand and fumbling with a pair of scissors with the other. His big dark eyes, gleaming with an unnatural but serious and adult-seeming sparkle, were gazing into the distance; his irregular lips, pressed together as if about to whistle, apparently held in the word that he, having coined it in his imagination, was about to express.

Semka was standing at the large writing desk with a big white sheepskin over his back (tailors had recently been in the village), his belt loosened, his hair disheveled, writing in crooked lines and constantly jabbing his pen into the inkstand.

I tousled Semka's hair; his fat face—with its protruding cheekbones and that matted hair and those surprised and sleepy eyes—looked at me in fright. It was so funny that I burst out laughing. But the children did not laugh with me.

Without changing his expression, Fedka touched Semka on the sleeve and told him to go on writing. "You must wait," he said, "we'll be done soon." (Fedka addresses me with the familiar form of *you** whenever he is agitated or gets carried away by something.) He continued his dictation.

I took away their notebook. Five minutes later they had seated themselves near a small food safe, and were helping themselves to potatoes and kvass. For some reason, they found the silver spoons hilarious, and roared with musical, childish laughter. Hearing them upstairs, an old woman also burst out laughing without knowing why.

"Don't slouch like that!" said Semka. "Sit straight, or you will eat to one side."

They took óff their fur coats. Spreading them out under the writing desk they lay down to sleep, all the time pealing with their charming, childish, peasant laughter.

I read over what they had written. It was a new variant of the previous story. A few things had been left out, and a few new artistic gems had been added. Again there was the same feeling for beauty, truth, and measure. Sometime later, one sheet of the lost manuscript was found. In the printed story, recalling the lost version, I combined the two versions from memory.

The writing of this story took place in early spring, before the end of the school year. For various reasons I was unable to try new experiments. When I gave the students proverbs a second time, the result was only one story. This was written by two of the less good and more spoiled children, sons of the domestic staff. "He Who Is Glad of a Holiday Is Drunk Before Daybreak" was printed in the third number of *Yasnaya Polyana*. The same phenomena were repeated with these boys and this story as had occurred with Semka and Fedka and the first story, only the degree of talent was not the same, nor was the level of enthusiasm and cooperation on my part.

In the summer we never have had and never will have school. We shall devote a separate article to the reasons teaching is impossible in our school during the summer months.*

---

* No such article appeared.—*Ed.*

For part of the summer, Fedka and some of the other boys lived with me. After a swim and tired of playing, they took it into their heads to work. I proposed that they write compositions, and gave them several themes. I told them an entertaining story about the theft of some money, a story of a murder, and a story of the marvelous conversion of a milkman to Orthodoxy. I also proposed writing the autobiography of a boy whose father is sent into the army, and to whom the father later returns a reformed, good man.

"I would write it like this," I said. "I remember that, as a child, I had a father, a mother, and some other relatives. I would tell who they were. Then I would write that I remember how my father went out on the town while my mother wept, and how he beat her; then how he was drafted into the army; how she wept; how life became worse; how father returned, and as if I didn't recognize him, he asked whether Matryona—his wife— was alive; and how everyone was happy, and we began to live well."

That was all I said at first. Fedka took a great liking to this theme. He immediately took up pen and paper and began to write. While he wrote I planted thoughts about the sister and about the grandmother's death. The rest he wrote himself; he didn't show me anything except the first chapter until it was all done.

When he showed me the first chapter and I began to read it, I could sense that he was terribly agitated. He held his breath while he watched my eyes scan the manuscript, trying to glean from them an expression of approval or disapproval.

When I told him it was very good, he flushed but said nothing. With excited but quiet steps he walked up to the desk, set the notebook down, and walked slowly out into the yard. Once outside he was wild and short-tempered with the other boys during the day, and whenever our eyes met he looked at me with grateful, tender eyes. By the next day he had forgotten entirely about what he had written.

I came up with a title and divided the story into chapters, here and there correcting mistakes made due to carelessness. The original version of the story is being published in pamphlet form under the title "The Life of a Soldier's Wife."

I am not speaking of the first chapter, although there are some inimitable beauties there, and although in it heedless Gordyei is represented exceedingly vividly and true to life—Gordyei, who is ashamed to confess his repentance and who regards it as proper to plead to the Town Council only for his son's welfare—despite this, the chapter is drastically weaker than all that follows. The fault is mine alone, for I could not hold back during the writing from making suggestions to Fedka and telling him how I might have written the chapter. If there is a certain triteness in the introduction, in the description of persons and dwellings, I alone am to blame for it. If I had left Fedka alone, I am sure he would have described the same actions subtly, more artistically, without using the accepted and truly impossible method of logically distributing the descriptions, which consists in describing first the dramatis personae—even giving their histories—then the locale and surroundings, all before describing the action itself.

The odd thing about it is that these various descriptions, which sometimes run to dozens of pages, acquaint the reader with dramatis personae much less effectively than would a careless but artistic detail dropped into an action already in progress, among characters totally unfamiliar to the reader. Thus even in this first chapter, Gordyei's singular phrase "That is all I need"—when he renounces everything and acquiesces to his fate as a soldier, and only asks the Town Council not to abandon his son—this phrase acquaints the reader much better with Gordyei than a description of his attire, physique, or his habit of frequenting the tavern, which I repeatedly pressed on Fedka. The same effect is produced by the words of the old woman, who always scolded her son, when in her grief she enviously remarks to her daughter-in-law: "That's enough, Matryona! What are we going to do? It was apparently what God wished! Look, you're still young—maybe God will bring him back to you. But me, I'm so old and so sick that I could die any minute."

In the second chapter there are still traces of triteness due to my tampering, but here again the profoundly artistic detail in the description of the pictures and of the boy's death redeems the whole enterprise. I prompted Fedka to say that the boy had thin little legs; I also suggested the sentimental details about Uncle Nefed, who makes the little coffin. But the mother's lament—expressed simply with "Lord, when will this burden end?"—presents the reader with the whole essence of the situation. That night, when the older son is wakened by the mother's tears, the mother responds to the grandmother's inquiry of what the matter is with the simple words "My son has died," and the grandmother gets up, makes a fire, and washes the little body of the dead infant son—all this is Fedka's own. It is all so compressed, so simple, so strong, that one word cannot be omitted, changed, or added. There are five lines in all, and those five lines paint a picture of that whole sad night for the reader—a picture reflected in the imagination of a six- or seven-year-old boy.

> My mother started crying about something in the middle of the night. Grandmother got up and said, "What's the matter? Christ is with you!"
> Mother said, "My son is dead."
> Grandmother lit a fire, washed the boy's body, put a shirt on him, girded him, and laid him in front of the icons. When it became light. . . ."

You see the boy, awakened by the familiar tears of his mother, emerging sleepily from under a caftan somewhere on the sleeping bunk, watching the goings-on in the hut with frightened and sparkling eyes; you see the exhausted wife, the soldier's widow—who but the day before had said "When will this burden end?"—repentant and so crushed by her infant son's death that she only says "My son has died"; not knowing what to do, she calls to the grandmother for help. You see the old woman, worn out by the sufferings of life, bent over, emaciated, with bony limbs, as she calmly takes hold of the work with hands used to labor; she lights a torch, brings water, and washes the baby; she puts everything in the right place and lays out the body, washed and dressed, under the icons. And you see the icons, and the sleepless night through to daybreak, as though you yourself were living through it, as that boy [the narrator] lived through it, looking out from under the caftan; that night rises before you in full detail and stays in your imagination.

In the third chapter there is less of my influence. The character of the sister belongs entirely to Fedka. Even in the first chapter he characterizes the relationship between the sister and her family in one sentence: "Only my sister worked—for her dowry, not for the family—she bought new clothes and was preparing to marry." This one detail depicts the girl for who she is: she cannot take part—and does not really want to take part—in the joys and travails of the family. She has her own legitimate interests; her only goal, decreed by Providence, is her future marriage.

One of our fellow authors, especially one who wants to instruct the people by offering them moral models worthy of imitation, would have certainly have stereotyped the sister by the [lack of] interest she takes in the common needs and sorrows of the family. This author would have made her a disgraceful example of indifference, or a model of love and self-sacrifice, and there would have been an idea of the sister, not a living person. Only a person who has profoundly studied and learned life could understand that for the sister the question of the family's bereavement, and of the father's conscription, was legitimately a secondary question: she has her marriage to think about.

This very thing, in the simplicity of his heart, the child, though a child, sees as an artist. If we had described the sister as a completely sympathetic, self-sacrificing girl, we would not have been able to imagine her at all, and we would not be able to love her as we love her now. Now there stands before me the dear, living figure of a ruddy, fat-cheeked peasant girl, running off in the evening to the round dance in shoes and a red cotton kerchief bought with the money she's earned, loving her family, but burdened by its poverty and gloom, which are in such contrast to her own mood.

I feel that the sister is good, if for no other reason than that her mother never complains about her or is aggrieved by her. Moreover, I feel that the sister—with her concern for clothes, with the snatches of hummed songs, the gossip she hears during the summer field work or on the street in wintertime—was the representative of mirth, youth, and hope during the sad time of the soldier's wife's loneliness. Fedka says rightly that their only joy is when the sister marries. It is therefore with good reason that he describes the wedding feast at such length and with so much love; it is with good reason that he makes the mother say after the wedding, "Now our ruin is complete." It is apparent that, by letting the sister go, they have lost the joy and merriment which she brought to the house.

The whole description of the wedding is unusually good. There are some details there that simply stagger one; remembering that it is an eleven-year-old boy who wrote it, you ask yourself, "Is it possible this was just an accident?" Behind the strong, compressed description you see just the eleven-year-old boy, no taller than the table, with his bright and intelligent little eyes, to whom nobody pays any attention, but who notices and remembers everything.

When, for example, the little boy wanted some bread, Fedka did not say that the boy asked his mother for it, but that he "bent his mother down." This is said not by accident, but because Fedka is recalling his own relationship with his mother at that stage of growth, and because he remembers how that relationship receded in the presence of others, and how familiar he and his mother were when it was just the two of them.

There is another thing he chose and noted down from the mass of observations he could have made about the wedding ceremony, because to him—and to each of us—it captures the whole character of the ceremony: when they are told "Kiss!" the sister grabs Kondrashka by the ears, and they begin to kiss. Then the death of the grandmother, her recollection of her son prior to death, and the special character of the mother's grief—all this is so sure and so compressed, and it is all strictly Fedka's own.

When I gave Fedka the plot of the story, I talked with him most about the father's return. I liked that scene, and told it to him in a trite and sentimental way. He, too, liked the scene and said: "Don't tell me anything! I know it all myself, I know it." He sat down to write, and finished the story in one sitting.

It will be interesting for me to know other judges' opinions, but I consider it my duty frankly to express my own. I have not come across anything like these pages in Russian literature. In the whole episode there is not one reference to its having been touching—everything is described simply, how it happened—there is only what is necessary for the reader to understand the characters and the scene.

Once home, the soldier says only three sentences. At first he braces himself and says: "Hello!" When he begins to forget the role he must play, he says, "Is this all the family you've got?" And everything is conveyed by the question, "Where is my mother?"

What simple and natural words these all are, and not one of the characters is left out! The boy is happy and even weeps; but he is a child, and so in spite of his father's tears he keeps examining his father's wallet and looking in his pockets. Nor is the sister forgotten. It's easy to see that ruddy woman, who, in her shoes and fine clothes timidly enters the room and without saying a word kisses the father. You see the embarrassed and happy soldier, who kisses everyone in succession without knowing who they all are, and who, upon learning that the young woman is his daughter, calls her to him again and kisses her a second time, not as a young woman but as a daughter whom he had once left behind without any thought.

The father has reformed. How many false and inept phrases could have been used here! But Fedka simply tells how the sister brings some vodka, but the father does not drink it. You just see the mother, breathing heavily, take the last twenty-three kopecks out of her purse.

With whispers she sends her daughter in the hall to go out for more, and deposits the copper money in her open hand.

You see the young woman who, raising her apron with her hand, has a half-bottle underneath it. Clumping her shoes and swinging her elbows she runs down to the tavern. You see her enter the house with a flushed face and take the bottle out from underneath the apron, and you see the mother place it on the table with an expression of self-satisfaction and joy, and how she feels both annoyed and happy that her husband has stopped drinking. And you see that he has truly reformed, because he will not drink even on this special occasion. You feel that the members of the family have become different people.

> My father said a prayer before he sat down at the table. I sat down beside him; Sister sat on the bench, and Mother stood by the table looking at my father. She said, "You know, you look so much younger without your beard." Everyone laughed.

Only when the others have all left does the real family discussion begin. Only then is it revealed that the soldier has become rich. He has become rich in the simplest and most natural way, as nearly all people in the world become rich—that is, through money that did not belong to him, which came into his hands through a lucky accident. Some of the readers of the story remarked that this detail was immoral, and that the perception of the state as a milk cow needs to be eradicated, not strengthened, among the masses. But to me this detail—its artistic truth aside—is particularly pleasing. The Crown's monies always get waylaid somewhere—why not in the hands of the poor, itinerant soldier, Gordyei?

We often encounter diametrically opposed conceptions of honesty in the masses on the one hand and the upper classes on the other. The demands of the people are particularly serious and strong in respect to the honesty of close relations—for example, the family, the village, or the commune. With outsiders—the public, the government, the treasury, and foreigners especially—the application of the common rules of honesty becomes vague. The same peasant who will never lie to his brother and who will endure all kinds of hardships for his family, who will take not an extra or undeserved kopeck from his neighbor or fellow villager—will strip a foreigner or a townsman like a linden switch, and will tell strings of lies to a nobleman and an official; if a soldier, that peasant will stab a captive Frenchman without the slightest remorse; and if state funds fall into his hands, he will not regard it as a crime—at least not before his family—to take advantage of them.

In the upper classes, on the contrary, quite the opposite occurs. A man from our class will just as soon deceive a wife, a brother, or a merchant with whom he has had dealings for dozens of years, or his servants, his serfs, and his neighbors. But when this man is abroad he is forever consumed by fear lest he cheat someone and always wants it pointed out to him to whom he owes money. This same gentleman will stiff his company and regiment to get money for his champagne and gloves, and yet will shower civilities on the captive Frenchman. This same man regards it as the greatest crime to make use of the Crown's money when he is penniless. But he only regards it as such, for typically he won't stand on such high ground when the opportunity presents itself, and will commit the very deed he regards as entirely underhanded.

I am not saying which is better; I am only telling it as it is, as it appears to me. I will only remark that honesty is not a conviction, and that the expression "honest convictions" is nonsense. Honesty is a moral habit; in order to acquire it, the only way is to start with our relationships with those closest to us. The expression "honest convictions" is, for me, absolutely meaningless: there are honest habits, not honest convictions.

"Honest convictions" is an empty phrase; for this reason those supposedly honest convictions which refer to the remotest conditions of life—to the Crown's monies, to the government, to Europe, to humankind—these things are not grounded in honest habit and are not informed by near and vital relations. Because of this, these "honest convictions"—or rather, these empty phrases—prove inadequate in relation to life.

I return to the story. The mention of the money taken from the Crown—which at first appears immoral—conversely has, in our opinion, a quite charming and touching character. How often a *littérateur* of our circles, his simple soul wishing to present his hero as the paragon of honesty, shows us the whole dirty and corrupt interior of his own imagination! Here, on the contrary, the author needs to make his hero happy: for happiness, the hero's return to his family might suffice, but the author must also wipe out the poverty that has been weighing so heavily on the family for so many years. From where was the hero to find necessary wealth? From the faceless State. Only to offer wealth, one must get it first—and this was the most lawful and clever way he could find.

In the same scene in which the money comes up, there is a tiny detail, one word whose novelty strikes me each time I read it. It sheds light on the whole picture, colors in all the characters and the relationships between them. This one word—used incorrectly, from the point of syntax—is the word *hastened*. A teacher of syntax would be obliged to say so. *Hastened* requires a modifier: "Hastened to do what?" the teacher must ask. But the story simply goes: "Mother took the money and hastened and carried it away to hide it." I wish I myself had chosen such a word, and I wish that language teachers might say or write such a sentence.

> When we had eaten, Sister kissed Father again, and went home. Then Father began to rifle through his wallet as Mother and I looked on. Mother saw a little book there, and says: "Oh, you have learned to read?"
> Father said, "I have."
> Then Father took out a big bundle from his bag and gave it to mother. Mother said, "What is this?"
> Father said, "Money."
> Mother was happy and hastened and carried it away to hide it. Then Mother came back, and said, "Where did you get it?"
> Father said, "I was an under-officer and had government money. I gave it to the soldiers, and what was left in my hands, I kept."
> My mother was so happy and ran around like a mad person. The day was over, and evening came. They lit a fire. My father took the book and began to read. I sat down near him and listened, and Mother held the torch. Father read the book for a long time. Then we went to bed. I lay down on the back bench with Father, and Mother lay down at our feet, and they talked for a long time, almost till midnight. Then we fell asleep.

Here again we have a noticeable but hardly striking detail that leaves a deep impression: how they go to bed. The father lies down with his son, the mother at their feet, and it's a long time before they tire of talking. How ardently, I think, the son must have pressed himself to his father's chest, and what joy and happiness it was for the son, falling asleep and waking again, hearing the two voices, one of which he had not heard for so long.

It seems as if it's all over: the father has returned, and there is no poverty. But Fedka was not content with this (his imaginary people are so alive, so deeply seated in his imagination). He felt the need to create a vivid picture of their changed life: how the woman is no longer alone, a grieving soldier's wife with small babies; how there is now a strong man in the house, who will take from his wife's shoulders the burden of grief

43

and grinding poverty; and how independently, firmly, and joyfully a new life begins.

He paints for us only one scene: the powerful soldier chops some wood with a notched ax and brings it into the house. You see the sharp-eyed boy, used to the groans of his feeble mother and grandmother, admiring the bared, muscular arms of his father with wonder, respect, and pride; the energetic swinging of the ax, simultaneous with the chesty sighs of masculine labor; and the block of wood, like a piece of kindling, split under the notched ax. You see this, and your mind is eased completely about the future life of the soldier's wife. "Now she will not be lost, the dear," I think to myself.

> In the morning, Mother got up, went over to Father, and said, "Gordyei, get up! I need some wood to make a fire in the stove."
>
> Father got up, dressed himself, put on his cap, and said, "Do you have an ax?"
>
> Mother said, "I have . . . it is notched—maybe it won't cut."
>
> My father took the ax firmly in both hands, walked over to the block of wood, stood it on end, swung the ax with all his might, and split the block; he chopped up some wood and carried it over to the house. Mother lit a fire in the hut and stoked it, and soon it grew light.

But to the artist, this seems paltry. He wants to show us another side of their lives, the poetry of happy family life, and so he paints the following picture for us:

> After daybreak, my father said: "Matryona!"
>
> My mother came up and said, "Well, what?"
>
> Father said, "I am thinking of buying a cow, five sheep, two horses, and a new house—this one is falling to pieces—well, that will take about 150 rubles."
>
> Mother, lost in thought a while, said, "Well, then we will spend all the money."
>
> Father said, "We will begin to work."
>
> Mother said, "All right, we'll buy all these things, but where will we get the lumber?"
>
> Father said, "Doesn't Kiryukha have any?"
>
> Mother said, "That's the trouble. The Fokanychevs have taken it all."
>
> Father thought a while, and said, "Well, we'll get it from Brantsev."
>
> Mother said, "I doubt if he has any."
>
> Father said, "Why wouldn't he? He's sitting on a forest."
>
> Mother said, "I'm afraid he will ask too much. He's such a beast."

Father said, "I will go to him with some vodka and maybe come to an understanding with him, and you bake some eggs in the ashes for dinner."

Mother got some dinner ready—she borrowed from her friends. Father took the vodka and went to Brantsev's, and we sat and waited for a long time. I felt lonely without Father. I began to ask Mother to let me go after Father.

Mother said, "You will lose your way."

I began to cry and wanted to go, but Mother slapped me, and I sat on the stove and cried more than ever. Then I saw Father enter the hut. He came toward me and said, "Why are you crying?"

Mother said, "Fedka wanted to run after you, and I gave him a beating."

Father walked over to me and he said, "What are you crying about?"

I began to complain about Mother. Father went up to Mother and pretended to beat her in jest, saying: "Don't beat Fedya! Don't beat Fedya!"

Mother pretended to cry. I sat down on Father's knees and was happy. Then Father sat down at the table with me at his side and shouted: "Mother, give Fedka and me something to eat—we're hungry!"

And Mother gave us some beef, and we began to eat. When we were done eating, Mother said, "What about the lumber?"

Father said, "Fifty rubles in silver."

Mother said, "That is not bad."

Father said, "It goes without saying that it's fine lumber."

It seems so simple: so little is said, and you see in perspective their whole domestic life. You see that the boy is still a child, who will cry one minute and the next will be happy; you see that the boy is unable to appreciate his mother's love, and that he has swapped her for the virile father chopping the block of wood; you see that the mother knows that it must be so, and is not jealous; you see the wondrous Gordyei, whose heart is overflowing with happiness.

You note that they ate beef. This is lovely comedy, which they all play knowing that it is a comedy, and which they are led to play by an excess of happiness. "Don't beat Fedka! Don't beat Fedka!" says the father, waving his hand at her. And the mother, who is used to unfeigned tears, pretends to cry, smiling joyfully at the father and son; and the little boy who climbs up on his father's knees is proud and happy, not knowing why—proud and happy, no doubt, because now they are all happy.

"Then Father sat down at the table with me at his side and shouted: 'Mother, give Fedka and me something to eat—we are hungry!'"

"We are hungry," he says and he seats Fedka by his side. What love and happy pride of love breathes in these words! There is nothing more lovely and heartfelt in the whole lovely story than this last scene.

But what do we mean to say by all this? What importance does this story—written, perhaps, by an exceptional boy—have pedagogically? They will tell us: "You, the teacher, may have unconsciously helped in the composition of this and other stories, and to define what belongs to you and what is original would be exceedingly difficult."

They will tell us: "We will admit that the story is good, but as literature it is of the one-dimensional variety."

They will tell us: "Fedka and the other boys whose compositions you printed are the happy exceptions."

They will tell us: "You yourself are a writer, and without knowing it you have been leading the students up paths that essentially cannot be taught by teachers who are not authors themselves."

They will tell us: "From all this it is impossible to derive a common rule or theory. It is merely partial evidence of an interesting phenomenon, nothing else."I shall try to give my own conclusions in such a manner as to answer all the objections I assume will be made.

Feelings of truth, beauty, and goodness are independent from degree of development. Beauty, truth, and goodness are only, in essence, concepts that express only a harmony of relations in our senses of truth, beauty, and goodness. A lie is only a non-correspondence of relations to our sense of truth; there is no absolute truth. I am not lying when I say that I saw the tables whirl about under the touch of my fingers if I believe it to be so, even though it is an untruth. But I am lying if I say that I have no money when, according to my own understanding, I do have money. A huge nose is not ugly in itself, but it is on a small face. Ugliness is only a disharmony in relation to beauty. If I were to give my dinner away to a beggar or eat it myself, neither would be bad in itself; but to do either when my mother is dying of hunger would create a disharmony of relations apropos my sense of goodness.

While rearing, educating, developing, or if you like influencing a child in any way, we ought to have—and consciously do have—one aim in mind: to attain the greatest harmony possible in terms of truth, beauty, and goodness. If time stood still, if children did not lead well-rounded lives, we should be able quietly to attain this harmony by adding things where there seems to be a lack, and by reducing where there seems to be too much. But the child is alive: every side of his existence strives to develop itself, tries to outstrip every other side, and for the most part we mistake the progress of individual sides of his being for the true goal, while neglecting the harmony of his development as a whole. In this lies the eternal mistake of pedagogical theories.

We see our ideal in front of us when in fact it is behind us. The necessary development of man is far from being a means of attaining that ideal of harmony that we carry in us; it is, on the contrary, an obstacle placed in our way by the Creator, the way toward the attainment of the highest ideal of harmony. In this necessary law of forward movement lies the concept of the fruit from the tree of knowledge, of good and evil, which our first ancestors tasted.

A healthy child is born into the world completely satisfying all the demands of unconditional harmony of relations to truth, beauty, and goodness that we carry within us; the child is nearer to other beings—to plants, to animals, and to Nature, which always represents to us that truth, beauty, and goodness we are searching for. In all eras and with all men, the child has been represented as a model of innocence, sinlessness, goodness, truth, and beauty. "Man is born perfect" in the great words of Rousseau, words that remain firm and true as stone. But each hour in life, each minute increases the volume, quantity, and extent of these relations that at birth are in full harmony, and each step and each hour threaten to violate that harmony, and each successive step and each successive hour threaten the now-disturbed harmony and give no hope for its restoration.

For the most part, educators overlook the fact that stages in childhood are models of harmony, and they assume that the child's development, which progresses independently according to unvarying laws, is the goal. Development is erroneously accepted as the goal because the same thing happens to educators that happens with bad sculptors. Instead of trying to stop an exaggerated local development or the development as a whole, instead of waiting for a new event to destroy a wrong that has arisen—just as a bad sculptor, instead of eradicating the superfluous, keeps adding more and more—so educators seem to be concerned only with not breaking the developmental process. If they ever think of harmony, they always try to attain it by approaching an unknown model in the future, and ignoring the model in the present and in the past.

No matter how abnormal a child's development may be, there is always left in that child the original traits of harmony. By assisting—not pushing—development, we can hope to achieve at least a sure approach to normalcy and harmony. But we are so sure of ourselves, we are so dreamily devoted to the false ideal of human perfection, we are so impatient with the imperfections near to us and so firmly believe in our ability to correct them, we so little comprehend and value the primitive beauty of the child, that as fast as we can we magnify and shore up what strike us as imperfections—we correct, we educate the child. This one side has to be made equal with the other, now a third has to be made equal with the first. The child develops further and further and all the time departs from the earlier prototype that has been destroyed, and attaining the imaginary model of human perfection becomes more and more impossible. Our ideal is behind us, not before us. Education spoils, rather than corrects, people. The more a child is "spoiled," the less one needs to educate him, the more liberty he needs.

It's impossible and absurd to teach and educate a child for the simple reason that the child stands closer than I do—and than any grown-up does—to that ideal of harmony, truth, beauty, and goodness to which I, in my pride, wish to raise him. The consciousness of this ideal lies more powerfully in him than in me. All he needs of me is the necessary material to fulfill himself, harmoniously and multifariously. The moment I gave Fedka complete freedom and stopped teaching him, he wrote a poetic work, one that is unique in Russian literature. And thus it is my conviction that we cannot teach children in general, and peasant children in particular, to write and to compose—particularly artistic works. All that we need teach them is how to set about writing.

If what I did in order to obtain this goal may be called a method, the method consisted of the following:

Give a wide variety of themes—not ones you've invented especially for children, but those that seem most serious and interesting to you, the teacher.

Give the children children's work to read, and give them only children's work as models, for children's compositions are always more correct, more artistic, and morally truer than adults' work.

Most important, when looking through a piece composed by a student, never make any comments about the neatness of the notebook, about penmanship, spelling, and above all, about sentence structure or logic.

Since the difficulty of composing stories doesn't lie in the volume, content, or artistic quality of the given themes, the sequence of themes need not be based on volume, content, or language, but rather on logistics: first, selecting one out of a large number of presented ideas and images; second, choosing the right words for clothing a particular image or idea; third, remembering that one idea or image and finding a place for it; fourth, not repeating or leaving out anything, and successfully unifying what comes before with what comes after; fifth, and finally, thinking and writing at the same time, without letting one interfere with the other. To attain this goal, I did the following: a few of the aspects of the work I at first took upon myself, gradually turning them over to the students' care. At first I chose the ideas and images I considered best. I kept these in mind, and pointed them out when appropriate. I consulted what had already been written, kept the students from repeating themselves, and played the role of scribe, leaving the students free to clothe the images and ideas in words. I had them make their own choices, then consult the written text themselves, until finally—as in the case of "The Life of a Soldier's Wife"—they had taken the entire process of writing into their own hands.

The village of Yasnaya Polyana

They Feed with the Spoon, Then Poke the Eye with the Handle

by Ignat Makarov, Vassily Morozov, and Leo Tolstoy

THERE ONCE WAS A BIG BLIZZARD. A woman got dressed and went out for water. She carried a pail; it took all her strength to pull her legs through the snow, and she could see nothing in front of her. Suddenly she came across something in the road and spilled the water. Taking fright, she cried out. Her husband asked from the window, "What are you shouting about?"

And she said, "Semyon, take a light and come out here quick. Something frightening is lying on the doorstep."

The peasant went out, looked around and said, "It's a man lying here, maybe frozen."

The woman said, "I will call our neighbor. Somebody will have to drag him away."

The man said, "Don't you wear a cross around your neck?"

The woman ran to the neighbor, her son's godfather. The neighbor came and said, "The man must've frozen to death. No need to touch him."

The neighbor's wife said, "Maybe he's just pretending, on purpose."

The woman said, "We must tell the village elder. He'll inform the district police superintendent about it."

The neighbor said, "Just touch him and they will take you to court straight away." But Semyon looked the man over, touched him, and saw that he was still alive.

Semyon said, "And you call yourselves Christians? Look at you!"

He grabbed the old man crosswise and dragged him into the hut.

He said to his wife, "Light a spill."

The wife got up to light a spill, growling under her breath, "He'll take any beggar that comes around into the house."

They laid him on the stove to warm up, and the old man came to and started to mutter something.

The man approached him and started to ask him questions: "Who are your people, Grandfather? Where are you from?"

But it was impossible to find out anything from the old man. The man told his wife to take off the old man's shoes, and he took the old man's fur coat off himself. The fur coat was poor and frozen; the sheepskin was worn bare and tattered. As the peasant was taking the old man's coat off, snow sprinkled out from it, and under the fur coat was a soldier's greatcoat, patched together from various rags. Underneath the greatcoat, his shirt was torn, and through it his body was visible. The peasant took off the greatcoat and thought, "Wearing that, it's no wonder that he froze." He said to his wife, "Here, hang the greatcoat and sheepskin on the top of the stove door so they'll dry quicker, and take his shoes off."

The woman snorted, snatched the clothes from his hands, and opened the oven door so hard that it hit the ground and the handle broke off. She went over to the old man and began to take his shoes off as if she were tearing his feet off. Suddenly, the old man let out a groan and started to speak in a soft voice, so the peasant could hear him.

"Oh, oh, gently, mamakins. I've got sores there."

The peasant yelled at his wife, "Gently, you bitch! Oh, my God, if it weren't for me, she'd be the death of him. . . ."

The old man's bast shoes were so frozen that when they began to thaw, they steamed, and a dirty trail of water flowed onto the woman's hands. The woman spat and flung the shoes at her husband. The man picked them up and shook his head, saying, "How did he not freeze to death? I suppose his feet must feel like ice right now. Oh! Life is bitter for so many, so many on this earth. . . ."

Then he rolled up the old man's cloth puttees, and put them in a place by the stove, and threw the mud-splattered bast shoes in the stove; he moved the man's feet at the middle, took the fur coat off him, and put it

---

* *Bast shoes*: crude wooden shoes worn by the Russian peasantry.
† *Cloth puttees*: cloth wrappings covering the legs up to the knee; sometimes called "leg rags."

over him. Lying on the stove*, the old man only grunted, "Oh, my God, oh-h-h-h!"

The woman covered herself with a caftan, heading towards the door, and the man said, "Are you off to the neighbors' again?"

She said, "No, to the yard!"

She slammed the door so hard even the lintel shook. But she had deceived her husband: she had slammed the door that led out to the yard, and then turned the other way, run out to the street in the direction of the neighbors. She arrived at the neighbors' house gasping for breath, and said, "Neighbor, talk my fool of a husband out of this. He's taken in some kind of stinking soldier. He takes them in and asks me to take their shoes off! You should see the shoes he was wearing—they were truly enough to make you sick!"

The neighbor said, "He's clearly lost his mind this time. How could this be? What if the old man dies? Then see what trouble it'll bring you."

This made the woman scareder still, bringing tears to her eyes. She said, "He'll bring ruin to our house. Come with me, neighbor, and talk him out of it."

The neighbor said, "Oh him, he cursed me out real good not long ago. Wouldn't listen, and now he'll probably turn me out of his hut. I won't go."

But the woman pestered him incessantly, and began to kiss his hands, "Come on, Godfather, for God's sake. For the love of Christ!"

The neighbor put on a woman's fur coat, went out, and said, "Maybe I'll bring him around somehow, and if I can't I'll curse him and go off."

Meanwhile, the peasant was sitting by the table with his hand in his gray beard. In the hut you could just hear the old man groan and the young boy, Seryozhka, on the ledge above the stove murmuring in his sleep (he was dreaming about a game), "Kids, catch, catch the bitch!" Meanwhile, the lambs in the doorway were crying, "*Baa! Baa!*" The man remembered his wife and thought that the storm might have carried her off again to the neighbor's house.

---

* The hut-like houses of the Russian peasantry (*izby*) typically had one or two rooms constructed around a central stove. The stove—very, very large by our standards—was for heat during the severe winters. All well as ovens for cooking, this central stove also had elevated "shelves" for sleeping (built-in pallets or bunks) and cabinets for storage. Hence in these stories—as well as in works by Gogol, Leskov, Goncharov, Chekhov, and other Russian authors—the peasants literally do "lie on the stove."

"Ech, the wretch! One of these days, I'll strangle her. And she didn't even let the lambs out to go to their mothers. If she got in the way of Savoska the corpse, he'd tear her hair out!"

He sat, and he sat, scratching the back of his head, and said, "And maybe in fact she really senses that there will be disaster! And indeed it could be that she's right. I'd better look in the old man's bag and see if there are any papers there."

He stood up, took the old man's bag, and began to look at what was in it: he saw two books—one thin, the other thick. The peasant said, "The thin one must be an ABC book and the thick one a psalter. This old man must know how to read and write." He put his finger on the pages of the thick book and came across some paper with a printed seal. Overjoyed, he said, "This must be the paper, all right." He turned it over in his hands and tried to make out what it said, saying, "If my Seryozha knew how to read and write, he'd jump up, tear this book out of my hands, read it from start to finish, and tell me exactly who this old man is."

He put the paper back between the same pages where he found it and continued looking through the old man's bag. He found a small cloth which he unrolled and also eight half-kopeck pieces, one old quarter-kopeck piece, and a medal. The man then said, "Maybe somebody robbed him somewhere. Things are such nowadays that they only have to find some money on somebody, their souls are so hardened, that they'll kill him right away for it. Oh, God our Savior, save us all from these evil men."

The man sighed, wrapped everything in the cloth again, and sat down on the bench. As soon as he had sat down, he heard the creaking of someone at the door. He said, "That must be my loose woman coming." The man had felt like saying, "Well, have you run around enough, bitch?" But suddenly in came the neighbor. The neighbor entered the hut, sat in the doorway, and said, "What's with you, Semyon, what do you have against your own family? What did you take that old man in for?"

Semyon only said, "Ech, you're a godless one!"

The neighbor said, "Yes, yes, godless. . . . You'll see. You'll see what will happen to you because of him."

Semyon said, "You'd have me throw him out on the street."

The neighbor said, "Now look here, my friend. You will make many, many people suffer because of him. First they'll take you to the local station, and after that to the district, and from the district they'll take you to town, and from town they'll take you to the police court. They'll mark you down in their books and send you off to prison, and there you'll sit until you die. It might be better if he had no papers, if he were one of those fellows without any official documents at all."

The man said, "Well, what will be, will be. If the Tsar himself punishes me, as I said, I won't throw the old man out."

Then the old woman let out a cry and said, "No, neighbor, you won't get to him. He's been stubborn like that since the beginning of time. Evidently he wants to play folly with his little children. How our son will suffer, O God!"

The neighbor said, "But what you should really do is look in his bag. Aren't there some papers? Did you at least find out what kind of a man he is?"

The man said, "I found a book in his bag and in the book a paper with a seal on it. Maybe that's what we need."

The neighbor sent word to his uncle to send Vanushka to make out what the paper said.

Vanushka came and began reading the paper, and the man said to his wife, "What are you doing fidgeting about there? Bring more light."

The neighbor said, "Never mind; he's young, he can read it through without it."

They began to read, and learned that the man had been a soldier in the Caucasus, had been in many battles, had been decorated with two medals by the Tsar, and had been wounded three times.

The neighbor said, "Even if he's got papers, there'll be a lot of trouble if he dies. Look here, neighbor! You've heard what happened in the town of Yagodnaya with one man. He took in some beggar and the beggar up and died. They took the man to court, found him guilty, and sent him to prison, and there he rotted, all because of a beggar. . . . They'll send you to prison too."

Semyon thought this over and said, "Get away from me. Get out of here, please."

The neighbor said to Semyon, "You are no longer my friend and neighbor!" He put on his hat and said to the woman, "Goodbye, my friend," and went out.

The woman began to cry, saying, "O my sweet little child, Seryozha. O-o-oh! We will both perish. . . . We will wander the earth with our belongings and our home will be destroyed." She howled with grief for a long time.

Then Semyon said, "Well, go ahead with your wailing. Get me some supper. I'm hungry."

The woman grumbled under her breath, "Let the first bite choke you," and she went to ladle out some cabbage soup. She started to act like a crazy woman: she rattled around with the long tool she used to get pots out from deep in the oven, and flung more wood into the stove. As she stuck the potholder into the stove she spilled the soup. She pulled the empty pot off the stove, and smashed it on the ground, so that the vessel broke into a thousand pieces.

Not knowing what happened, Semyon said, "There you go, gorging yourself again. You're such a pig, but you don't want to dirty your hands."

Then Semyon got up from the bench and went to find himself something to eat—he fumbled around and found Seryozhka's little pot of kasha in the oven and ate it up. Then he went over to the old man to see whether he was alive. The old man had thawed out, and was tossing about in his sleep. Then the peasant made a bed for himself, put out the lamp, and lay down by the front of the stove. He put on his fur coat, and laid his head on his wife's caftan. As soon as he had fallen asleep, the woman pulled the caftan out from under his head, so that he struck it against the bench. He then said, "Oh, you are anathema. God!" But he left off quarreling with her after that.

He felt underneath the front of the stove to see if there was something to lay under his head, and found the old man's tattered puttees. He put them under his head and went back to sleep. Suddenly a dream came to him. It seemed an old goat was coming toward him, and the goat had sores on its legs, and the goat was halfway between a goat and the old man. The goat said, "I thank you, Semyon, for saving my life. For saving me, I will do something good for you." Semyon felt sorry for the goat. Then all of a sudden he saw his wife climb down from the stove, mount the goat, and grab hold of its horns, bending its head back towards its spine. This made Semyon feel even sorrier for the poor goat, and yelled out, "Stop it!" And Seryozha, it seemed, started wailing, saying, "Mama, please, don't hit the goat, I feel so sorry for him." The peasant woke up and said: "O Lord! What did I dream?" He turned on his side, scratched his back, and said, "It's time to take a bath so my back won't be so itchy.

I suppose the old man is even worse off, though." Then the peasant fell back asleep.

All became very quiet in the hut. All one could hear was the peasant and his wife snoring, the half-asleep Seryozhka occasionally letting out an "Ahhh," the cockroaches falling off the sleeping bunk, and the sheep coughing from the heat, stamping their hooves, and looking for something to drink. Outside the blizzard had quieted down and frost had set in; the moon was shining. The night watchman walked up the street through the snow, making crunching sounds with his feet and rapping his truncheon on the gates.

II.

The next morning, the old man was the first one in the hut to come to his senses. He began groping around for his puttees and bast shoes and wondering whether or not they were in the oven. He bent over and felt around in the stove for them. His arms weren't long enough, and the oven was too narrow. He bent over still further. The stove door came off and the old man fell off the stove, causing the little lambs to shy up close to their mother as they watched him. The lambs thought someone was teasing them—they screwed up their courage and began jumping over the prostrate old man. He lay there awhile, wheezing, before he got up. Then the peasant woke up and saw the old man lying in the middle of the hut. The peasant got up, sat himself on the bench and said, "What happened, Grandfather, did you hurt anything?"

The old man said, "No, nothing. I'm feeling better now."

The old man felt fresher than the day before. Meanwhile, Seryozhka had woken up and had fixed his gaze on the old man from his bunk. He was thinking, "Yesterday he wasn't here with us." The old man said, "Boy, don't be afraid of me—come here and I'll give you a kopeck to keep." The old man reached into his bag, pulled out the folded rag, extracted a quarter-kopeck piece from it, and gave it to the boy. The boy took the quarter-kopeck piece as everyone watched. The peasant asked, "Grandfather, don't you want something to eat?"

"Thank you, you're a good man. God will not forget you."

The peasant cut off a piece of bread from a round loaf, salted it, and gave it to the old man. Serozhka asked, "Grandpa, would you like us to bring you some water to drink?"

"There's a good boy, bring some to please God."

The old man started to eat, scattering crumbs all around. The woman started a fire to warm up the hut, and went off to the pond to wash Seryozhka's underclothes. The peasant went to feed the cattle, and dropped by the neighbors' to shoot the breeze. Seryozhka, meanwhile, lost his shyness and took interest and pleasure in the old man, all the time feeding him more and more—he got him potatoes and showed him where the milk was kept in a little pit. He said, "Help yourself, Grandpa."

The old man said, "Thank you. But I won't. Better that your father or mother give it to me." The woman and her husband arrived and began to get lunch ready. The man said, "Akulina, serve us some cabbage soup. Come on over here and sit down, Grandfather."

The old man crawled over to the bench with some difficulty, like a small child. When the woman saw that the old man had sat down next to her husband, she was vexed, even gnashing her teeth. She said, "Let's take in some more beggars. There's plenty of those devils roaming around on the face of the earth. You can't support them all by charity. Better to buy a new oven door."

The peasant said, "You broke it yourself. You buy a new one. Go buy a piece of canvas to cover it with."

The woman said, "And then where will you get your shirts, you evil man?"

The woman got angry and refused to sit down to eat. The peasant said, "The bigger the lips, the smaller the belly," and they again began cursing each other.

The old man became embarrassed and started to get up from the table. But Seryozhka filled his spoon and brought it up to the old man's mouth, saying, "Eat, Grandpa," and poured the soup all over his beard and even spilled some on his chest. The old man said, "O my stars, there's a good boy."

They went on eating the cabbage soup and the potatoes. The peasant said, "Akulina! Pour us some milk."

The old man wanted to get away. But Seryozhka grabbed him by the finger and shouted, "Grandpa! Milk, milk!"

The woman got a small cup and placed it in front of Seryozhka and said, "Gorge yourself, you imp, till your sides burst." She bent over Seryozhka, whispered something, and threatening him with her finger said, "You look out, if you give any of this milk to that old devil, I'll flog the daylights out of you with a switch."

As soon as she turned away, Seryozhka took the cup, stood up on the bench, and poured it straight down the old man's throat saying, "Drink up, Grandpa, quick so Mama won't beat me."

Half the milk went down his throat, and half onto his beard, his shirt, and onto the ground. The old man only mumbled—his mouth was too full for him to say anything. A crumb dropped into his throat, and he belched—which embarrassed him still more. The peasant burst out laughing, and said, "Attaboy, Seryozha, you mustn't forget your elders."

And Seryozhka also burst out laughing at "Grandpa."

The woman almost started laughing too, and said to herself, "Look at how you gorged yourself, you stinking, rotten beggar." Then she gushed with laughter.

The old man got up from the table. He sighed and sat to one side of the stove, covering himself with his hands and saying nothing.

III.

Summer came. The old man's strength returned to him. The peasant said, "Grandfather, go watch over the horses."

The old man rejoiced in the fact that they were sending him off to work. He took his little ABC book, mounted a gray horse, and rode off. Just then Seryozhka woke up and yelled out, "Grandpa, help me down from my sleeping bunk, or I'll fall."

The mother said, "Look at what habits you've gotten into, you imp."

The father laughed, "Seryozhka, say goodbye, your grandpa has gone." And the father got out a kopeck piece of his own and gave it to his son, saying, "Here you go. Grandpa left this for you, for the milk you gave him to drink."

Seryozhka grabbed the kopeck piece to put it under the bench. It slipped through his fingers and hit the floor, making a ringing sound. Seryozhka leapt up wanting to dash off after the old man, but he did not know which way to run. He shouted, "Grandpa's gone! Grandpa's gone!"

The peasant became frightened. "God knows where he'll run to," he thought. He said, "Seryozha, don't run off. Your grandfather's in here— as a joke he hid in the chest." Serezhka turned and rushed toward the chest, opened it, and saw that it held only a loaf of bread. Cockroaches were running over the bread. He yelled at the top of his lungs, "Grandpa,

Grandpa!" This made the father sorry for him, and the father said, "That's enough. Want to know where your grandpa is?"

"Tell me."

"He's watching over the horses."

"Take me there, Dad."

The father said, "Do you know where Vanka looked after them? Do you know the Puzikov Heights?"

"I know it. Say, give me a lump of porridge to bring to him."

Seryozhka put the lump of porridge inside his shirt, took a small knife, and ran off with the little knife flashing. The father watched him go until he turned into a small black spot like a tiny insect. "Look at how accustomed to the old man he's become. They're inseparable."

Seryozhka ran up to the Puzikov Heights all out of breath. The old man saw him, said, "Oh, my dear boy," and kissed him.

Seryozhka took the lump of porridge, put it in a kerchief, and said, "Here, Grandpa, cut it, and make me a pipe from it."

"Fine, my boy. I'll do it, I'll do it." The old man ate the porridge, took his ABC book, and began to read. Seryozhka said with amazement, "Grandpa, who are you talking to?"

"I'm saying my prayers."

Seryozhka took the book and drew it toward him: "What's this? What's this?"

The old man said, "That's a sin. That's a sin, Seryozha. Don't touch it, it's reading. A priest will come and cut off your ear, and you will cry."

"Then I'll hide in the chest, where you were."

"God will find you there, and drag you out by the leg."

"But where is he? God?"

"He is here with us no longer."

Surprised, Seryozhka fell silent. Then he said, "Give me the book so I can talk with it."

"Well, what of it. I'll teach you."

The old man showed Seryozhka the big words, sharpened a stick to use as a pointer, and began using it to direct the boy's attention, telling him "Say after me, *az . . . buki.* * Say it again. *Az.* Try harder."

---

* Russian children (and adults) learned the alphabet with the aid of mnemonic devices for each letter. *Az . . . buki . . . vedi* is the equivalent of the A, B, C in English.

Seryozhka was too scared to touch the book, and shrank back from it. The old man gave him the pointer and said, "Take it." But Serezhka was still too scared to touch the book, and screwed up his eyes, saying, "But the priest will cut off my ear, Grandpa, won't he?"

The old man said, "He will if you monkey about. He'll grab you by your little ear, and it will hurt a lot." The old man taught Seryozhka one line from the book. The sun was low in the sky. The old man said, "Seryozha, let's go!"

The old man started to try catching a horse, but the horse wouldn't be caught. Serezhka yelled out, "Grandpa, Grandpa! He'll kill you, and who will I learn my ABC from?"

The old man finally caught the horse, mounted it, and said, "Give me your hand." Seryozhka said, "Don't foul it up. *Az, buki, vyedi.*" Seryozhka kept repeating this the whole time they were riding home. All of a sudden some kids on horseback shouted, "Hey, Seryozhka, what are you up to?"

But Serezhka just kept mumbling "*Az . . . buki*" the whole time. The kids asked, "What's that?"

He said, "I'm learning reading." Then they arrived home. Seryozhka kept repeating, "*Az . . . buki, az . . . buki.*" The old man said with surprise, "What a good boy you are, Seryozhka! I'll buy you a bun to eat. Only why did you throw the kopeck on the floor? It rolled under the floorboards."

Serezhka said, "This is *az*, and that's *buki.*"

They had supper, went to sleep, and the whole time Serezhka kept droning on "*az . . . buki.*" He shouted, "Grandpa, give me the pointer! Come and read, Mitka, or the priest will cut off your ear!" Morning came and Serezhka said, "Dad, how about my teaching you to read?"

The father said, "Well, teach me."

Serezhka then said, "Say after me—*az.*"

Serezhka had a good laugh at his father, nearly splitting his sides with laughter. Serezhka said, "Say *buki.*"

The father said, "*Ruki.*"*

Serezhka said, "*Vedi.*"

The father said, "*Breden.*"†

And Serezhka shouted, "Grandpa! Dad doesn't know how to speak!"

---

* *Ruki*: the Russian word for *hands.*
† *Breden*: Russian for *dragnet.*

IV.

Autumn came. Semyon still had not sent the old man away. One day Semyon went to town to buy bread. His wife bought white bread and vodka, filled the samovar, and called the neighbor. She said to herself, "What am I to do with that old man? He'll tell my husband everything."

So she said, "Emilyanych, what are you lying around for, go watch over the white-legged colt. That filthy horse likes to run away at a moment's notice."

But the old man's back was hurting him. He said nothing to the woman, only moaning, "O God the Father!"

The woman said, "You eat our bread, but won't watch over the animals. You eat like a man, but are a boy when it comes to working."

The old man simply put on his fur coat and said, "I would go, but today I have no strength, and my back is hurting."

This made the woman even more angry, and she said, "It doesn't hurt when you eat, just when you walk."

The old man started to get down from the stove, and accidentally caught his foot on the chamberpot and knocked it over. When the woman saw this, she yelled at him with even more venom, "Oh, you rotten devil! You really want to do evil. No wonder they kicked you out of the army, you devil."

The old man thought to himself, "I don't want to embarrass myself with this woman," and he took his coat and got dressed on the porch.

As he was doing this, his coat caught on the samovar in the dark. The samovar fell over, the top broke off, and the water poured out of it. The old man didn't know what to do. As soon as the woman sensed that the old man had overturned the samovar, she went into a frenzy—she leaped up and started to pick up the samovar. The old man wanted to help, but got all tangled up. She gave him a rude shove in the shoulder and he bumped his head against the lintel. The woman said, "Vanish, you damned tramp! You eat our bread, and then do things like this, all out of spite."

The old man did not go to the horses. Instead he put on his coat and went back into the hut. He said nothing to the woman—he got his bag and began to pack all his belongings in it. His book was under the icons. He leaned over the table to get it. The woman shied away from him. The old man fetched his psalter, putting it in the bag with the ABC book beside it. The woman started to scrape something as if she didn't notice anything, and thought to herself, "What's he going to do? Better make sure he doesn't steal anything." Just then the neighbor came in, and said, "What are you up to, Grandfather? Are you ill?"

The old man said, "What did you say?"

"Why are you shaking all over?"

The old man did not try to talk with the neighbor; he put his belt on, crossed himself, put his bag over his back, took the ABC book in hand, and began to pray before the icons.

The neighbor said, "Where are you off to, Grandfather?"

The old man said nothing. So the neighbor said to the woman, "Look, friend, you'll be in hot water with Semyon over this."

The woman said, "All because of that rotten tramp. He'll beat me, too. It's all the same in the end."

The old man bowed to both of them and said, "I thank you for all your kindness." And then he left the hut.

The woman jumped up and went to the porch to see where the old man was going. Seryozha was playing with some kids in the street. When he saw his grandfather, he ran up to him. "Where are you going, Grandpa? Take me with you."

The old man took the boy, kissed him, and said, "Goodbye, my dear boy, I'm going home. Seryozha, here's my ABC book, I'm giving it to you."

Seryozha began to cry; he grabbed the old man's coat and would not let go. But the woman leapt up, grabbed Seryozha by the hand, and said, "What are you crying about this beggar for?" She pulled the boy away, saying, "Let go of him, or you'll become rotten, too."

Seryozha, sobbing, asked the old man, "Why are you leaving, Grandpa?"

The old man said, "I'm leaving because *they feed with the spoon, then poke the eye with the handle.*"

The woman tore Seryozha away, and led him back into the hut. The old man went limping off along the side of the street. Seryozha climbed up to his sleeping bunk and cried all night without stopping. The woman began drinking vodka with the neighbor. After they'd drank some, the neighbor asked, "What will you tell Semyon when he asks about the old man?"

The woman said, "I'll tell him that he went to the devil. I only hope he doesn't run into him on the street. Who's going to tell him what really happened?"

Just then they heard someone riding up outside. The woman hid the half-bottle of vodka. The peasant unharnessed his horse, came in the hut, looked around, and said, "Where's Emilyanych, hasn't he come home yet?"

The woman said, "God knows where he is. He lay about and lay about and then went off somewhere. . . ."

The peasant hung his hat on a hook, took his belt off, sat down at the table, and said, "Seryozha, Seryozha! Come down here and see what I brought you from town."

He pulled a new dish out of his shirt. Seryozha went up to his father, still crying.

The father asked, "What's the matter?"

"Grandpa left."

"Why did he leave?"

"Mamma drove him away."

The woman said, "It was high time he left."

The man started to ask, "Did he say anything as he was leaving?"

Seryozhka said, "He said, 'I'm leaving because you feed me with a spoon, then poke me in the eye with the handle.'" Then the boy broke down into tears and refused to take the dish his father had brought him.

Semyon was furious, shaking with rage. He said to his wife, "You've really done it now, you bitch! You've disgraced my house, you wretched woman!"

The neighbor pleaded with him, "Leave her alone, forgive her, she won't do it again."

The peasant shouted, "Get out of my house, and don't let me catch a whiff of you here ever again. No one can tell me what to do with my wife."

The neighbor left. The peasant sat at the table, eating his supper. Seryozhka was so frightened that he would not leave his place by the stove, but he stopped crying.

The village of Yasnaya Polyana

The Life of a Soldier's Wife

by Vassily Morozov

I.

THE LITTLE that I remember, I was seven and we lived in a poor corner of town, my father, mother, grandmother, my sister, and me. I remember as through a dream how my grandmother loved me more than my mother. Grandma wore an old, white caftan and a long,worn-out wool skirt, and wore an old rag tied around her head. Whenever I started to run off anywhere, she would say, "Don't hurt yourself, Fedya!"

My mother was meek. Father would often knock her around when he would come home drunk. She would cry some and say nothing. She would tie her hair up in a calico kerchief. She went barefoot in summer and wore bast shoes in wintertime.

My father was about thirty years old, of average height, barrel-chested, and had a small beard. He dressed in a short blue jacket and wore the kind of cap the men wear at the post-mail stations.

I was afraid of him. When I was naughty, he would beat me and curse me out something awful. Whenever he started to beat me, I would run straight to my grandmother, and she would protect me. My sister would always look through my hair for lice, so whenever my head began to itch, I would go seek out my sister. From the little I remember, our house was falling down, and we had propped it up. Our house was already cramped inside, but the braces made it even more so. I also remember how I would climb on the supports with my friend Taraska. My grandmother would say, "Don't climb on the supports, or the house will fall down." Taraska and I would go out in the yard to hunt for bird nests. I wasn't afraid of anything. I grabbed the wicker fencing and leaped up on the netting. Then I grabbed for a stick with both hands, trying to climb further, but the stick broke and I went flying towards the ground upside down. As ill-luck would have it, a post was lying there—I fell right on it with my cheek and I screamed bloody murder. Since then I've had a scar on my cheek.

The yard was cramped and bare, with rotting straw scattered about it. In the yard there was one old, lopsided horse. We had no cows, but we had two sheep and one lamb. I often slept with the lamb; he sometimes soiled on me—but I didn't mind at all. We ate dry bread and drank water; we had no one to do work for us. My mother was big with child, Grandmother was always around the stove and always had headaches. Only my sister worked—for her dowry, not for the family—she was preparing to marry. She sometimes bought new clothes. And as for my father, it went without saying, whatever he earned went towards drink.

I remember Uncle Nefed came to us—he was the village elder—and started to curse my father out over something. I only heard Nefed say, "Everyone's paid their poll tax but you. Look, brother Gordyushka! They'll call a meeting and send you off to the army."

I heard him mention something about a pillow.* I was afraid my father would be shot—I grabbed my pillow and put it on Nefed's knees and said, "Here, here it is, take the pillow, but don't send my father off to the army." Everyone laughed.

The village elder said, "Look, Gordyei, whatever money you make, you spend at the tavern, but your son feels so sorry for you that he will give up his throw pillow for you." My father threw up his hands in dismay and went outside.

Then Grandmother said to Nefed, "That's just what he wants to do— leave his home and family, without a care in mind."

Father wasn't afraid of anything, and I remember that he kept going to the tavern all the same. A month later the village elder called a meeting. A crowd of people gathered in our yard, and they started shouting: "He should be sent off to the army!" My mother and sister stood next to the people. I ran up to them and asked, "Why are you crying?" Mother took me by the hand, crying even more. She said, "They want to send him off to be a soldier, and you're not even sad. . . ."

Then they sent Uncle Yefim to fetch my father. Uncle Yefim brought him back, and he was drunk. I said, "Ma, what will they do with him there?"

My mother said to me, "The soldiers will bayonet him."

---

* The Russian words for *poll tax* and for *pillow* are very close in sound.

I felt so bad that I broke down and started to cry. Uncle Nefed looked at my father and said, "Well, what will your sentence be?"

The crowd said, "Into the army with him!"

My father threw up his hands again and said, "That's what I deserve, just don't forget my son."

Then they brought up a cart for him. They put my father in the cart and began to drive off. Mother grabbed Father around the neck and burst into tears. The cart drove off quietly as my mother and my mother's sister Agafya and old Tatyana followed on foot. All of them were crying. I sat on my father's knee. Then we drove to the church, my father and all our relatives prayed to God, and my father made me get down from the cart. We said good-bye; my mother and all our relatives began to burst into sobs and cried all the way home.

When we got home, Grandmother sat by the window and cried, and my mother collapsed on the bench and sobbed until dinnertime. Grandmother tried to calm my mother, saying, "That's enough, Matryona! What are we going to do?" Grandmother sighed. "It was apparently what God wished! Look, you're still young—maybe God will bring him back to you. But me, I'm so old and so sick that I could die any minute."

My mother said, "Mama! Oh, I feel sick, I feel sick!" and she broke down crying.

Then Grandmother said, "Well, what are we going to do now? There's no bringing him back now, you know."

My sister sat on the step in front of the stove and cried: her eyes were red from tears. From that point life became harder, at least three times worse than it had been when father was there: there was nothing to eat, we sold the sheep for bread and we sold my cute little lamb. Only the lopsided mare was left. And then she broke her leg.

II.

A month after my father was sent off to the army, my mother had a baby. Grandmother went for the midwife. Then she borrowed some grain from her father-in-law and sent her son for the priest. She lit a fire in the stove and began to make kasha. My sister went off to gather people for the christening. She brought back people and a loaf of bread. The relatives began to set the table, covering it with a tablecloth. When everything was ready, they brought benches. Everybody took a place by the table. A priest came and read from some sort of book. They handed him the baby boy and filled a tub with water. Then the priest went and thrust the boy into the water. I thought that the priest wanted to drown him and cried out, "Give the boy here!"

But Grandmother slapped me and said, "Don't cry out, or I'll give you a tanning." I quieted down. The priest dipped the baby in the water three times, and then gave him to Aunt Akulina. Auntie cloaked him in calico and gave him to Mother.

Then everyone sat down at the table; Grandmother put out two bowls of kasha for the guests. Everybody began to eat. When everybody had eaten their fill, they got up from the table, thanked my grandmother, and they all left. I went up to my mother and asked, "Ma! What is his name?"

Mother said, "Same as yours." The baby boy was thin, with skinny little legs, and seemed to scream all the time.

Mother said, "Lord, when will this burden end?"

A week passed. Grandmother said, "Well, thank the Lord for the fact that we celebrated his christening." But the boy kept getting weaker and weaker.

My mother started crying about something in the middle of the night. Grandmother got up and said, "What's the matter? Christ is with you!"

Mother said, "My son is dead."

Grandmother lit a fire, washed the boy's body, put a shirt on him, girded him, and laid him in front of the icons. When it became light, Grandmother went out to look for Uncle Nefed and told him what had happened. Uncle Nefed brought some planks and began to make a coffin—he made a little coffin and put the dead boy inside it. Then Mother sat down and began wailing in a thin voice, telling each one of her woes, and she went on crying for a long time. Then Uncle Nefed took the boy and went off to bury him.

III.

The only joy we had came when my sister married. They found her a groom named Kondrashka. When it came time for the two of them to wed, a loaf of white bread was brought, and much vodka. Everyone sat down at the table, my mother as well. Then Uncle Ivan filled a glass with vodka and presented it to my mother. Mother drank it. Then he cut a slice of bread and handed it to her.

I stood by the table. I had a hankering for a piece of bread. I bent Mother down and whispered in her ear. Mother burst out laughing, and Uncle Ivan said, "What does he want? His own little loaf?" And he went and cut me a big slice from the loaf. I then got up and went to the larder with my sister.

Uncle Nefed poured another glass and offered it to Mother. Mother said, "No, I don't want any more." But Uncle Ivan pestered her and my mother finally took the glass and drank it. When everyone had left, Uncle Ivan said, "Well, tomorrow we'll start."

"Fine," Mother said, and Uncle Ivan went home.

I got up early the next morning. I saw that my sister was dressed up in new fur slippers, a fancy dress, and a new fur hat. Then I saw that Mother was also dressed up. She lit a fire in the stove, and Kondrashka's mother was washing some beef to cook. When the house was nice and warm, a lot of people came over, until there was no space left. Then I saw three troikas drive up and the bridegroom Kondrashka appeared in a new caftan and a top hat, and he drove right into our yard. Then the bridegroom got down from the cart and went into the house. They led my sister up to him and he took her by the hand. The two were given places at the table, and then the women honored the guests by thanking them one by one, and the women did this for a long time. Then the two got up from the table, prayed to God, and left the house. They walked out to the troika, and Kondrashka helped my sister up into the cart and then sat next to her. Then they crossed themselves and drove off.

I went out into the street, and I watched them as they galloped off towards the church and disappeared from view. Then I went back into the house, and Mother gave me a little piece of bread. Then I sat by the window waiting for them to come back. I asked my mother, "When will Sister come back?" Then I heard someone yell, "The wedding party's coming!" This cheered me up and I went to look.

I saw a big crowd of people outside the entryway standing there playing some song. "Why were you so long in coming?" I asked. Then the troikas drove up into the yard and the bridegroom got down and lifted my sister out of the cart. They came inside. I wanted to sit at the table, but many people were sitting there, so I sat next to a rolling pin. Then Uncle Gerasim said, "Get away from the table." I got scared and wanted to flee. But Grandmother said, "Show him your rolling pin and say, 'And what's this?' He'll give you money." So I showed him the rolling pin and said, "And what's this?" Gerasim said, "I'll give you a lashing." "And I'll get you with this rolling pin," I said. Then Gerasim poured a glass of vodka and handed it to me with some money. I drank the vodka and took the money. Everyone was given vodka, and then they got up from the table.

Then people started to play songs and to dance. Mother gave me some beef to eat. They handed some vodka to Uncle Gerasim and he drank a little and then pronounced, "Kiss!" My sister grabbed Kondrashka by the ears and they began to kiss. They played music for a long time. When they finally stopped playing the guests all left, and the bridegroom took my sister home with him.

My mother said, "Now our ruin is complete!"

A year passed. We had almost nothing to eat. My mother went and asked the village elder for flour, and after that every month they gave us two pounds of flour. Half a year later my grandmother became very sick. She just lay in bed and kept saying, "Never will I see Gordyei again," and she would cry all the time. Then she would say to my mother, "God be with him. If God grants that he come home, you mustn't quarrel with him."

A month later my grandmother died; my mother was left all alone. They came and lay my grandmother in front of the icons; my mother sat next to her body and began to cry. I remember how my mother cried and said, "Oh, my dearest mother, for whom have you left me, so bitter and ill-starred—what am I going to do? What reason do I have to keep going?" My mother cried like this for a long time. They brought a coffin and put my grandmother in it. They went out to get a priest. The priest came and recited a service for the dead. Then they took her off to bury her. My mother cried all the way to the funeral. When the funeral was over, my mother came home and I saw that she was very pale.

There were only two of us left—my mother and me—and we lived in extreme poverty. Six years had gone by since my father was sent off to the army; I was twelve years old by then. One day my mother sent me out to feed the lopsided mare. I watched over her for a long time. Some soldiers came passing by. I saw that one of them looked a lot like my father. He came up to me and asked, "Where are you from?"

I said, "From Yasnaya."

"So, do you know Matryona Shintyakova?"

I said, "I do."

"Has she married anyone?"

"No."

Then I asked, "Have you seen my father? He's in the army. His name is Gordyei Shintyakov."

"Yes, I've seen him. We served in the same regiment."

Then I noticed tears well up in the soldier's eyes, and he began to cry. I led him to our house. He prayed to God and said, "Hello!" Then he took off his coat, sat on the bench by the door, and began to look around. Then he said to my mother, "Well, is this all the family you've got?"

My mother said, "That's it."

This made the soldier cry, and he asked, "Where is my mother?"

Mother ran up to Father and said, "She died a long time ago."

I ran up and started to kiss Father. My father cried, and in spite of the fact that he was crying, I looked around in his bag and in his pockets. In the bag I found two fine medals, and I slipped them inside my shirt. Then people came and they all began to kiss my father. Father stopped crying and looked at the people, hardly recognizing any of them. Then my sister came and kissed my father.

My father asked, "Whose young woman is this?"

Mother laughed and said, "See, he can't even recognize his own daughter!"

Father called my sister to him again and kissed her, and asked my mother whether Sister had married a long time ago.

My mother said, "Yes, it was a long time ago now."

Then the people went home, all except my sister. Mother lit a fire in the stove and fried up some eggs, and sent my sister with an empty bottle for vodka. She came back with the vodka and set the bottle on the table.

My father said, "What's that?"

My sister said, "Some vodka for you."

Father said, "No, I've given up drinking."

Mother said, "Well, thank God that you've stopped." Then she served us the eggs. My father said a prayer before he sat down at the table. I sat down beside him; Sister sat on the bench, and Mother stood by the table looking at my father. She said, "You know, you look so much younger without your beard." Everyone laughed.

When we had eaten, Sister kissed Father again, and went home. Then Father began to rifle through his bag as Mother and I looked on. Mother saw a little book there, and said: "Oh, you have learned to read?"

Father said, "I have."

Then Father took out a big bundle from his bag and gave it to Mother.

Mother said, "What is this?"

Father said, "Money."

Mother was happy and hastened and carried it away to hide it. Then Mother came back, and said, "Where did you get it?"

Father said, "I was an under-officer and had government money. I gave it to the soldiers, and what was left in my hands, I kept."

My mother was so happy and ran around like a mad person. The day was over, and evening came. They lit a fire. My father took the book and began to read. I sat down near him and listened, and Mother held the torch. Father read the book for a long time. Then we went to bed. I lay down on the back bench with Father, and Mother lay down at our feet, and they talked for a long time, almost till midnight. Then we fell asleep.

In the morning, Mother got up, went over to Father, and said, "Gordyei, get up! I need some wood to make a fire in the stove."

Father got up, dressed himself, put on his cap, and said, "Do you have an ax?"

Mother said, "I have . . . it is notched—maybe it won't cut."

My father took the ax firmly in both hands, walked over to the block of wood, stood it on end, swung the ax with all his might, and split the block; he chopped up some wood and carried it over to the house. Mother lit a fire in the hut and stoked it, and soon it grew light.

After daybreak, my father said: "Matryona!"

My mother came up and said, "Well, what?"

Father said, "I am thinking of buying a cow, five sheep, two horses, and a new house—this one is falling to pieces—well, that will take about 150 rubles."

Mother, lost in thought a while, said, "Well, then we will spend all the money."

Father said, "We will begin to work."

Mother said, "All right, we'll buy all these things, but where will we get the lumber?"

Father said, "Doesn't Kiryukha have any?"

Mother said, "That's the trouble. The Fokanychevs have taken it all."

Father thought a while, and said, "Well, we'll get it from Brantsev."

Mother said, "I doubt if he has any."

Father said, "Why wouldn't he? He's sitting on a forest."

Mother said, "I'm afraid he will ask too much. He's such a beast."

Father said, "I will go to him with some vodka and maybe come to an understanding with him, and you bake an egg in the ashes for dinner."

Mother got some dinner ready—she borrowed from her friends. Father took the vodka and went to Brantsev's, and we sat and waited for a long time. I felt lonely without Father. I began to ask Mother to let me go after Father.

Mother said, "You will lose your way."

I began to cry and wanted to go, but Mother slapped me, and I sat on the stove and cried more than ever. Then I saw Father enter the hut. He came toward me and said, "Why are you crying?"

Mother said, "Fedka wanted to run after you, and I gave him a beating."

Father walked over to me and said, "What are you crying about?"

I began to complain about Mother. Father went up to Mother and pretended to beat her, in jest, saying: "Don't beat Fedya! Don't beat Fedya!"

Mother pretended to cry. I sat down on Father's knees and was happy. Then Father sat down at the table with me at his side, and shouted: "Mother, give Fedka and me something to eat—we're hungry!"

And Mother gave us some beef, and we began to eat. When we were done eating, Mother said, "What about the lumber?"

Father said, "Fifty rubles in silver."

Mother said, "That is not bad."

Father said, "It goes without saying that it's fine lumber."

The School at Yasnaya Polyana

by Leo Tolstoy

A General Sketch of the School's Character

We have no beginners. The youngest class reads, writes, and solves problems in the first three operations of arithmetic, and reads sacred history*, so that the course of study is divided in the following way: 1) reading mechanics and graded reading; 2) writing; 3) penmanship; 4) grammar; 5) sacred history; 6) Russian history; 7) drawing; 8) drafting; 9) singing; 10) mathematics; 11) natural sciences; 12) religion.

Before saying anything about the instruction, I must give a short sketch of what the Yasnaya Polyana school is, and of its current stage of development. Like any living organism, the school not only varies with each year, day, and hour, but also is subject to temporary crises, hardships, illnesses, and bad moods. The Yasnaya Polyana school passed through such a crisis last summer. The causes were many. In the first place, as is always the case, all our best students left us, and we met them only occasionally as they worked in the fields and pastures; second, new teachers had come to the school, and new influences began to be felt; third, all summer long every day brought new visiting teachers who were taking advantage of the summer vacation. Nothing impedes the regular progress of the school more. One way or another, our teachers change their ways for the new audience.

We have four teachers. Two older ones have been teaching in the school for two years, and are accustomed to the students, their work, and to the freedom and the external disorder of the school. The two new teachers—themselves both fresh from school—are lovers of external order—schedules, bells, and so forth—and have yet to grow into the life

---

* Tolstoy uses this term throughout for the class in Bible study.

of the school as have the first two. What for the first two seems reasonable, necessary, unavoidable—like the features of a beloved yet homely child, grown up before one's eyes—to the two new teachers sometimes appears as a failing needing correction.

The school is housed in a two-story stone building. Two rooms are devoted to classrooms, one to an office, and two to the teachers. Under the roof hangs a bell, with a cord attached to the clapper; in the hall downstairs there are parallel and horizontal bars, while in the upstairs hall there is a workbench. The staircase and the floor of the halls are covered with snow or mud; here also hangs the class schedule.

The order of study is as follows: at about eight o'clock in the morning, the teacher who lives at the school—a lover of external order and the school administrator—sends one student, who nearly always stays overnight with him, to ring the bell. In the village, people light fires. From the school, the fires have long been visible in the windows, and half an hour after the bell, in the mist and rain, or in the slanting rays of the autumn sun, dark figures appear by twos and threes, or singly, on the hillocks (the village is separated from the school by a ravine). The students' feeling of being herded up has long since disappeared. There's no need to wait and shout: "Hey, kids! To school with you!" The students know this time that the word *school* is neuter—as are the words for many other sorts of things—and strange to say, for that reason they no longer need a push from the crowd. When the time comes, they just go. It seems to me that each day their personalities are becoming more independent, and this independence is due to the strength of their personalities and the sharpness of their characters. I have never noticed the students playing on their way to school—unless it is one of the youngest, or a student who has just transferred from another school. The children bring nothing with them, neither books nor notebooks. There is no homework.

Not only do they carry nothing in their hands, they carry nothing in their heads. They are obliged to remember not a single lesson, nothing of what they were doing the day before. They are not troubled by the thought of upcoming lessons. They bring only themselves, nothing but their sensitive natures and their belief that school today will be as joyful as it was yesterday. They do not think of their classes until the classes begin. No student is scolded for tardiness, and they never are tardy; except for some of the older ones whose fathers now and then keep them

The Yasnaya Polyana school

home to work. In such cases these older ones arrive at school after running full speed, all out of breath.

If the teacher has not yet arrived, the students gather near the staircase, pushing one another off the steps or skating on the frozen ice of the smooth road, while others go to the classrooms. If it is cold, they read, write, or play.

The girls do not mingle with the boys. When the boys start something with the girls, they never single out one, but address the girls collectively: "Oh, girls, how come you don't skate?" or "The girls, I guess, are frozen," or "Now, girls, all of you against one of me!" Only one of the girls, a girl from the manor about ten years old, with great all-around ability, is beginning to stand out from the herd of girls. This girl alone the boys treat as their equal—as a boy, except for a delicate shade of politeness, condescension, and reserve.

Let us suppose that according to the course schedule the lowest and youngest class first has mechanical reading; second, graded reading; and third, mathematics. The teacher comes into the room, where on the floor lie squealing children, shouting, "The pile is not big enough!" or "Guys, you're crushing me!" or "That's enough! Don't pull my hair!" and so on.

"Petr Mikhailovich!" a voice at the bottom of the heap calls out to the teacher as he enters. "Tell them to stop!"

"Good morning, Petr Mikhailovich!" shout the others, continuing their romp.

The teacher takes the books and gives them to the students who have gone to the bookcase with him. The students lying on top of the pile also ask for books, but without getting up. Little by little the pile becomes smaller. As soon as the majority have books, the rest run to the bookcase and cry out, "Give one to me too! Give me the book from yesterday; give me the 'Koltsovian book' (our name for Koltsov's collected works)!" etc. If there are two left who, all hot from the struggle, are still rolling on the floor, the students sitting with books will yell at them: "Why are you bothering us? We can't hear anything! That's enough!" The excited ones submit, and out of breath, gather up their books. For a brief moment, while sitting at their books, they are still so agitated that they keep swinging their legs. But then the martial spirit takes flight, and the spirit of reading reigns in the room. With the same enthusiasm with which one student was pulling Mitka's hair, he is now reading the Koltsovian book, almost clenching his teeth, his eyes flashing, seeing nothing around him, only his book. To tear him away from reading would take as much effort as it previously took to get him away from fighting.

They sit wherever they like: on benches, tables, the windowsill, the floor, and in the armchair. The girls always sit together. Friends and neighbors from the same village—especially the younger ones (they have the most camaraderie)—always sit next to each other. As soon as one of them decides to sit in one corner, all his friends—who are jostling one another and diving under benches—creep to the same place to sit near him. As they look around, their faces express the kind of happiness and contentment they might as if sitting in those seats would make them happy for the rest of their lives. The large armchair that somehow found its way into the room is the object of envy for the more independent types—the girl from the manor and others. As soon as one of them makes up his mind to sit in the chair, another gleans his intention from his looks, and the two lock horns. One squeezes the other out, and the victor sprawls himself out, his head way below his back, and goes on reading—

like the rest, totally absorbed in reading. During class time I have never noticed any students whispering, pinching their neighbors, giggling, snorting into their hands, or complaining about each other. When a student who has studied with a sexton or a student from a district school comes to us with a complaint, he's told: "Why don't you pinch him back?"

The two lower classes meet in one classroom, while the advanced class goes to the other. The teacher comes. In the lower class, all surround him—at the blackboard, sitting or lying on the benches and tables. If a student is reading, all surround him. If it is a writing lesson, the students seat themselves in a more orderly fashion. Periodically they stand to look over each other's notebooks, or to show their own to the teacher.

According to the course schedule, there are to be four lessons before lunch, but sometimes there are only three or two, and sometimes these are entirely different subjects. The teacher may begin with arithmetic and next go to geometry, or he may start with sacred history and finish with grammar. At times the teacher and students become so absorbed that instead of one hour the class lasts three hours. The students will call out, "More, more!" and yell at the students who are tired of the subject. "If you're tired, go join the babies," they'll cry, contemptuously.

The students all meet together for religion class, the only regularly scheduled class we have because the teacher lives two versts* away and comes only twice a week. All the students also meet together for drawing class. Before these classes the students are animated. There is fighting, shouting, and the most pronounced kind of external disorder: some drag benches from one room to another; some fight; some (the children of the domestic staff) run home for bread, which they roast in the stove; someone is taking something away from someone else; someone is doing gymnastics. Just as with the bustle in the morning, it is much easier to have them calm themselves down to a natural order than it would be to force them to do so. With the present spirit of the school, it would be impossible to stop them physically. The louder the teacher shouts—this actually happened—the louder they shout. His voice only excites them. If you successfully stop them, if you transport them in another direction, the small sea begins to heave less and less as it calms itself. For the most part there is no need to say anything. Drawing class, everybody's favorite,

---

* *Verst*: a Russian measure of distance equivalent to 0.6629 of a mile

starts at noon, when the children are hungry after three hours' work. The benches and tables have to be carried from one room to another, and there is a terrible hubbub; but in spite of this, as soon as the teacher is ready, the students are, too, and if one of them delays the start of class, the others take it out on him.

I should explain myself. In presenting a description of the Yasnaya Polyana school, I do not mean to offer a model of what's needed and what is good for a school, but simply to furnish a true description of the school. I assume that such descriptions have their use. If I succeed in the following numbers [of the journal, *Yasnaya Polyana*] in presenting a clear account of the school's evolution, it will become understandable to the reader why the present character of the school is as it is, why I regard this order to be good, and why it would be absolutely impossible for me to change it even if I wanted to. The school has evolved freely from the principles introduced into it by teachers and students. In spite of the predominant influence of the teacher, the student has always had the right not to come to school, and—if he or she does come—the right not to listen to the teacher. The teacher has the right not to admit a student, and can bring to bear all the force of his influence on the students, or the society surrounding that student—in other words, the other schoolchildren.

The farther the students progress, the more the teaching branches out, and the more necessary the need for order becomes. Because of this, in the normal, noncompulsory development of the school, the more educated the students become, the more capable of order they become and the more strongly they themselves feel a demand for it, and the greater the teacher's influence on them is in this regard. In the Yasnaya Polyana school this rule has always been confirmed—constantly, from the day of its founding. At first it was impossible to subdivide things into classes, subjects, recess, or lessons: everything naturally blended together, and all efforts at separation proved futile. Now we have students in the lower class who demand that the program be adhered to, who are unhappy when they are disturbed in their lessons, and who constantly shoo away the little children who run in when they are working.

In my opinion, this external disorder is useful and shouldn't be changed, however strange and inconvenient it might seem to the teacher. I often find myself talking about the advantages of our system. About the supposed inconveniences I'll say the following. First, this disorder, this free order, seems terrible to us only because we are accustomed to something quite different—so have we been educated. Second, in this and in many other cases, force is used only due to haste and to a lack of sufficient respect for human nature. We think that the disorder is growing greater and greater and that it has no limits—it seems we have no other means of stopping it except the use of force—whereas we only need to wait a little, and the disorder (or animation) calms down naturally, by itself, growing into an order much better and more solid than what we might have come up with.

Schoolchildren—small though they are—are people, and as people they have the same needs we do, and they follow the same trains of thought. They all want to learn, and come to school for this reason alone, and so they will naturally arrive at the conclusion that they must submit to certain conditions in order to learn. Although they are little people, they form a social unit, united by one idea. "And where three are gathered in the Lord's name, there shall the Lord be with them!" When they submit only to natural laws, such as result from their natures, they do not revolt and grumble, but when they submit to your premeditated interference, they will not believe in the legality of your bells, schedules, and regulations.

How often have I seen, when children fight, the teacher rush up to tear them apart, and this only makes the separated enemies glare at each other. But even the presence of a stern teacher does not prevent them from rushing at each other to inflict a still more painful kick! How often do I see some Kiryushka, with clenched teeth, fly at Taraska, pull his hair, knock him down, trying if it costs him his life to maim his enemy—and a minute later, Taraska is laughing with Kiryushka on top of him. It is so much easier to square accounts in a personal way: less than five minutes have passed and the two are fast friends sitting next to each other.

The other day, between classes, two boys got into a fistfight in the corner: one, about nine years old, a remarkable mathematician in the second class; the other, a short-haired manorial servant's son, an intelligent but vengeful, tiny, black-eyed boy nicknamed Kyska (Kitty). Kyska had grabbed the mathematician's long hair and jammed his head against the wall; the mathematician in vain tried to get hold of Kyska's closely cropped bristles. Kyska's little black eyes were triumphant; the mathematician could scarcely restrain his tears and kept saying: "Well, well! What? What?" He was obviously in a bad way, and trying to find a way to screw up his courage. This lasted for quite a while, and I was in a

A drawing by one of the Yasnaya Polyana students. The figure on far left is Tolstoy; the culprit in these shenanigans is the student called Taraska.

quandary as to what to do. "They're fighting, they're fighting!" the boys shouted, crowding around. The smaller boys laughed, while the big ones—without separating the two combatants—exchanged serious looks. This, combined with the silence, did not escape Kyska. He understood that he was doing something bad. He began to smile criminally, and gradually let go of the mathematician's hair.

The mathematician got away, and pushed Kyska so that he fell, hitting the back of his head against the wall. The mathematician walked away satisfied. Kyska burst into tears, made after his enemy, and punched him with all his might. The blow landed harmlessly on his fur coat. The mathematician wanted to pay Kyska back, but just then several disapproving voices were heard.

"Well, he's fighting a little guy!" cried the spectators. "Run, Kyska!"

The matter ended thus, and it was as though it never happened, except, I suppose, for the fact that both were left with the dim consciousness that fighting is unpleasant, because it caused both pain.

It struck me that I had observed here the sentiment of justice that guides a crowd. How often such matters are settled and you don't know on the basis of what law, and yet the settlement satisfies both sides. How arbitrary and unjust in comparison are all the usual educational methods used in such cases!

"You are both guilty, get down on your knees!" says the educator, and the educator is wrong because one of them is guilty and that guilty one is now victorious. And as he kneels and chews on his pent-up rage, the innocent one is doubly punished.

Alternatively, "You are guilty of having done this or that, and you will be punished," says the educator, and the punished boy hates his enemy that much more, because the despotic power of the teacher, whose legal authority he does not recognize, is on the side of his foe.

Or, "Forgive him, as God commands, and be better than he," says the educator. You say to the student: "Be better than him. He just wants to be stronger—you be better."

Or, "Both of you are wrong: ask each other's forgiveness and kiss and make up, children!" This is worst of all, on account of the lie and the artificiality of the kiss, and because the quieted bad feeling only flares up anew.

Leave them alone if you are not a father or a mother sorry for your child, and therefore always right when you pull away by the hair the one who has given your son a beating. Leave them alone and see how clear and manageable everything will become, while at the same time complicated and various, like all unconscious relations in life. It may be that teachers inexperienced in such disorder, or free order, will think that without the teacher's interference such disorder may result in physical injury, and so forth. In the Yasnaya Polyana school there have been only two cases of injury since last spring. One boy was pushed down the steps and skinned his leg to the bone (the wound healed up in two weeks), and another boy's cheek was scorched by burning rubber, and the burn healed in two weeks. No more often than once a week does somebody start crying, and then not from pain but from anger or shame. With the exception of these two cases, we cannot recall any beatings, bruises, or bumps for the whole summer among the thirty or forty students left on their own.

I am convinced that the school should not interfere in matters of education that belong to the family; that the school does not and should not have the right to reward and punish; that the best policy and administration of a school consists in granting students full freedom to study, and to settle their disputes as they see fit. I am convinced of this, and yet, in spite of it, the old habits of the educational schools are so strong in us that we frequently depart from this rule in the Yasnaya Polyana school. Last semester, in November, there were two cases of punishment.

During drawing class, the incoming teacher noticed a boy who was shouting and furiously striking his neighbors without cause. Not finding it possible to calm the boy with words, the teacher ordered him out of his seat and took away his slate—that was his punishment. During the rest of the lesson the boy was bathed in tears. This was the very boy whom I had not admitted when the Yasnaya Polyana school first opened—I had considered him a hopeless idiot. The boy's main characteristics were obtuseness and meekness. His mates never let him in their games, laughed and mocked him, and would say with surprise: "What an oddball Petka is! If you hit him—even the little fellows hit him—he just picks himself up and walks away."

"He has no heart at all," one boy said to me.

If such a boy as Petka had been driven to such rage that the teacher was forced to punish him for it, the punished boy was certainly not the guilty party.

Another case: in the summer, while the school building was being renovated, a Leyden jar disappeared from the storage closet. Later, some pencils and books disappeared when there were no longer any carpenters or painters working in the building. We asked the students: the best ones, those who had been with us the longest, our oldest friends, blushed and looked so timid that any examining magistrate would have taken their embarrassment for certain proof of their guilt. But I knew them, and could vouch for them as for myself. I understood that the notion that they were suspects offended them, deeply and painfully. A boy whom I will call Fyodor, talented and tender by nature, was all pale, and he trembled and wept. They promised to tell me when they found out who did it, but they refused to make a search.

A few days later the thief was revealed: a manorial boy from a distant village. He had used his influence on a peasant boy from the same village as he, and the two had hidden the stolen objects in a small trunk. The discovery of the crime produced a strange effect on the others: something like relief and even joy, but, with these feelings, contempt and compassion for the thief. We proposed that the students should choose the punishment. Some demanded that the thief be flogged, but that they themselves should do it. Others said that a label with the inscription *thief* be sewn on his clothes. This punishment, to our shame, had been used by us earlier, and the very boy who had the year before worn the label *liar* was the most persistent in this demand. We agreed on this punishment, and while a girl sewed it on, the students all watched the punished boys with evil joy, and made fun of them. They demanded that the punishment be intensified: "Take them through the village! They can keep the labels on until the holidays."

The punished boys wept. The peasant boy, who had been swayed by his comrade—a talented storyteller and joker—was a white-skinned, chunky little tot. He cried his heart out. The other, the main culprit, a hook-nosed boy with a plain-featured yet an intelligent face, was pale. His lips trembled; his eyes looked wildly and spitefully about at the jubilant crowd. Now and then his face became unnaturally distorted, as if on the verge of tears. His cap, its peak torn, was set on the back of his head. His hair was disheveled, and his clothes were dusted with chalk. All this wounded me and everybody else as much as if we were experiencing this type of behavior for the very first time. The whole group's hostile attention was focused on the thief. He was painfully conscious of this. As he walked home—head bent, eyes to the ground, with a peculiarly criminal gait, I thought—the crowd of children ran after him, teasing him in a somehow unnaturally and strangely cruel manner. It was as if an evil spirit were leading them, against their will, and something told me it was not good. But the matter stayed as it was, and the thief wore the label for a whole day. From that time on, it appeared, the punished boy studied poorly, and he was no longer involved in games and conversations with his mates outside of class.

Some time later I came into the classroom, and the students all with certain horror announced to me that the boy had stolen again. He had taken twenty copper kopecks from the teachers' room and had been caught when he tried to hide the money under the stairs. We again hung a label on him, and the monstrous scenario began all over again. I began to admonish Petka, in the way that all educators admonish. A much older student was present at the scene, a big talker, and he began to admonish Petka as well, repeating words which he no doubt had heard from his father, a *dvornik*.* "You steal once, you steal twice," he said smoothly and gravely. "It becomes a habit, and leads to no good." I began to feel

---

* *Dvornik*: a peasant who worked a groundskeeper on an estate of the nobility. A *dvornik* had somewhat higher status than common laborer.

annoyed. I felt almost rage toward the thief. I looked at the face of the punished boy, now even paler, showing more and more cruelty. For some reason I recalled convicts I had seen and suddenly felt such shame and disgust that I tore off the stupid label, told the boy to go wherever he pleased, and suddenly I was convinced—not by reason, but with my whole being—that I did not have the right to torment the unfortunate boy and that I couldn't treat him the way the *dvornik*'s son and I wanted to treat him. I was convinced that there are secrets of the soul, hidden from us, which only life can spur to action, not "morality lessons" or punishments.

What bosh! The boy had stolen a book. By a whole, complicated road of feelings, thoughts, and erroneous conclusions, he had been led to take a book belonging to someone else, that he for some reason locked up in a chest—and I stuck a piece of paper on him with the word *thief*, which means something altogether different! For what? What is shame? To punish him by shaming him, they'll tell me. To punish him by shaming him? What for? What is shame? Is it really known that shame destroys the inclination to steal? Maybe it encourages it. Maybe what showed on his face was not shame. Indeed, I know for certain that it was not shame, but something quite different, which might have always slept in his soul, and which there was no need to evoke. Maybe there, in the world—the "real world," the world of the Palmerstons, Cayenne*—in the world where what is unreasonable is reasonable, that which is real is, well. . . . Let the people who are themselves punished invent the rights and obligations of punishment. Our world of children—of simple, independent people—must remain pure, free from self-deception and the criminal faith in the legality of punishment, the self-deception of believing that the feeling of revenge becomes justified as soon as you call it punishment.

Let us continue with the description of the daily order of instruction. At about two o'clock the hungry children run home. In spite of their hunger, they linger a few minutes to find out what grades they received. At the present time grades don't give anyone precedence, but they do occupy the students a great deal.

"I have five plus, and Olgushka got a big, fat zero! And I got four!" they shout.

---

* *Palmerstons, Cayenne*: reference unknown. Our best guess is that Cayenne may refer to French Guyana and its penal colonies, and that the Palmerstons may a criminal gang.—*Ed.*

Grades are, for the students, a measure of their work, and the students express dissatisfaction with grades only when they believe a grade has been given unfairly. There is trouble when a student has tried hard, and a teacher, by oversight, gives him or her a lower grade than he or she deserves. That student will not give the teacher any peace and will weep bitter tears if he or she cannot get the teacher to change it. When deserved, bad marks remain without protest. Grades, by the way, are left with us only from the old ways, and are beginning to fall into disuse.

For the first lesson after lunch recess the students assemble just as they do in the morning, waiting for the teacher in just the same way. This first lesson is generally in sacred or Russian history, for which students of all levels meet together. This lesson generally begins at dusk. The teacher stands or sits down in the middle of the room, and the crowd gathers around him as if forming an amphitheater—some students on benches, some on tables, some on windowsills.

All the evening lessons, especially this first one, have a peculiar character of calm, dreaminess, and poetry distinctly different from the morning classes. You come to the school at twilight: no lights are visible in the windows and it is almost quiet. Only the fresh tracks of snow on the stairs, a weak rumble stirring beyond the door, and some kid clinging to the staircase, going up two steps at a time while clutching the banister, prove the students really are at the school. You walk into the room. It is already dark behind the frozen windows; the best students are jammed together near the teacher. Lifting up their little heads, the good ones look straight in the teacher's mouth. The independent manorial girl always sits with an anxious face on the high table—and, it seems, swallows every word. The weaker students, the small fry, sit farther away. They listen attentively, even seriously, and behave just like the big kids, but in spite of this attention, we know that they will not be able to relate a single thing the next day, even though they will remember some things. Some press on others' shoulders, and some actually stand up on the table. Occasionally one pushes his way into the very center of the crowd, where he busies himself with drawing some sort of figures with his nail on somebody's back. Seldom will one of them look back at you. When the teacher is telling a new story, all listen in silence; when there is a review for a test, ambitious voices are heard here and there, unable to resist helping the teacher out. By the way, if there is an old story they like, they ask the teacher to repeat it all in his own words, and won't let anyone interrupt him. "What is the matter with you? Can't you hold it in? Keep quiet!" they will call out to the upstart. Interruptions of the character and the artistic quality of the teacher's story are painful for them. Lately, this story has been that of Christ's life. Each time, they asked to have the whole story told to them. If this whole story is not told to them, they themselves supply their favorite ending: the episode of Peter denying Christ, and of the Savior's passion.

You would think they were all dead. There is not a stir—have they fallen asleep? You walk up to them in the semidarkness and look some little fellow in the face—he sits there, his eyes drinking in the teacher, brows furrowed in concentration. For the tenth time he brushes away the arm of his companion, which is pressing down on his shoulder. You tickle his neck, he does not even smile; he moves his head, as though to chase away a fly, and again returns to the mysterious and poetic story: how the veil of the church was torn and it was made dark on earth—and he feels both dread and joy.

But the teacher has finished the story, and all rise from their places. Crowding around the teacher, they try to outshout one another in the effort to tell everyone else what they have retained. The clamor increases—it takes all the teacher's strength to follow them all. Some students are forbidden to talk, because the teacher is sure that they have understood everything. But these students are not satisfied: they approach the teacher, and if he has gone they approach one of their mates, or a stranger, or even the man who stokes the fire—walking from corner to corner in twos and threes they beg everybody to listen to them. It is rare for only one to retell the story. They divide themselves up into groups according to the strength of their voices, and tell the stories together, encouraging and correcting one another, and waiting their individual turns. "Come on, let's do it together," says one to another, but one knows the first can't keep up, so that student goes to another group. As soon as they have had their say, they quiet down. Lights are brought, and a different mood comes over the children.

Generally in the evenings, and in the lessons that follow this first one, the shouting and hubbub is less, and the teacher's authority and confidence are much greater. The students' distaste for mathematics and analysis is especially evident, as is their passion for singing, reading, and, most of all, stories. "What's the use of doing mathematics and writing? Better to tell us a story, about the earth or even history, and we will listen," they say. At about eight o'clock eyes begin to get heavy; the children begin to yawn; the candles burn more dimly—they are seldom trimmed. The older children prop themselves up, but the younger, less astute ones doze off, leaning their elbows on the table, to the pleasant sound of the teacher's voice.

Sometimes, when though the classes are interesting there have been too great number of them (sometimes classes last seven long hours a day) and the children are tired—or before the holidays, when at home the ovens are readied for a steam bath—suddenly, without saying a word, two or three boys will suddenly rush into the room during the second or third afternoon class-hour, hurriedly collecting their caps.

"What's up?"

"Going home."

"What about the lesson? There's still singing class!"

"But the kids say they are going home," says one, slipping away with his cap.

"But who says so?"

"The kids are gone!"

"How is that?" asks the perplexed teacher, having prepared the lesson. "Stay!"

But another boy runs into the room, with an excited and anxious face.

"What are you staying here for?" this boy angrily attacks the one staying back, who, indecisive, pushes the cotton batting back into his cap. "The boys are way down there—I guess as far as the smithy."

"They've gone?"

"They have."

And both run away, yelling from behind the door: "Goodbye, Ivan Ivanovich!"

And who are these boys who decided to go home, and how did they decide to? God knows. Who they are exactly never will be revealed. They did not come to a quorum, did not conspire, but some boys simply wanted to go home. "The kids are going!"—and their feet rattle on the stairs and one rolls down the steps like a cat, leaping and tumbling in the snow. Racing with one another along the narrow path, the children bolt for home.

Such occurrences take place once or twice a week. They are aggravating and disagreeable for the teacher—who will not admit that? But at the same time who will not admit that due to these events the five, six, and even seven lessons a day for each class—which the students attend of their own accord and with pleasure—take on that much more significance? Only by the recurrence of these cases can one be certain that the instruction, however insufficient and one-sided, is not entirely bad or harmful. If the question were put like this: Which would be better, that one such occurrence should not take place the whole year, or that this should happen for more than half the lessons?—we would choose the latter. I, for one, have always been glad to see these things happen several times a month at the Yasnaya Polyana school. In spite of the frequently repeated statements to the students that they may leave anytime they wish, the influence of the teacher is so strong that, of late, I have been afraid that the discipline of the classes, schedules, and grades might, imperceptibly to the students, so restrict their liberty that they would submit to the cunning of the nets of order set by us, and that they may lose their right to choice and protest. Their continued willingness to come to school, in spite of the liberty not to come, does not, I think, by any means prove the special qualities of the Yasnaya Polyana school—I think the same thing would be evident in the majority of schools, and that the desire to study is so strong in children that in order to satisfy it they will submit to many hard conditions and will forgive many shortcomings. The possibility of such escapades is useful and necessary as a means of insuring that the teacher doesn't fall into the worst and coarsest errors and abuses.

In the evening we have singing, graded reading, discussions, physics experiments, and composition. Of these, their favorite subjects are reading and experiments. During reading, the older ones find room on the large, star-shaped table—they lie with their heads together, feet apart—one reads and the others all narrate the text to each other. The younger children plant themselves in twos with their books, and if they can understand the text, they read it as we do—by getting close to the light and making themselves comfortable—and apparently they get pleasure from this. Some, trying to unite two kinds of enjoyment, seat themselves opposite the burning stove, warming themselves while they read. Not all are permitted to participate in the physics experiments, only the oldest and best, and the most intelligent students from the younger class. This lesson has assumed for us a most nocturnal and fantastic character, very close to the mood produced by reading fairy tales. Here the fairy-tale element becomes real, everything becomes personified for the students: the pith-ball* that is

---

* *Pith ball*: This is the Russian. What exactly this *pith ball* is, we do not know.—*Trans. and Ed.*

repelled by the sealing wax, the deflecting magnetic needle, the iron filings scurrying over the sheet of paper underneath which the magnet is
guided. These present themselves to the students as living creatures. The
most intelligent ones, who understand the cause of these phenomena,
become excited and talk to the needle, the ball, and the filings: "Come on,
you! Where are you going? Hold on! Off! Roll it!" and so on.

Generally the classes end around eight or nine o'clock, if woodshop
does not keep the boys longer, and then the band of them runs shouting
into the yard, and from there they begin scattering in groups to all corners of the village, calling to one another from a distance. Sometimes
they undertake to ride into town on the large sleighs that stand by the
gate. Hitching up the sleighs, they crawl in and disappear screaming into
snowdrifts, leaving here and there along the road the black spots of children who have tumbled out. Outside the school, in the open air, new relations between the students and teachers establish themselves, despite all
the liberties granted the students in school. The greater liberty, simplicity, and trust between the students and teachers outside the school are
our ideal for what we should strive for *in* the school.

Recently we read Gogol's "Elf-king" with the oldest class. The last
scenes had a powerful effect on them and stirred up their imagination.
Several in the crowd tried to look like witches, recalling the previous
night.

It had not been not cold out—a moonless winter night with clouds in
the sky. We stopped at the crossroads. The older, third-year students
stopped near me, inviting me to accompany them further; the younger
ones looked at me a while and sped downhill. The younger ones had
begun to study with a new teacher, and I no longer had the rapport with
them that I had with the older boys.

"Come on, let's go to the preserve (a small forest some two hundred
paces from the house)," said one of them. Fedka, a small boy of ten with
a tender, impressionable, poetic, and bold nature, was the most persistent in his demands. Danger seems to be his main recipe for enjoyment.
In the summer it always made me shudder to see him swim out to the
very middle of the pond, which is some 350 feet wide, with two other
boys, and now and then disappear in the hot reflections of the summer
sun. Fedka would then swim over the deepest part, turning on his back
and sending up a spout of water, calling out in a thin voice to his companions on the shore so that they could see what a fine fellow he is.

Fedka knew that there were wolves in the forest, and therefore he wanted to go to the preserve. The others chimed in, and so the four of us headed off to the forest. Another boy, who I'll call Semka—a lad of about twelve, healthy both morally and physically, who goes by the nickname of Vavilo—walked ahead and kept calling to someone in the distance in ahigh, shrill voice. Pronka, a sickly, meek, and exceptionally talented boy—the son of a poor family andsickly, I think, mainly due to an insufficient diet—walked alongside me.

Fedka was walking between Semka and me, talking away in his extremely soft voice, first telling us how in the summer he had watched over some horse here and then saying that he was not afraid of anything. "Suppose something should jump out at us?" he asked, insisting that I answer. We did not go into the forest itself—that would have been too scary—but even at the forest's edge it had become darker. We could hardly see the path, and lights in the village were hidden from view.

Semka stopped and began to listen closely. "Stop, boys! What is that?" he said suddenly.

We grew silent, but nothing was audible; nonetheless, our fear increased.

"Well, what would we do if a wolf jumped out and came right at us?" Fedka asked.

We began to talk about robbers in the Caucasus. They recalled a story about the Caucasus I had told them long before, about the Abreks, the Cossacks, and Hadji Murad. Semka went ahead of us, taking long steps in his big boots and evenly swaying his strong back. Pronka tried to walk beside me, but Fedka pushed him off the path. Pronka, who probably always submitted to such treatment on account of his poverty, ran up alongside me only during the most interesting passages, even though he sank knee-deep in the snow as he did this.

Anyone who knows anything about peasant children has noticed that they are not accustomed to any kind of affection—tender words, kisses, being touched, and so on. I happened to see a lady in a peasant school who, wishing to treat a peasant boy kindly, said, "Come, darling, let me kiss you!" She actually kissed him, and the kissed boy was so embarrassed and offended because he couldn't fathom why this should be done to him. A boy of five years of age is above these caresses—he is already a "lad." Therefore I was quite struck when Fedka, walking by my side, suddenly

A winter view of Yasnaya Polyana village

touched me during the scariest part of the story, first lightly, then holding two of my fingers with his whole hand. He would not let them go. The moment I grew silent, Fedka demanded that I keep talking, and he did this in such an imploring and agitated voice that I could not help but give in to his wish.

At one point Fedka yelled, "Don't get in my way!" at Pronka, who had run ahead. He had become carried away to the point of cruelty. He felt both terror and joy as he held onto my fingers, and no one should dare interrupt his pleasure.

"Come on, more, more! That's right!"

We passed the forest and began to approach the village from the other end.

"Let's go farther," all cried when the lights of the village became visible. "Let's keep going!"

We walked in silence, now and then sinking in the loose, untrodden path. The white darkness seemed to sway before our eyes; the clouds were low, as though falling upon us. There was no end to the whiteness on which we crunched alone through the snow. The wind rustled through the bare tops of the aspens, but where we were, behind the forest, it was quiet.

I finished my story with the Abrek being surrounded, beginning to sing songs, and then throwing himself on his dagger. All were silent.

"Why did he begin singing when they surrounded him?" asked Semka.

"Didn't you hear? He was getting ready to die!" Fedka replied dolefully.

"I think it was a prayer he sang," added Pronka.

All agreed. Fedka suddenly stopped. "How was it you said they cut your aunt's throat?"* he asked, having not had enough terror for one day. "Tell us! Tell us!"

I told them once more the terrible story of the murder of Countess Tolstoy, and they stood silently around me, gazing into my face.

"The fellow got caught!" said Semka.

"It must have really frightened him to walk through the night, while she lay with her throat cut," said Fedka. "I would have run away!" and his grip moved up on my two fingers.

We stopped in the grove beyond the threshing floors at the end of the village. Semka picked up a stick from the snow and began hitting the frozen trunk of a linden tree with it. The hoarfrost fell off the branches onto his cap, and the lonely banging resounded through the forest.

"Lev Nikolaevich," said Fedka (I thought he wanted to say something about the countess), "why do people learn singing? I often really wonder why they sing."

God knows what made him leapfrog from the terrors of murder to this question, but through everything—the sound of his voice, the seriousness with which he wanted an answer, the silent interest of the other two boys—I could feel a real and legitimate connection between this question and the previous conversation. Whether or not the connection consisted in my explaining the possibility of crime from ignorance (I had talked to them about this), and Fedka's act of transferring himself into the murderer's soul and then recalling his own favorite occupation (Fedka has a charming voice and immense musical talent), or whether the connection consisted in his feeling that the time had come for the conversation to

---

* Avdotya Maximovna, Tolstoy's aunt, had been murdered by her serf cook in 1861.

become heartfelt and that in his soul questions were bubbling up demanding solutions, Fedka's question did not surprise any of us.

"What is drawing for? And what is the good of writing?" I asked, positively not knowing how to explain to him what art is for.

"What is drawing for?" Fedka repeated thoughtfully. He was actually asking me what art is for. I did not dare and did not know how to explain it to him.

"What is drawing for?" said Semka. "You draw everything, so you know how to make things from it."

"No, that's drafting," said Fedka. "But why do you draw figures?"

Semka's healthy nature was not at a loss: "What is a stick for? What is a linden for?" he asked, still hitting the linden tree with his stick.

"Yes, what is a linden tree for?" I asked.

"To make rafters with," replied Semka.

"What is it for in the summer, when it has not yet been cut down?"

"For nothing."

"No, really," Fedka kept at it, "why does a linden grow?" And we began to talk about how there is a usefulness to things, and about how there is also beauty and how art is beauty, and we all understood each other, and Fedka understood fully why a linden grows and why people sin. Pronka agreed with us, but he understood beauty in more moral terms—as goodness. Semka, with his great intelligence, understood correctly, but did not see beauty without usefulness. He was dubious. This often happens with people of great intelligence who feel that art is a force, but at the same time feel in their souls no need of that force. Like them, Semka wanted to approach art with his intellect, and he tried to start the fire [of art] in himself by himself.

"Let's sing 'He Who' [a hymn] tomorrow. I remember my part," said Semka. Semka has a fine ear, but no taste or gracefulness in his singing.

Fedka understood completely that the linden is beautiful because of its leafiness, and that it is pleasing to look at in summer—and apart from that, nothing else is needed. Pronka understood that it is a shame to cut down a linden, because like us it is alive: "Drinking birch sap is just the same as drinking blood." Semka said almost nothing, but made it clear that he did not think there was much use in a linden when it is rotten.

It feels strange to me to repeat what we said on that evening, but I remember we talked through everything, it seemed to me, there is to say on the subjects of utility and of physical and moral beauty.

We headed for the village. Fedka had not let go of my hand—from gratitude, I thought. We were so close to one another that night, as we had not been for some time. Pronka walked beside us along the wide village street.

"Gosh, a light is still burning in Mazanov's house!" Pronka said. "As I was going to school today, Gavryukha was coming from the tavern," he added, "drunk, beyond drunk! The horse was all in a lather and he kept tanning her hide—these things always make me feel sorry. They do! What does he beat her for?"

"The other day Father gave his horse free rein, coming from Tula," said Semka, "and the horse took him into a snowdrift, but he was drunk and asleep."

"Gavryukha kept whipping her across the eyes. I felt so sorry," Pronka said again. "What did he beat her for? He got down and whipped her."

Semka suddenly stopped.

"They are asleep," he said, looking through the windows of the black, crooked hut where he lived. "Won't you walk a little more?"

"No."

"Goooood-bye, Lev Nikolaevich!" Semka suddenly shouted, and, as though forcibly tearing himself away from us, he ran for his house quick as a lynx, raised the latch, and disappeared.

"So you will take us home? First one, then the other?" asked Fedka.

We walked on. In Pronka's house there was a light on. We looked through the window: his mother, a tall, beautiful, but haggard-looking woman with black brows and eyes, was sitting at the table and cleaning potatoes. In the middle of the room hung a candle; one of Pronka's brothers, the mathematician in the upper class, was standing at the table, eating potatoes with salt. The hut was tiny, dirty, and black.

"So you're not lost after all!" the mother yelled at Pronka. "Where have you been?"

Pronka gave a meek, sickly smile while looking at the window. The mother guessed that he was not alone, and immediately changed her natural expression to a poorly feigned one.

Now only Fedka was left.

"The tailors are at our house, so there is a light on," he said in the soft voice he had used that evening. "Good-bye, Lev Nikolaevich!" he added softly and tenderly, and began to knock with the ring on the locked door. "Let me in!" his thin voice rang out through the winter quiet of the village.

A long time passed before they let him in. I glanced through the window. The hut was a large one. Legs and feet could be seen on the stove and on the benches. His father was playing cards with the tailors—some copper coins were lying on the table. A woman, the boy's stepmother, was sitting near the torch-stand, looking greedily at the money. One tailor, a real scoundrel, held his cards on the table, bending them like bark and looking triumphantly at his partner. Fedka's father, his collar unbuttoned, was scowling from the mental strain and vexation, fumbling with his cards in indecision and waving his toughened peasant hand over them.

"Let me in!" Fedka called.

The woman got up and went to open the door.

"Good-bye!" Fedka said once more. "Let's always take walks like that."

* * * *

I see honest, good, liberal men, members of charitable societies, who are ready to give and do give one-hundredth of their fortunes to the poor, who have established schools, and who, reading this, will say, "It is no good," and shake their heads. "Why develop them forcibly? Why give them feelings and understandings that will make them hostile to their surroundings? Why take them out of their own way of life?" they will say. I am talking about those who regard themselves as leaders, and who will say, "A fine state it will be, when everybody wants to be thinkers and artists, and nobody wants to be a worker."

It should be said straightaway that people do not like to work, and that therefore there must be people who act as slaves, working for the rest of society. Is it good, is it bad, is it necessary to lead the working people out of the conditions they live under? Who knows? And who can lead them out of their surroundings? This can hardly be achieved by rote, or by a simple recipe. Is it good to add sugar to flour, or pepper to beer?

Fedka does not feel burdened by his ragged little caftan, but moral questions and doubts torment him, and you want to give Fedka three rubles, a catechism, and a tract on the usefulness of labor, and the humility that you yourselves cannot tolerate. He does not need the three rubles: he will find and take them when he needs them. And he will learn to work without your help, just as he has learned to breathe. He needs what life has brought you, your own life and that of ten generations not crushed by work. You have been able to seek out leisure, to seek, think, suffer—so give him the things you have gained by suffering, that is what he wants. But you, like an Egyptian priest, hide yourselves from him in a secretive veil and bury in the ground the talents that history has passed down to you. Fear not: nothing human is injurious to man. Do you doubt this? Give yourselves up to your feelings, and they will not deceive you. Have faith in Fedka's nature, and you will become convinced that he will only take in as much as history has enjoined you to give him, the benefits of what years of suffering and experience have worked in you.

The school is free, and the first students to enter were from the village of Yasnaya Polyana. Many of these students have left the school because their parents did not consider the instruction to be good; many, having learned to read and write, stopped coming and began working for the railroad (the chief line of work in our village). Children were brought from other, poorer villages nearby, but because of the inconvenience of travel and of board (in our village, the minimum is two silver rubles a month), they were soon taken out of our school. From farther villages, some well-off peasants, flattered by the fact that the school was free and by the rumors circulating that the teachers were very good at the Yasnaya Polyana school, began to send their children. But this winter, when schools were opened in the villages, these parents took their children out again and put them in the local schools, which charge tuition. This left in the Yasnaya Polyana school the children of the Yasnaya Polyana peasants—who come to school in winter, but who, in summer, from April to mid-October, work in the fields—and the children of the estate groundskeepers, clerks, soldiers, manorial servants, tavernkeepers, sextons, and rich peasants, who are brought from a distance of thirty and even fifty versts.

In all there are about forty students, but rarely more than thirty come at a time. The girls are ten years old and account for only six [actually fifteen—*Ed.*] percent of the student body, as we have only five or six of them.

Boys age seven to thirteen are the norm. In addition to these, every year we have three or four adult students who come to us for a month and sometimes the whole winter, and then leave. For these adult students, who come to school one at a time, the school's lack of order is very inconvenient: on account of their years and their feeling of dignity, they cannot take part in the school's animation, nor can they free themselves of their contempt for the youngsters, and so they remain entirely alone. The school's animated nature is what really impedes them. They generally come to finish a course of instruction begun elsewhere, having some knowledge under their belts and the conviction that learning is essentially rote learning—which they have heard somewhere, and with which they have experience. In order to come to school, they had to overcome their own fear and embarrassment, and to endure family quarrels and the scorn of their mates. "Look at the gelding, going to study!" On top of this, they feel that every day spent at school is a day of work lost—a loss of livelihood—and so the whole time they are at school, they are in an irritable state of haste and zeal, which is more detrimental to study than anything else.

During the time I am writing about, we had three adult students, of whom one is studying now. An adult student is like someone whose head is on fire: the moment he finishes writing he puts his pen down with one hand and grabs a book with the other. He begins to read while standing up; take the book away from him, and he picks up the slate; take that away from him, and he is completely at a loss. There was one laborer who studied with us this fall, and at the same time tended the fires at the school. He learned to read and write in two weeks, but this was not learning but a disease, a kind of binge. Passing through the classroom with an armload of wood, he would stop with the wood still in his arms, bend over a boy's head and spell *s, k, a—ska,* and then go to his place. If he made a mistake, he looked at the children with envy, almost with malice. When he was free just to study, we could not do anything with him: he clung hard to the book, repeating *b, a—ba, r, i—ri,* and so forth, over and over, and in this state he lost all ability to learn anything else. When these adult students had to sing or draw, or listen to a history lecture or watch science experiments, it was apparent that they were submitting to cruel necessity, and they waited like starving people torn away from their food for the moment they could once again seize their spelling books. Remaining true to the rule, I have not forced the children to study ABC when they do not want to, and so I do not insist that a grown person learn drafting when in fact he wants to do ABC's. Each takes what he or she wants.

In general, the adults, who started their studies elsewhere, have not yet found a place for themselves in the Yasnaya Polyana school, and their instruction proceeds poorly: there is something morbid and unnatural in their relationship to the school. I have seen the same phenomenon with adult students in Sunday schools, and so any information regarding the successful free education of adults would be a very precious acquisition for us.

The popular view of our school has changed a great deal since its beginning. To speak of earlier days we would have to discuss the history of the school; these days people say that in the Yasnaya Polyana school, "They teach everything and all the sciences, and there are some awfully smart teachers there—they say they can make thunder and lightning! What's more, the children learn well—they have begun to read and write." Some of them—rich workmen from nearby estates—send their children to school out of vanity, "to enroll them in the full science, so that they may practice division" (division in arithmetic is the highest conception they have of scholarly wisdom). Some fathers assume that science is very profitable; most send their children to school without thinking much about it, submitting to the spirit of the times. Of these children, who form the majority, the most encouraging to us are those who have just been sent to school and who have become so fond of study that their parents now submit to the children's desires. These parents unconsciously feel that something good is being done with their children and have made up their minds not to take their children out of school.

One father told me that he once burned a whole candle while holding it over his son's book, and hugely praised both his son and the book. It was the Gospels. "My father," a different student told me, "now and then listens to a fairy tale, and laughs and goes away. If it is something divine, he sits and listens until midnight, holding the candle for me."

A new teacher and I visited a student's house. In order to show the boy off, I had him solve an algebra problem for the teacher. The mother was busying herself over the oven, and we forgot all about her; we listened to her son quickly and seriously rework the equation, saying "$2ab$ minus c equals d, divided by 3," and so forth. The mother kept her face covered with her hand the whole time. Forcibly restraining herself, she finally broke into laughter, but she was unable to explain to us what she was laughing about.

Another father, a soldier, once came to fetch his son. He found the boy in drawing class, and when the father saw his son's artwork, he began to address the boy with the formal instead of the familiar form of *you**, and decided not to give him the mess tins he had brought as presents.

The common opinion is, I think, as follows: they teach everything there (just as they do with the gentry children)—many things, some useless—but they also teach them to read and write in a short time, so it is all right to send them our children. There are also ill-intended rumors circulating among the people, but they carry little weight. Two worthy boys recently left the school, for the alleged reason that we do not teach writing. Another father, a soldier, wanted to send his boy to us. After examining one of our students and finding that the boy read the Psalter haltingly, the soldier decided that the school's instruction was bad, and only its reputation was good. A few of the Yasnaya Polyana peasants still fear that old rumors will prove true: they imagine that there is some ulterior motive to the instruction, that without a moment's notice somebody will slip their boys in a cart and haul them off to Moscow.

The parents' dissatisfaction with the absence of corporal punishment and order at the school has now almost entirely disappeared. I have often had occasion to observe the dumbfoundedness of a father come to fetch his son, when he sees students running about, making a ruckus, and fighting. He is convinced that naughtiness is harmful, and yet he believes that we teach well, and he is at a loss as to how to reconcile the two things.

Gymnastics classes now and then cause the parents to reassert their belief that exercise has a harmful effect on the stomach and the bowels, so that "the food won't go through." They believe that especially after fasting—or in the fall, when the vegetables get ripe—gymnastics do the most harm, and the old women cover up their pots and explain that gymnastics are the cause all the children's "naughtiness and twisting."

For some parents, though a minority, even the spirit of equality in the school causes dissatisfaction. In November we had two girls, the daughters of a rich innkeeper, who wore little women's coats and caps. The two

---

* Russian has two forms of the second person pronoun, the formal *vy* and the informal *ty*. *Ty* is routinely used with children—especially with one's own. Hence the father's use of *vy* here presumably signifies a nod to his son's "instant adulthood"—and to his intellectual superiority.

at first kept themselves apart, but then began to mix with the others; forgetting their tea and teeth cleanings with tobacco, they began to study well. Their father, dressed in a Crimean sheepskin coat, all unbuttoned, entered the school and found the girls standing in a crowd of dirty bast-shoed boys, who were leaning over the girls and touching the girls' caps as they all listened to what the teacher was saying. The father was offended and took his girls out of the school, though he did not divulge the cause of his dissatisfaction.

Finally, there are students who leave the school because their parents, who have sent their children to school in order to worm their way into someone's good graces, take them out when the need of gaining that person's favor has passed.

And so—there are twelve subjects, three grades, forty students in all, four teachers, and from five to seven lessons each day. The teachers keep diaries of their work, from which they report to one another on Sundays, and make their plans accordingly for the coming week. These plans are not carried out each week, but change to conform with the needs of the students.

Reading Mechanics

Reading forms part of the language instruction. The problem of teaching language consists, in our opinion, in guiding students to understand the contents of books written in the literary language. The knowledge of literary language is necessary because the good books are only in that language.

Earlier on, soon after the Yasnaya Polyana school was founded, there was no subdivision of reading into reading mechanics and graded reading*, for the students read only what they could understand: their own compositions, words and sentences written on the board, and then Khudiakov's and Afanasiev's fairy tales. I then decided that if the children were to learn to read, they had to like reading, and in order to like reading, it was necessary that the reading matter be intelligible and interesting. That seemed clear and rational, yet the basic idea was false. In the

---

* Tolstoy uses these two terms throughout this chapter. By "reading mechanics" he means learning the alphabet, learning to spell and to read, etc; "graded reading" is the reading of (presumably) progressively more difficult texts.

first place, in order to go from reading from the board to reading books, it became necessary to devote individual attention to each student, with whatever the reading material might be, to help each one with the mechanics of reading. Given our modest number of students and the lack of subdivision, that was possible, so I could with little effort help the children make the transition from reading on the wall to reading in a book. With the arrival of new students, however, that became impossible. The younger ones could not yet read and understand fairy tales: the simultaneous jobs of putting the words together and understanding their meaning were too much for them. Another inconvenience was that the graded reading ended with fairy tales, and whatever book we tried—whether *Popular Reading*, *The Soldier's Reader*, Pushkin, Gogol, Karamzin—it turned out that the older students had the same difficulty the young ones encountered with the fairy tales: they could not fulfill the dual tasks of reading and understanding what they read, though they understood a little when we read to them.

At first we thought that the difficulty was only with the students' imperfect mechanics, so we invented "reading mechanics"—reading for the process of reading. The teacher would trade off reading with the students, but things stayed the same, and the same bewilderment arose with reading *Robinson Crusoe*. In the summer, the transitional stage of our school, we hoped to be able to overcome these difficulties in the simplest and most commonly used way. Why not admit it: we yielded to false shame when faced with visitors. (Our students read much worse than those who had studied the same amount of time with a sexton.) A new teacher proposed introducing reading aloud from the same set of books, and we agreed to it. Having set our minds to the false idea that the students must by all means read fluently this year, we changed the class schedule to include reading mechanics *and* graded reading. We made the students read about two hours a day from the same books, and this was very convenient for us.

But this one deviation from the principle of student freedom led to lies, and to one error after another. We bought some booklets—fairy tales by Pushkin and Ershov—sat the students on benches, and had one read aloud while the others followed along. To verify that the others really were following, the teacher asked them questions, by turns. For a while we thought everything was going well. You come to the school, the students all sit properly on benches, one reads, the rest follow. The one who reads says, "Bles-síngs, my Queen Fish!" and the others—or the teacher— correct him: "Blés-sings, my Queen Fish!" All follow. "Ivanov, read!" Ivanov hunts for the right place and reads. All are busy, the teacher can be heard, every word is pronounced correctly, and the students read quite fluently. You would think all is well. But look closer: the one who is reading is reading the same thing for the thirtieth or fortieth time. (A printed sheet does not last longer than a week; it is terribly expensive to buy new books each time, and there are only two books peasant children understand: fairy tales by Khudiakov and by Afansiev. Besides, a book that has been read once in class is familiar not only to the students, but to their families, who are tired of it as well.) The reader becomes timid, listening to his lonely voice amid the silence of the room; all his effort is directed toward observing all the punctuation marks and accents, and he acquires the habit of reading without understanding the meaning, for he is burdened with other demands. Those listening do the same, and, hoping always to fall on the right spot when called upon, they evenly guide their fingers along the lines, become bored and distracted by other things. The meaning of what is being read does lodge in their heads at times, against their will; sometimes it doesn't, as it is really of secondary concern.

The main harm lies in the eternal battle of cunning and trickery between the students and the teacher that develops under a certain order, and which did not exist in our school before this. The only advantage of this method of reading—learning the correct pronunciation—meant absolutely nothing to our students. Our students had been learning to read from the board: all knew that you write *kogo* but say *kago*.* To teach stops and stresses [inflection] from punctuation marks is something I consider to be useless, because every five-year-old child correctly uses punctuation marks if he or she understands what he or she is saying. Thus it is easier to teach a child to understand what he or she reads from a book (which the child must achieve sooner or later) than it is to teach him or her to sing—as though from musical notes—the punctuation marks. But it seems so convenient to the teacher!

The teacher always involuntarily strives to select the method of instruction most convenient for himself or herself. The more convenient

---

* In Russian, *o* vowels are generally pronounced with as short *a*'s if unstressed.

the method for the teacher, the more inconvenient it is for the students. The manner of instruction is correct only when the students are satisfied.

Thanks to the school's vitality of spirit, especially when the old students returned to it from working in the fields, reading this way fell into disuse on its own; the students grew bored and got up to mischief, and became slack with their work. Above all, the students' reading of stories, which we used to evaluate their success in reading mechanics, proved that there had been no progress: in five weeks we had not taken one step forward, and many had fallen behind. The best mathematician of the first class, R—, who derived square roots in his head, had forgotten how to read to such an extent that we had to read with him syllable by syllable. We abandoned reading from the booklets and racked our brains to discover a method for teaching the mechanics of reading. The simple notion that the time was not ripe for good reading mechanics—that there was no urgent need for it at the present time, and that the students themselves would find the best way, when the need arose—only came to us a short time ago. The following became clear in the course of that search:

During the reading lessons, now divided into "graded reading" and "reading mechanics," the worst readers pair off and take some book (sometimes fairy tales, sometimes the Gospels, sometimes song collections or an issue of *Popular Reading*). They then read in twos, focusing on the process of reading only. They understand what they read if the book is a fairy tale, and we insist that the teachers ask them questions even though the class is called "mechanical reading." Sometimes the students, mainly the poorer ones, take the same book several times in a row, open it to the same page, read the same old story, and memorize it on their own, in spite of the teacher's explicit prohibition of this. Sometimes these poorer students come to the teacher or to an older student and ask him or her to read with them. The better readers, students in the second class, are less fond of reading in company, and less often read for the process of reading; if they memorize anything, it is a poem, not a tale in prose.

With the oldest students the same phenomenon is repeated, with this one difference, which struck me last month. In graded reading class, these students get one sort of book, which they read by turns, and then as a group they relate the contents. This class was joined in the fall by a very talented boy, Ch—, who had studied for two years with a sexton and who therefore had outstripped them all in reading. He reads as well as we do, and so during the graded reading the students understand—at least a lit-tle—when Ch— reads. Even so, each of them wants a turn as reader. The moment a bad reader starts to read, however, all express dissatisfaction—especially when the story is interesting—they laugh, get angry, and the bad reader is ashamed, and there are endless arguments. Last month one of the students declared that, whatever it might take, within a week he would read as well as Ch—; others promised the same, and suddenly reading mechanics became the favorite subject. They would sit reading an hour or an hour and a half at a time without tearing themselves away; though they did not understand the books, they began to take them home. The students made more progress in three weeks than anyone might have expected.

What happened with the Yasnaya Polyana students is the exact oppo-site of what generally takes place with those who learn to read. Generally, a person learns to read, but there is nothing for him to read or under-stand; here, as it turned out, the students had convinced themselves that there was something to read and understand and that they did not read well enough, so they strove to become better readers.

We have now completely abandoned reading mechanics and conduct business as described above. Each student is free to use whatever method he or she is most comfortable with, and, strange to say, they have made use of all the methods I am acquainted with: 1) reading with the teacher; 2) reading for the reading process; 3) reading with memorization; 4) reading in groups; and 5) reading to understand content.

The first method, used by mothers the world over, is generally used not at school but in the home. It consists of the student's coming and ask-ing to read with the teacher, whereupon the teacher reads, demonstrating with every syllable and word. This is invariably the very first rational method a student will request, and that a teacher involuntarily hits upon. In spite of all the means supposed to streamline instruction and presum-ably facilitate the teacher's work with a large number of students, this method will always remain the single best method for teaching people to read, and to read fluently.

The second method of teaching reading is also a favorite one, which everyone has practiced. It consists in giving a student a book and leaving it entirely to him to spell out and understand as well as he can. The stu-dent who has learned to read by syllables so fluently that he does not feel the need to ask the instructor to read with him, but feels self-sufficient, always acquires the passion for the process of reading so ridiculed in Gogol's "Petrushka"—and on account of that passion his reading skills improve. God knows what shape this kind of reading takes in his mind, but the student does get used to the letter forms, to the process of combining syllables, to the pronunciation of words, and even to understanding what he reads. I have more than once been convinced, through experience, that our insistence that a student must understand what he or she reads is a step backward. There are many autodidacts who have learned to read well in this way, although the defects of this system should be obvious to everybody.

The third method of teaching reading consists in learning by heart prayers, poems, and, generally, anything printed, and in pronouncing what has been memorized by following the printed text.

The fourth method is one that has proved harmful in the Yasnaya Polyana school: learning to read from a few books only. This arose by itself in our school. At first we did not have enough books, and two students would read together from one book. Then they became fond of this, and when they were told, "Read!" students of precisely the same ability would pair off, or sometimes form groups of three, with one book. One would read while the others would follow and correct his or her reading. You could disturb them only by rearranging them, because they knew exactly how their abilities matched up. Taraska immediately would ask for Dunka, and would tell another to look elsewhere: "You come here to read, and you go to your partner." A few of them did not care for reading in groups, because they did not need to.

The advantage of this approach lies in the greater accuracy of pronunciation and the greater room for understanding possible for whoever is not reading, but following along; yet on the whole, using this method becomes harmful the moment it—or, for that matter, any other method—is extended to the whole school.

A fine and even more favored method of ours is the fifth, graded reading: that of reading books with ever-growing interest and comprehension.

All the methods described above came into use quite naturally in our school, and in one month we made considerable progress.

The business of the teacher is to offer the choice of all known and unknown methods that can make the business of learning easier for the student. It is true that with a certain method—say, reading from one book only—instruction becomes easy and convenient for the teacher, and lends an air of seriousness and correctitude. But with the lack of order in our school it seems not only difficult, but strikes many as impossible. How, they will ask, to gauge what each student needs, and how to decide whether the needs of each are warranted? How can one help but be lost in this heterogeneous crowd, which is under social rule? To this I will reply: the difficulty lies in our inability to relinquish our old view of school as a disciplined company of soldiers, commanded today by one lieutenant and tomorrow by another. For the teacher who has adapted to the liberty of the Yasnaya Polyana school, each student represents a separate character, putting forth separate demands that only the freedom of choice can satisfy. If it had not been for our school's freedom and external disorder—which seems so strange and impossible to some—not only would we never have come on these five methods of reading, we would never have known how to use and apportion them according to the needs of the students, and therefore would never have attained the brilliant results we have achieved of late. How often have we had occasion to observe the bewilderment of visitors to our school, who wanted to study our method of instruction for two hours—two hours we do not have—and in the course of those two hours tell us all about their own method! How often have we listened to the same visitors, advising us to introduce some method or other, which, unbeknownst to them, was being used at that very moment in our school, but merely had not been codified as a despotic rule!

Graded Reading

As I've said, reading mechanics and graded reading in actuality have merged into one subject. For us, though, reading is still subdivided into these two categories due to the differing aims of reading mechanics and graded reading. It seems to us that the aim of the first is mastering the art of fluently forming words from certain signs, while the aim of the second is learning the literary language. For the study of the literary language we naturally conceived the means which seemed the simplest—but in reality were the most difficult. We thought that after the students learned to read the sentences they wrote on the board we needed to give them fairy tales by Khudiakov and Afansiev, then something more difficult and complex in its language, then something more difficult still, and so on, up to the language of Karamzin, Pushkin, and the Code of Laws. But this supposition, like the majority of our suppositions—and all suppositions—never came to pass. From what the students wrote on the board, I succeeded in advancing them to the language of fairy tales, but when we tried to take them from fairy tales to the next stage, we couldn't find a transitional "something"—it doesn't exist in literature. We tried *Robinson Crusoe*, but it was no good: some of the children wept in despair because they could not read it or understand it. I began to tell the story in my own words, and they began to believe in the possibility of coming to grasp the meaning of the text. They were able to get a handle on the story, and finished *Robinson Crusoe* in a month, but with much boredom and, in the end, near-disgust. The labor was too great for them. They gleaned things mostly through memory: they remembered passages from the story if they retold them in the evenings of the days we read. But not one of them could master the whole book on his or her own. Unfortunately, they remembered only certain words they couldn't understand, and began to use them pell-mell, as half-educated people do. I saw that something wasn't good, but what help to offer, I had no clue. To justify myself and to clear my conscience, I began to give them all kinds of popular imitations to read, such as "Uncle Naum" and "Aunt Natalya." I knew in advance that they would not like them—and my supposition came true. These books bored the students out of their minds, especially when they were asked to relate the contents.

After *Robinson Crusoe* I tried Pushkin, namely his story called "The Gravedigger." Yet when I did not help them, they were less successful with it than with *Crusoe*, and they found "The Gravedigger" much duller. The author's appeals to the reader, his frivolous relationship to his characters, his humorous characterizations, and his sparse, incomplete use of detail all so failed to jibe with the students' needs that I finally gave up on Pushkin, whose stories I had previously assumed to be well constructed, simple, and therefore intelligible to the people.

I next tried Gogol's "The Night Before Christmas." Aided by my reading aloud, it pleased them at first, especially the adult students, but as soon as I left them alone they could not understand anything and became bored. Even when I read, they did not ask to hear anything a second time. The wealth of color and the fantastical and capricious nature of the story's structure were contrary to their needs.

Then I tried reading Gnyedich's translation of the *Iliad* to them, and the reading produced only a strange bewilderment. The students assumed that the text had been written in French, and they did not understand a thing unless I retold the plot in my own words. But even then the poem's plot did not stick in their heads. The skeptic Semka, a sound, logical soul, was struck by the picture of Phoebus Apollo flying down from Olympus, his sheath of arrows rattling on his back, but it was apparent he did not know where to put this image.

"How come he didn't smash to pieces when he flew down from the mountain?" Semka kept asking me.

"They believed he was a god," I answered.

"A god? But weren't there many of them? Then he was not the real God. It is no joke to fly down from such a mountain—he must have been smashed all to pieces." Semka tried to prove this by motioning with his arms.

I tried George Sand's "Gribouille," *Popular Reading,* and *The Soldier's Reader*—all in vain. We try everything we can find and everything they send us, but now we try everything almost without hope. I sit at school and unseal a package containing a book supposed to be popular reading, fresh from the post office.

"Uncle, let me read it! Me!" several voices cry, and the children reach out their hands, "So I can understand it."

I open the book and read: "The life of great Saint Alexei presents us with an example of the fire of faith, of piety, of untiring activity, and of ardent love for one's country, for which this holy man did such important service"; or, "Since long ago Russia has been noted for the frequent appearances of gifted autodidacts, but all the same this does not explain everything"; or, "Three hundred years have passed since Bohemia became dependent on the German Empire"; or, "The village of Karacharovo, spreading out at the foot of the mountains, lies in one of the richest grain-producing provinces in Russia"; or, "Broadly lay, and laid out, was the road, the footpath"; or a popular exposition of some sort of natural science on one sheet, half of which is taken up with the author's flattering appeals to the peasantry. You give a book like this to one of the children, and his eyes grow dim, and he begins to yawn.

"No, I can't understand it, Lev Nikolaevich," he will say as he returns the book.

For whom and by whom are these books written? This remains a mystery. Of all the books of this type we read, the only exception to the rule was "The Grandfather" by Zolotov, which enjoyed great success both in the school and at home.

Some of these are simply inferior works, written in bad literary language. Finding no readership in the general public, they are foisted on the masses. Others, worse still, are written not in Russian but in some newly invented language supposed to be the language "of the people," something akin to the language in Krylov's fables. Still others are reworkings of foreign books intended for the people, but not popular. The only books that the masses can understand—and that suit their tastes—are not those written for the people but those that originate from the people: namely, fairy tales; proverbs; collections of songs, legends, verse, and riddles; the recent collection by Vodovozov; and so forth. One cannot believe, without seeing it firsthand, with what constant pleasure these types of books are read, without exception—even *Sayings of the Russian People, bylinas**, songbooks, Snegirev's proverbs, chronicles, and all the monuments of ancient literature. I have observed that children have a greater liking than adults for reading these sorts of books: they read them several times over, learn them by heart, delight in taking them home, and in their games and conversations they give each other nicknames taken from the ancient *bylinas* and songs. Grown-ups—either because they are less natural, or because they have gotten a taste for showing off their knowledge of bookish language, or because unconsciously they feel the necessity for knowing the literary language—are less partial to reading such works, preferring those in which the words, images, and thoughts are unintelligible to them.

However much the children like books of this kind, the goal that we set for ourselves, probably erroneously, is still out of their reach: the same gulf between these books and the literary language still remains. So far we have glimpsed no means to find our way out of this quandary. We are constantly making new experiments and new postulations, trying to discover our error. We ask all who are truly familiar with these questions to inform us of their theories, experiments, and solutions. The insolvable question for us is this: The education of the people requires the opportunity and desire to read good books, but those books are written in a language which the masses do not understand. In order to learn to under-

---

* *Bylinas*: traditional Russian epic poems, on historical subjects.

stand, one must read a great deal; in order to read with pleasure, one must understand what one is reading. In what lies the error, and how can we find a way out of this conundrum?

Maybe there exists an intermediary literature that we do not recognize; maybe we need to study the books circulating among the people, and how the people view these books, and this will reveal to us the paths by which individuals from the people come to achieve an understanding of the literary language.

We devote a special department in our journal to studying this question, and we ask all who understand the importance of this matter to send us their articles on the subject.

Maybe this is due to our [the aristocracy's] isolation from the masses, and to the compulsory education of the upper classes, and only with the passage of time will we see the appearance not of a chrestomathy* but a whole intermediary literature. This new transitional literature might be composed of all the books now in circulation, and arrange itself organically into a course of graded reading. It may be too that the masses do not understand and do not wish to understand our literary language because there is nothing for them to understand, because our literature is not good for them, and because on their own they are making a literature for themselves. This last proposition, which of all of them strikes us as the most on the mark, is based on a perceived shortcoming—connected not to the heart of the matter, but to our fixed idea that the aim of language instruction is to raise students to a knowledge of the literary language and that the ultimate goal is to get them there as quickly as possible. It is very possible that the subject we dream of, graded reading, will appear of itself, and that the knowledge of the literary language will come to each student naturally, just as we constantly see with people who read the Psalter, novels, and legal documents for days on end, not understanding what they read, but who in this way come to learn the literary language.

Supposing this to be so, the one thing we don't understand is why all the books now being published are so bad and not to the people's taste, and what the schools should do in the meantime. For there is one proposition that we cannot admit: that having decided in our minds that knowledge of the literary language is useful, we are teaching the masses the

---

* *Chrestomathy*: a digest or reader for students.

literary language against their will, by forced explanations, recitations, and "din learning,"* as French is taught. We must confess that we have tried to do this repeatedly in the last two months, and we have invariably encountered an insurmountable loathing in the students, thus proving to us the error of our ways. These experiments convinced me that explaining the meaning of words and parts of speech is absolutely impossible even for a talented teacher. (We won't mention the favorite explanations used by untalented teachers, such as "a throng is a certain small synedrion"† and so on. When explaining any word to students—for example, the word *impression*—you either substitute another unintelligible word in place of the one in question, or give a whole series of words, whose connection is as incomprehensible as the word itself.

Nearly always it is not the word that is unintelligible, but that the student does not have the concept expressed by the word. The word is nearly always ready when the idea is present. Besides, the relation of the word to the idea, and the formation of ideas, are such a complex, mysterious, and delicate process of the soul, that every intrusion appears as a rude, clumsy force that impedes the process of development. It is easy to say, "Understand!" But how many different things can one understand when reading the same book? In spite of not catching two or three words in a sentence, a student may grasp a fine shade of thought, or its relation to what precedes it. You, the teacher, insist on one side to the understanding, but a student does not need all of what you want to explain to him. At times he will understand, but not know how to prove it to you, dimly guessing at what you want. Meanwhile, he has grasped something quite different, something of great use and importance to him. You'll badger him for an explanation, and as he is on the verge of expressing in words what impression the words have made on him, he falls silent, or begins to speak nonsense, fabrications, and deceits, all the while trying to discover what you want from him and to adapt himself to your wishes. Or he invents a difficulty that wasn't there before and labors over it. But the general impression the book has produced on him—the poetic feeling that helped him divine the meaning—is cowed, and hides itself away.

---

* "Din learning": learning through constant aural bombardment.
† *Synedrion*: From the Greek, a synonym of *sanhedrin*. An ancient Jewish judicial council composed of 23 members.

We read Gogol's "Elf-King," rephrasing each passage in our own words. Everything went well until we came to the third page, which had the following sentence: "All those learned people, both of the seminary and of the *bursa**, who bore a certain traditional hatred to each other, were exceedingly poor in means of subsistence, and besides, uncommonly gluttonous, so that to ascertain what number of flour and suet dumplings each of them got away with at supper would have been a nearly impossible affair, and therefore the voluntary contributions of the well-off landowners would not have been sufficient."

TEACHER: Well, what did you read? (Nearly all the children are very well educated.)

BEST STUDENT: In the *bursa* the people were all gluttons, poor, and at supper got away with a lot of dumplings.

TEACHER: What else?

STUDENT (a smart aleck with a good memory, who says anything that comes into his head): An impossible affair, the voluntary contributions.

TEACHER (*angrily*): You must think. It was not that. What is an "impossible affair"?

Silence.

TEACHER: Read it once more.

They read. Another boy, with a good memory, added a few more words he could recall: "The seminary, the feeding of the well-off landowners would not have been sufficient." No one understood anything. They began to talk absolute nonsense. The teacher kept after the boy.

TEACHER: What is an "impossible affair"?

He wanted them to say that "It was impossible to ascertain."

A STUDENT: The *bursa* is an impossible affair.

ANOTHER STUDENT: Very poor, impossible.

They read the passage once more. The hunt for the word the teacher needed was like a search for a needle in a haystack. They got every word except *ascertain*, and they became utterly discouraged. I—the teacher I speak of—did not give in, and insisted that they take the whole passage apart, but this time they understood even less than when the first student tried to relate its contents. And after all, there wasn't much to understand. The carelessly constructed and lengthy passage gave nothing to

---

* *Bursa*: commercial exhange.

the reader. Its essence was simple enough—the poor, voracious people made off with the dumplings—that was all the author really wanted to say. I made a fuss about the form, which was faulty, and by striving to get at it, I ruined class for the rest of the afternoon, and had trampled to death a mass of budding flowers, of multiple understandings.

Another time, in much the same sinful and ugly manner, I wasted much effort trying to explain the meaning of the word *implement* to a student, with the same disastrous result. The same day, in drawing class, a student (Ch—) challenged his teacher, who decreed that the drawing books should have "Romashka's drawings" written in them. Ch— said that the students themselves had drawn in the books, and that Romashka had only invented the figure they'd used, so that they could write "Romashka's creation," but not "Romashka's drawing." Just how the distinction of these ideas had come into his head—the same way participles and introductory clauses now and then pop up in their compositions—will remain a mystery to me, a mystery best left alone.

It is necessary to give a student the opportunity to acquire new words and ideas from the general context of language. When that student hears or reads an unknown word in a sentence he or she understands, and then encounters it in another sentence, the student dimly begins to grasp a new idea, and by chance will come to feel the need to use the new word. Once used, the word and the idea become the student's property. But consciously to present the student with new ideas and forms of a word is, in my opinion, as impossible and fruitless as teaching a child to walk by teaching him or her the law of equilibrium.

Every such attempt fails to push the student forward. Instead it holds students back, moving them further from the assumed goal that the teacher tends with something like the rude hand of a man who, wishing to help a flower to open, tears the flower open by its petals, trampling everything around it.

Writing, Grammar, and Penmanship

We taught writing in the following way. Students learned to recognize and draw the letters simultaneously, to spell and write words, to understand what they had read, and to write it down. They all stood at the board and used chalk to mark off spaces for themselves. Then one student would dictate whatever came to him or her while the others wrote. If there was a large number of students, we had them divide up into smaller groups. As we continued, they would all take turns dictating, and they all read over one another's writing. The students wrote the letters as they appear in print, and at first corrected mistakes with incorrectly formed syllables and the separation of words, then mistakes of transposing vowels—using *o* not *a*, then *yat* not *ye*, and so forth. Our classes in writing moved ahead quite naturally. Every student who has learned to make the letters is possessed by a passion for writing, and first the doors and then outside walls of the school and of the huts in which the students live become covered with letters and words. The students' greatest pleasure is to write out whole sentences, such "Marfutka had a fight with Olgushka today."

To organize this class, the teacher had only to show the students how to conduct business together, just as a grown-up person teaches youngsters any game. In fact, writing class has been conducted the same way for two years, and every time with as much liveliness as a good game. Here we have reading and pronunciation and writing and grammar. With our approach to writing we achieve quite naturally the most difficult thing in the initial study of language: the faith in the stability of the word forms, not only of the printed word, but also when spoken—that is, *one's own words*. I think that every teacher who has taught language, not merely by using Vostokov's grammar, has come across this difficulty. For example, you want to draw a student's attention to a particular word, the word *me*, let's say. You hear a student say this sentence: "Mikishka pushed me off the stairs."

"Whom did he push down?" you ask. You have the student repeat the sentence, hoping he or she will say "me" again.

"*Us*," says the student.

"No, how did you say it before?"

"We fell down the stairs because of Mikishka," the student says, or, "When he pushed us, Praskutka flew down, and I after her."

You are looking for the accusative singular in its correct ending. But the student does not see anything different in the words he used. And if you were to take out a book or to repeat this student's words, he would be parsing with you not the living word, but something altogether different. When this same student dictates, every word of his is caught on the fly by the other students, and is written down.

"How did you say it? How, exactly?" The dictating student is not allowed to change a single letter. Endless debates ensue when one student writes something down one way and another writes the same thing another way. Very soon the student who is dictating begins to reflect on what he or she is going to say, and begins to understand that there are two things in speech: form and content. The student says some sentence one word at a time, thinking only of meaning. The others question him or her—"How?" "What?"—and the student, repeating the sentence several times silently, becomes sure of the form and of the parts of speech, and fixes them, using language.

Thus the students learn to write in the third class (the lowest one). Some write in cursive, others with letters as they appear in print. Not only do we *not* insist on their writing in script, but if there were anything that we would allow ourselves to prohibit, it would be that the students write in script, for its illegibility ruins their handwriting. They get used to script in a natural manner: one picks up a letter or two from an older student; then others learn them, frequently using them together with the letter forms from print (e.g., u*nc*le); and in less than a week, they are all writing in script. With penmanship, the same thing happened this summer as with reading mechanics: the students wrote very poorly, and the new teacher had them copy out models of handwriting from a book (again an easy and convenient exercise for the teacher). The students lost interest, and we were forced to abandon penmanship. We were unable to come up with a method for improving the students' handwriting; the first [highest] class discovered that method on its own. Having finished writing in sacred history class, the students started asking if they could take their notebooks home. These notebooks were soiled, torn, and horribly scribbled in. The neat and tidy mathematician R— asked for clean paper, and began to rewrite from his sacred history notebook. They all liked this idea: "Give me some paper! Let me have the copybook!" Penmanship soon came into fashion, and has sustained its popularity in the highest class. The students took their copybooks, placed them in front of the models they copy from, copied out each letter, and began to compete with one another. In two weeks they made great progress.

As children, nearly all of us were made to eat bread at the table, which we did not like, and yet now we eat everything with bread. Nearly all of us were made to hold the pen with outstretched fingers, and we held a pen with fingers bent because our fingers were short, and now we stretch out our fingers. The question becomes: Why did they torment us so, when what is necessary comes later quite naturally? Doesn't the desire and the necessity of knowledge of anything—of any subject at all—come in much the same way?

In the second class, the students write compositions on slates, from stories read aloud to them in sacred history class, and these they later rewrite on paper. In the third, lowest, class, the students write whatever they can think up. In addition, in the evenings the youngest ones write out single sentences, which they all compose together. One writes and the others all whisper among themselves, noting the writer's mistakes. They wait for the endings, where they can catch the writer out on a *yat* written where a *ye* should be, a preposition in the wrong place—and sometimes, they fabricate the rules. It gives them the greatest pleasure to write correctly and to correct the mistakes of others. The older ones take any letter that falls into their hands and look to correct any mistakes they can find. They do their utmost to write well, but they can't stand grammar and language analysis. In spite of our past bias for analysis, we admit it now only in small doses, or the students will fall asleep or skip class.

We have made various experiments with teaching grammar, and we must confess that not one of them has attained our goal: to make it entertaining for the students. In the second and first classes, this summer the new teacher attempted to explain the parts of a sentence. At first, a few students took an interest in them as in charades or riddles. Often, after class, the students hit on the idea of asking one another riddles, and they amused themselves by stumping one another with questions such as "Where is the predicate?" They considered this to be the same as a traditional riddle, such as "What sits on the bed to sleep, hanging down its feet?" The applications to actual writing were none; if there were any, they were more erroneous than correct.

The same thing happens with the letter *o* when it's used in place of *a*. You tell a student it is pronounced *a* but written *o*, and the student goes and writes *robota, molina* [*work, raspberry*] instead of the correct *rabota, malina*.* You tell the student that two predicates are separated by a

---

* In Russian, an unstressed *o* is pronounced like a short *a*. The students, thinking of this rule, are inverting it.

comma, and the student writes *I want, to say,* and so on. It is impossible to ask that he or she should each time identify what is the modifier in each sentence, and what is the predicate. And though the student may learn these things in the process of searching, he or she loses all instinct for writing the rest of the sentence correctly. This is not to mention the fact that when analyzing syntax, the teacher is constantly compelled to outfox students, and also to deceive them—and they sense this well enough. For example, we came across the sentence, "On earth there are no mountains." One student said that the subject was *earth*, another said *mountains*, and we the teachers announced that it was an impersonal construction. The students fell silent out of politeness; it was clear that they knew full well that our answer was far stupider than theirs, and we inwardly agreed.

Convinced of the fact that syntactical analysis was not the right approach, we tried analyzing morphology—in parts of speech, declensions, and conjugations. We also asked one another riddles about the dative, infinitives, and adverbs. The result was the same tedium, the same abuse of our teacherly influence, and the same lack of tangible results. In the upper class they always correctly write *ye* in the dative and prepositional cases, but when they correct this mistake in the younger students' work, the older ones are never able to give a reason for why they are doing so, and they must be reminded of the cases and declensions in order to remember the rule: "*Ye* in the dative." The youngest students, who have not yet heard tell of parts of speech, frequently shout *sebye ye*, without knowing why they've done so, but are obviously happy to have guessed right.

Recently I tried an exercise on my own with the second class. It was one that I, like all inventors, got carried away with, and it seemed unusually apt and rational to me until I found that it had no grounding in practice. Without naming the parts of the sentence, I had the students write sentences. Sometimes I gave them themes—in other words, the subjects of the sentences—and then I would have them, by asking questions, expand the sentences by adding new predicates, subjects, direct objects, and adverbial modifiers. "The wolves are running." When? Where? How? What kind of wolves are running? Who else is running? They run, but what else do they do? It seemed to me that by getting used to answering questions, which entailed adding this or that part of speech, the students would assimilate the parts of a sentence and the parts of speech. So they did, but they became bored and asked themselves inwardly what the point of all this was, so I was forced to ask myself the same question, and found no answer. Neither adult nor child likes to surrender his or her living word to mechanical dissection and disfiguration. There is a certain feeling for self-preservation in the living word. If the living word is to develop, it seeks to develop independently and only in conformity with real-life conditions. The moment you want to catch that word, to tighten it up in a vise, to plane off the edges, and to give it the "adornments" your ideas deem necessary, the vital thought and meaning connected with the word compress themselves and conceal themselves. You are left with nothing in your hands but an empty shell, on which you may exercise all your cunning, but will achieve absolutely nothing in terms of teaching students how to use that particular word.

Up to this point, the second class has continued with syntactical and grammatical analysis, doing these exercises in which the students expand sentences, but the going is sluggish and my assumption is that the practice will soon peter out on its own. In addition, we do the following language exercises, not at all connected to grammar:

1) We give them words to form sentences out of (*Nikolai, wood, learn*). They write, "If Nikolai had not been chopping wood, he would have gone to learn," or "Nikolai chops wood well, we must learn from him," and so forth.

2) We compose poems to a given meter, an exercise that particularly amuses the oldest students. The verses turn out something like this:

At the window sits a man
In a torn sheepskin coat
In the street a man hawks
Nice red eggs, the old goat

3) An exercise that is very successful in the lowest class is this: we give the students first a noun, then an adjective, then an adverb, then a preposition. With each word, one of the students goes out of the room. The rest must each form a sentence that uses the given word. The student who went out must then guess the word.

All these exercises—writing sentences from given words, composing verse, and word games—have one common goal: to convince the student that *a word is a word*, and each word has immutable laws, variations, endings, and the endings have a system—a conviction that does not enter their minds until some time has passed, and is essential before they learn grammar. They like exercises like these; exercises in grammar breed tedium. What a strange and remarkable thing it is that grammar is boring, when there is nothing easier.

As soon as you stop teaching grammar by the book, beginning with definitions, in half an hour a six-year-old child begins to decline, conjugate, recognize genders, numbers, tenses, subjects, and predicates, and you feel that that child knows it all as well as you do. (In our parts, there is no neuter gender; all neuter words—*gun, hay, butter, window*—are given feminine endings, everything is "she," and the rules of grammar don't apply. The oldest students have known all the rules of grammar for three years, and yet they make mistakes with gender and the correct endings. They wean themselves from these mistakes only through the corrections you make and through reading.) Why do I teach them all this, when they know it as well as I do? Whether I ask them what the genitive plural feminine of *great* is, or where the predicate is and the modifiers are, or what the root of the verb *to fly open* is—they are unsure only of the nomenclature, otherwise they will always use the adjective correctly in any case and number you please. Hence they know declension. They will never say a sentence without a predicate, and will not mix it with the object. They have a natural sense for the roots of words, and are more conscious than you of the laws by which words are formed, because no one coins new words more than children. Why then, this nomenclature, and our demand for philosophical definitions that are out of their reach?

The only explanation for the necessity of grammar—apart from the demand for exams—may be found in its application to the regular exposition of ideas. In my experience I have not uncovered this application, and I do not see it in the examples of those who do not know grammar and yet write correctly—and in the examples of candidates in philology who write ungrammatically—and I can scarcely find any evidence that the Yasnaya Polyana students apply their knowledge of grammar to anything practical. It seems to me that grammar by itself is a useless exercise in mental gymnastics, and that language—the ability to read, write, and understand—comes by itself. Geometry and mathematics in general also at first appear to be nothing more than mental gymnastics, but the difference is that every proposition in geometry, every mathematical definition, leads to further endless deductions and applications. In grammar, meanwhile, even if we should agree with those who see in it an application to language, there is a tenuous link to those further deductions and applications. As soon as a student masters language by one path or another, all applications of grammar shear off and drop away as something dead and lifeless.

Personally all of us are not yet able to renounce completely the tradition that grammar—in the sense of being the laws of language—is necessary for the regular exposition of ideas. It even seems to us that the students have a need for grammar, and that the laws of grammar are actually inside the students—as yet unconscious of them—waiting to get out. But we are convinced that grammar, as we understand it, is not at all the grammar that students need, and that some great historical misunderstanding underlies this custom of teaching grammar. The child learns that the word *sebye* [*himself* or *herself*] ends with letter *ye* not because it is the dative form of the word, however often you may told him or her this, and not merely because the child is blindly imitating what he or she has seen in writing a few times before. The child is generalizing from these examples, only not in the form of the dative, but in some different way. We have a student at Yasnaya Polyana who transferred here from another school. This student has an excellent knowledge of grammar, but is unable to distinguish between the third person and the infinitive reflexive. Another of our students, Fedka, has no understanding of the infinitive, but never makes mistakes because he circumvents problems with infinitives by adding the word *will*.*

In the Yasnaya Polyana school we recognize the legitimacy of all known methods for the study of language—including the study of grammar. We employ these methods if the students accept them gladly and if they accord with our own knowledge. At the same time we recognize none of the methods as exclusive, and we are continually trying to find new methods. We are as little in accord with Mr. Perevlessky's method—which failed to survive a two-day experiment at Yasnaya Polyana—as with the very widespread opinion that the only method to learn language is

* We have omitted a passage here, as it would be comprehensible only to speakers of Russian.

through writing—although writing forms the chief method of language instruction at the Yasnaya Polyana school. We seek and we hope to find.

Compositions

In the first and second classes, the students choose composition topics themselves. A favorite subject is the history of the Old Testament, which they write about for two months after the teacher has gone through it in class. The first class recently began to write about the New Testament, but not as successfully as about the Old; they even made more spelling mistakes—they did not understand it so well.

With the first class we also tried giving themes. The first themes that naturally occurred to us were descriptions of simple object such as grain, houses, villages, and so forth. But to our great surprise, asking this of our students nearly drove them to tears, and in spite of the writing instructor's help—the teacher had subdivided the description of grain into descriptions of its growth, milling into flour, and flour's uses—the students emphatically refused to write on these sorts of themes, or, if they did write, they made the most inexplicable and outrageous mistakes with spelling, with language, and with meaning. Then we tried having them describe events of all kinds, and they were as happy as if we had given them a present. The favorite approach in schools—describing everyday objects such as pigs, pots, and tables—turned out to be far more difficult than for the students to write whole stories directly from memory. This very mistake repeats itself in all the other subjects of instruction: the simplest and most general subject is what seems easiest to the teacher, whereas for the students only complex and living subjects seem easy.

All textbooks in the natural sciences begin with general laws, language textbooks with definitions, history textbooks with outlines of historical periods, and even geometry textbooks with definitions of the concepts of space and the mathematical point. Nearly every teacher, guided by the same line of thought, gives as a first composition the definition of a table or bench, without taking the trouble to consider that in order to define a table or bench one has to possess a certain level of a philosophical-dialectical development, and that the same student who cries over the composition about a bench can write excellent descriptions of feelings of love or anger, of Joseph meeting with his brothers, or of a cries over the composition about a bench can write excellent descriptions of feelings of love or anger, of Joseph meeting with his brothers, or of a fight with a schoolmate. The students naturally choose subjects such as real-life events, personal relations, and stories they have overheard.

Writing compositions is the students' favorite form of schoolwork. The moment the oldest ones get hold of a pencil and paper outside of school, instead of they writing "Dear Sir . . . ," they write some fairy tale of their own. At first I was vexed by the clumsiness and lack of structure of their compositions. I had given the students the inspiration necessary to write, but they misunderstood me, and everything went badly. It was as if the only thing they deemed essential was writing without mistakes. But now, with the passage of time, in the natural course of events, we frequently hear expressions of dissatisfaction from the students when a composition meanders, has frequent repetitions, or jumps from one subject to another. It is hard to define what their demands actually are, but they are definitely legitimate. "Clumsy!" some of them will shout when listening to a friend's composition; some of them will not read their own compositions after they have heard another student's that is good; some tear their writing notebooks from the teacher's hands, dissatisfied because it sounds different from what they wanted, and they will read it aloud themselves. The students' individual characters are beginning to express themselves so distinctly that we have experimented with making the students guess whose composition we have been reading, and the students in the first class can guess right every time.

Due to lack of space, we must save for another time describing our teaching of language and of other subjects, as well as giving extracts from the teachers' diaries. Here we give examples of writing from two students in the first class—as they wrote them, without changes in spelling or punctuation. Their compositions in sacred history we hope to offer in a future issue [of *Yasnaya Polyana*].

Here are two compositions by B— (a very poor student, but an original and lively boy): one about Tula [a large provincial town not far from Yasnaya Polyana] and another about his studies. The composition about his studies went particularly well. B— is eleven years old; this is his third winter at the Yasnaya Polyana school, but he had some schooling before coming to us.

About Tula

The other Sunday I went again to Tula. When we arrived, Vladimir Aleksandrovich and Vaska Zhdanov says to us go to the Sunday school. We went, and went, and went, and barely found it, we come and we see that all the teachers sit. And there I saw the teacher the one that taught us botany. So I say good morning gentlemen! They say good morning. Then I went up to class, stood at the table, and I got so bored, that I left and walked around Tula. I went and went and I see a woman selling *kalachi.** I began to take my money out of my pocket, when I took it out I began to buy some loaves, I bought them and went away. And I saw also a man walking on a tower and looking where it is burning. I am through with Tula.

Composition on How I Have Been Studying

When I was eight years old, I was sent to the cattle yard at Grumy. There I studied well. And then feeling lonely, I began to cry. The woman takes a stick and began to beat me. And I cried out even more. And a few days later I went home and told everything. And they took me away from there and gave me to Dunka's mother. I studied well there and they never beat me there, and I learned the whole alphabet there. Then they sent me to Foka Demidovich. He beat me horribly. Once I run away from him, and he saw me caught. When they catched me they led me to him. He took me, stretched me out on a bench and took into his hands a bundle of rawds [*sic*] and began to beat me. And I screamed my lungs out, and when he had beat me he made me read. And he himself listens and says: "What? You son of a bitch, just see how badly you read! Ach, what a swine you are!"

Now here are two compositions by Fedka: one on the given theme (grain); another on a topic of his own choosing, his trip to Tula. (Fedka has been with us three winters. He is ten years old.)

On Grain

Grain grows from the earth. In the beginning grain is green. When it grows up a little, ears sprout from it and the women reap it. There is also grain like grass, which cattle eat very well.

That was it. Fedka sensed that it was not good, and was not happy with it. About Tula he wrote the following, which is uncorrected.

About Tula

When I was small, I, was about five years old; then I heard the people went to this Tula and I myself did not know what this Tula was. So I asked Father.

---

* *Kalach* (sing.), *kalachi* (pl.): rolls made from white flour.

Dad! what is this Tula that you go to, it must be fine? Father says: It is. So I say, Dad! take me with you, I will see Tula, Father says well all right, maybe Sunday I will take you. I was happy and began to run and jump on the bench. After these days came Sunday. I just got up in the morning and Father was already hitching the horses in the yard, I put my shoes on and began to dress myself. The moment I was dressed and went out into the yard, Father had already hitched the horses. I sat down in the sleigh and I drove off. We drove, and drove, and made it fourteen versts. I saw a tall church and I cried: Father! Look at that tall church! Father says: there is a church that is not so tall but more beautiful, I began to ask him, Father let us go there, I will pray to God. Father went. When we came, suddenly they rang the bell, I was frightened and asked father what it was, or whether they were beating drums. Father says: no, mass is starting. Then we went to church to pray to God. When we were through praying, we went to the market. And so I walk, and walk and stumble, I kept looking around. So we came to the market, I saw they were selling *kalachi* and wanted to take without money. And Father says to me, do not take, or they will take your cap off you. I say why will they take it, and father says, do not take without money, I say well give me ten kopecks, I will buy me a small *kalach*. Father gave me, I bought three *kalachi* and ate them up and I say: Father, what fine *kalachi*. When we had bought everything, we went to the horses and watered them, gave them hay, when they had eaten, we hitched up the horses and went home, went into the hut and undressed myself and began to tell everybody how I was in Tula, and how Father and I were in church, and prayed to God. Then I fell asleep and I dream like Father was again going to Tula. I immediately woke up, and I saw all are asleep, then I went to sleep.

Sacred History

From the founding of the school even up until now the instruction in religious and Russian history has been carried out in this following way: The children gather around the teacher, and the teacher—guided by the Bible, or in Russian history by Pogodin's *Norman Period*, and Vodovozov's collection—narrates the stories and then asks questions. Then all the students begin talking at the same time. When there are too many voices speaking at once, the teacher stops the students and has them speak one at a time; the moment one hesitates, the teacher lets the others have a go. When the teacher notices that some have failed to understand, he makes one of the best students go over the problematic passage for the benefit of those who have not understood.

This approach was not invented, but evolved on its own, and it has been equally successful with anywhere between five or thirty students, provided the teacher follows it truthfully: that he not allow the students to interrupt or to repeat things, and does not permit the shouting to get out of hand, but instead regulates that stream of merry animation and competition just as much as he needs to.

In the summer, when we frequently have visitors as well as changes in our teaching faculty, we changed procedures, and our history instruction was much less successful. The general level of noise baffled the new teacher. It seemed to him that those who were telling the story through the noise would not be able do it alone, in quiet, and that the students only wanted to make noise. Above all, he felt uncomfortably warm and claustrophobic in the mass of kids pressing up on his back and staring into his open mouth. (In order to understand better, the children have to be close to the person speaking, to see every change of facial expression, every movement. I have more than once observed that passages are best understood when it occurs to the narrator to add an apt gesture or intonation.)

The new teacher decided to have the students sit on benches and answer one at a time. The student called upon to recite would be silent and embarrassed, and the teacher, looking askance, with the *sweet* expression of submitting to fate, or with a meek smile, would say, "Well, and then? Well done, very well!" and so forth—following the Socratic method that we all know so well.

I am convinced, moreover, that in practice there is nothing more harmful to a child's development than this type of one-on-one questioning and the type of authoritarian relation between teacher and student that arises from it. Nothing incenses me more than the spectacle of a big person tormenting a little one, having no right to do so. The teacher knows that the student feels tortured as he or she stands there blushing and perspiring before him. The teacher feels uncomfortable and bored, but he lives by the rule that students must always answer one at a time.

And why students must be singled out, nobody knows. Perhaps just in order to force the child to recite a fable in the presence of his or her Excellency. Experts will probably tell me that without this it is impossible to determine a given student's knowledge. To this I answer that it is really impossible for an outsider in an hour's time to determine what a student knows, while the teacher always feels his ability to assess a student's knowledge—without the student having a chance to respond, and without examinations—should go unquestioned. It seems to me that this method of one-on-one questioning is a recurrence of an old superstition. Long ago, the teacher, who made students learn everything by heart, could not in any other way determine students' knowledge but by making them repeat everything word for word. Then it was found that rote learning was not the same thing as knowledge, and the students were recasting things in their own words; but the method of calling on students one at a time, at the teacher's whim, was not changed. The fact is that at any time and in any circumstance students can repeat all the words of the Psalter or of a fable, but that in order to glean the contents of a text and to render it in their own words, students must be in a receptive mood.

Not only in lower school and high school, but even in the universities, I believe examinations should not be given unless they are done so according to a strict system of memorizing notes. In my college days (I left the university in the year 1845*), I studied for my examinations not word for word but sentence for sentence. The only times I received high marks were from those professors whose notes I had learned by heart.

Visitors, so detrimental to learning in the Yasnaya Polyana school, have been very useful to me in one way. They made me completely convinced that the recitation of lessons and the examinations are a remnant of superstitions from the medieval school, and that with the present order of things they are woefully inappropriate and exceedingly harmful. Often, carried away by childish vanity, I wished in an hour's time to show off the students' knowledge to an honored guest. The result was either that the visitor was convinced that the students knew things they did not in fact know (I diverted him with some hocus-pocus) or that the visitor supposed that the students did not know what they in fact knew very well. Such a tangle of misunderstandings developed between me and the visitor—a clever, talented man and a specialist in his business—all in an absolute freedom of relations! What, then, must occur when directors come to make inspections and so forth—not to mention the disorder to the teaching process and the contradictory ideas in the students' minds that such evaluations produce.

At the present time I am convinced that to make a résumé of all of a student's knowledge is as impossible for the teacher as it is for an outsider,

---

* It was actually 1847—*Ed.*

just as it is impossible to make a résumé of my own knowledge, or yours, in respect to any sort of science. If a forty-year-old man were to sit for a examination in geography, it would be just as stupid and strange as when a ten-year-old child does. Both of them have to answer the same way—by memory—and in an hour of time it is impossible to find out their actual knowledge. In either case, it would be necessary to spend months with them in order to find out what they really know.

Where examinations are introduced (by "examinations" I mean any required answering of questions), there only arises a new useless subject, one that requires special efforts and special talent. This subject is called "preparation for examinations or lessons." A high school student studies history and mathematics, but principally *the art of answering questions at the examinations*. I do not regard this art a subject that is useful in education. I, the teacher, evaluate my students' knowledge as correctly as I evaluate my own—although neither the students nor I report on our lessons. If an outsider wants to evaluate our knowledge, let him or her live with us awhile so he or she can see the results of our knowledge, and its applications to life. This is the only way, and all efforts to hold examinations are only a deception, a lie, and an obstacle to learning. In education, there is but one independent judge, the teacher, and the teacher should be answerable only to the students.

During history lessons the students answer all at once not so that someone (the teacher) might verify their knowledge, but because they feel the need to strengthen by means of verbalization the impressions they have received. This summer neither the new teacher nor I understood that; we saw it only as a way to verify their knowledge, and so we found it more convenient to verify it one student at a time. At the time I was unable to fathom that this was the reason this class was so tedious and bad, but my faith in the rule of student freedom saved me. The majority began to lose interest, three of the boldest boys were invariably the ones who answered all the questions, and the three most timid were constantly silent, wept, and received zeros.

During the summer I neglected our classes in sacred history, and the teacher, a lover of order, had full liberty to seat the students on benches, to torment them one by one, and to make noises about the stubbornness of the children. Several times I advised this teacher to let the children leave the benches during history lessons, but he took my advice as a sweet and pardonable eccentricity (just as I know in advance that my advice will be taken by the majority of readers), and this order prevailed until the old teacher returned. That summer the teacher made entries in his teaching diary such as: "I cannot get anything out of Savin." "Grishin did not tell a thing." "Petka's stubbornness is a surprise to me—he has not spoken a word." "Savin is even worse than before." Et cetera.

Savin is a ruddy, chubby boy, with gleaming eyes and long eyelashes, the son of a *dvornik* or a merchant. He wears a weatherbeaten sheepskin coat, small boots that are not his father's, a red cotton shirt, and trousers. The sympathetic and beautiful personality of that boy especially struck me because he was the top student in arithmetic class by dint of his imagination and his lively, enthusiastic nature. He also reads and writes not at all badly. But the moment the teacher asks him a question he presses his pretty head of curly hair to one side, tears appear on his long lashes, and he looks as if he wants to hide from everybody, and it is evident that he is suffering intolerably. If he is made to learn something by heart, he can recite it, but he is not able—or has not the courage—to express anything in his own words. It is due either to some fear inspired by his former teacher (a teacher involved in church work); to lack of confidence in himself; to his awkward standing among his fellows—who, in his opinion, are beneath him; or to his vexation that only in this area does he lag behind the rest. This is all because he once showed himself in a poor light in some teacher's eyes, or because his little soul was offended by some careless word that escaped from that teacher. It could be all these causes acting together—God knows. But his bashfulness, though not a good feature in itself, is certainly inseparably connected with everything that is best in his childish soul. It is possible to knock all that out with a physical or moral stick, but the danger is that all his precious qualities, without which the teacher would find it hard to lead him on, would be knocked out at the same time.

The new teacher listened to my advice, freed the students from the benches, allowing them to crawl wherever they pleased, even on his back, and that same day all began to speak so much better. The teacher made the following entry in his diary: "Recalcitrant Savin said a few words."

There is in a school something that is hard to put one's finger on, something that more or less refuses to submit to a teacher's control, something absolutely unknown to the science of pedagogy, and that is the spirit of the school. This spirit is subject to certain laws and to the negative influence of the teacher—that is, the teacher must avoid doing certain things so as not to destroy that spirit. The spirit of the school, for example, is always in inverse relation to the compulsion and order, in inverse relation to teacher interference in the students' thought processes, in direct relation to the number of students, in inverse relation to the duration of lessons, and so on. This spirit of the school is something that is rapidly communicated from student to student, and even to teachers. It is something that is palpably expressed in the tones of voice, in the eyes, the movements, the intensity of competition—something very tangible, necessary, and extremely precious, and therefore something that ought to be the goal of every teacher. Just as the saliva in the mouth is necessary for digestion, but is disagreeable and superfluous without food, so this spirit of intense animation, though tedious and disagreeable outside of class, is a necessary condition for the intake of mental food. This essential spirit or mood is something that is impossible to invent and prepare artificially—nor is it necessary to do so, for it always makes its appearance of its own accord.

In the beginning of our school I made such mistakes. The moment a boy began to learn poorly and unwillingly, when the dullness that is a common condition of school came over him, I would say, "Jump! Jump awhile!" The boy began to jump; he laughed and the others laughed with him; and after jumping the student was a different boy. But after having repeated this jumping several times, it turned out that when I told the boy to jump he was overcome by a greater anguish, and he began to weep. He saw that he was not in the mood he should be in, and yet he was not able to change how he felt, but he did not want anyone to try to help him. Children and adults both are receptive only when in a state of excitement. Therefore, to regard the happy spirit of a school as an enemy, an obstacle, is a grave mistake—one that we make far too often.

When the animation in a large class is so strong, however, that it interferes with a teacher's efforts to conduct class—when the teacher cannot be heard and cannot hear the students—how can one not feel tempted to raise one's voice with the children and try to subdue that spirit? If the animation is directed towards the subject at hand, the lesson, then nothing could be better. But if the students' animation directs itself elsewhere, the fault is with the teacher, who did not manage things properly. The problem for the teacher—which nearly every good teacher fulfills unconsciously—consists in constantly feeding this animation, and then gradually reining it in. You ask one student, and another wants to answer: the students know the answers—they bend toward you, and looking at you with both big eyes; they can scarcely keep their words back; they eagerly follow the person telling the story, and will not forgive him or her a single mistake. Ask them, and they will give you impassioned answers: what they tell you will forever impress itself on their minds. But if you deprive students of this intensity, keep them silent for half an hour, they will start to pass the time by pinching their neighbors.

Another example: Walk out of a class in one of our rural schools—or in a German school—where the students are quiet, and leave orders that the students are to proceed with their work, and half an hour later listen at the door. The class will be animated, but the animation is directed toward so-called "mischievousness." We have often done the following experiment with our classes at Yasnaya Polyana. Leaving it in the middle, when the hubbub was at the loudest, we would go outside and listen awhile at the door. We found that the children continued to tell the stories, correcting and competing with one another. Instead of becoming naughty without us, frequently they would quiet down entirely.

Just as with the order of seating the students on the benches and asking them questions singly, even so with this order there are simple rules which one must know and without which the first experiment may be a failure. One must watch the criers who repeat the last words said, only to increase the noise. It is necessary to see to it that the charm of the noise should not become their main purpose and problem. It is necessary to test some students, as to whether they are able to tell everything by themselves, and whether they have grasped the whole meaning. If there are too many students, they ought to be divided into a number of divisions, and the students ought to tell the respective story to each other by divisions.

There is no need to fear if a newly arrived student does not open his or her mouth for a month. All that is necessary is to watch whether he is busy with the story or with something else. Generally a newly arrived student grasps only the material side of the matter, and is all rapt in observing how the students sit and lie, how the teacher's lips are moving, how they all cry out at once; if he is a quiet boy, he will sit down just as the others do; if he is bold, he will cry like the rest, without getting the meaning of what is said, and only repeating the words of his neighbor. The teacher and his companions stop him, and he understands that something else is meant. A little time will pass, and he will begin to tell a story. It is difficult to find out how and when the flower of comprehension will open up in him.

Lately I had occasion to watch such an opening of the bud of comprehension in a very timid girl who had kept silent for a month. Mr. U— was telling something, and I was an outside spectator and made my observations. When all began to tell the story, I noticed that Marfutka climbed down from the bench with the gesture with which storytellers change the position of hearer to that of narrator, and came nearer. When all began to shout, I looked at her: she barely moved her lips, and her eyes were full of thought and animation. Upon meeting my glance, she lowered hers. A minute later I again looked around, and she was again whispering something to herself. I asked her to tell the story, and she was completely lost. Two days later she told the whole story beautifully.

The best proof that the students of our school remember what is told them is found in the stories which they themselves write down from memory.*

* * * *

Our discussion has referred to the teaching of sacred and Russian history; natural history; geography; some areas of physics, chemistry, zoology; and in general, all subjects with the exception of singing, mathematics, and drawing. About our current instruction in sacred history I should say the following:

First of all, why did we choose to study the Old Testament before anything else? Not only did the students and their parents ask for a knowledge of the Old Testament, but I also discovered that of all things I had tried to communicate orally to my students in the course of three years, nothing stuck in the students' minds as well as the Bible. I have observed the same thing in all the other schools I have visited. I have tried the New Testament, Russian history and geography, I have tried the favorite subject of our time—explanations of phenomena in Nature—but the students soon forgot all that and listened to my lectures without enthusiasm. On the other hand, they remembered the Old Testament

---

* As proof, Tolstoy goes on to quote three students' retellings of Bible stories: Abraham's sacrifice of Isaac, Jacob taking Esau's birthright, and Joseph and the multicolored coat. We have omitted these passages here; see Leo Wiener (*Tolstoy on Education*, pp. 302–307)—*Ed.*

gladly, and they were able to retell the stories from it with enthusiasm both at school and at home. It left such an impression upon the children that two months after it had been told to them, they were able to write, from memory, Old Testament stories in their notebooks, with hardly anything left out.

It seems to me that the book from childhood for one race will always be the best book of childhood for every man. It seems impossible to me to put another book in its place. It strikes me as harmful to change or shorten the Bible as is done in Sonntag's textbooks, et cetera. Everything—every word in it—holds truth, truth as revelation and truth as art. Read about the creation of the world in the Bible and in one of these abridged "Sacred Histories," and you will be unable to fathom the transformation that has taken place. From the Sacred History you can learn otherwise only by memorizing, whereas the Bible presents the child with a majestic and living picture, one which he or she will never forget. The omissions in the Sacred History are quite arbitrary and only impair the character and beauty of Holy Scripture. Why, for example, do all the sacred histories omit the passages that describe how when there was nothing, the Spirit of God was borne over the abyss, and how God surveyed His creation and saw that all was well and that now there was morning and evening? Why do they leave out that God breathed the eternal spirit into the soul through the nostrils; that having taken out a rib from Adam, he filled up the place with flesh, and so forth? Let uncorrupted children read the Bible, and then you will understand to what extent it is necessary and true. It may be tha we should not let the Bible get into the hands of spoiled young ladies of the nobility, but I did not leave out a single word when reading the Bible to peasant children. Nobody giggled behind somebody's back, and all listened with sinking hearts and natural awe. The story of Lot and his daughters, the story of Judas, provoke horror, not laughter. . . .

How comprehensible and clear, particularly for a child, everything is, and, at the same time, how stern and serious! I can't understand what kind of an education would be possible if it were not for that book. And yet it seems when we learn these stories only in childhood and then partially forget them—what good are they to us? And wouldn't it be the same if we did not know them at all?

This seems so only so long as you do not teach others—when you have a chance to watch all the elements of *your own* development at work in other children. It seems possible to teach the children to write and read, to give them a conception of history, geography, and natural phenomena, without the Bible and prior to reading the Bible. And yet that is not done anywhere—everywhere the first things children learn are stories and excerpts from the Bible. The first relation between teacher and student is based upon that book. Such a universal phenomenon is not accidental. My absolutely free relation to the students, in the beginnings of the Yasnaya Polyana school, helped me to find an explanation for this phenomenon.

A child, or adult, entering school (I make no distinction between students ten, thirty, or seventy years of age), brings with him his familiar things in life, as well as his favorite views on life. In order for a person of any age to begin to learn, it is necessary for that person to like learning. In order that this person should like learning, he must recognize the falseness and insufficiency of his view of things and he must divine the new world-view that the instruction opens to him. Not one adult or child would be able to learn if his future learning presented itself to him only as the art of reading, writing, and counting; not one teacher would be able to teach, if he did not have in his power a greater world-view than what the students have. In order that the student may entirely surrender himself to the teacher, one side of the shroud—the shroud that has been concealing from him all the charm of that world of thought, knowledge, and poetry that learning can introduce to him—must be lifted. Only by being under the spell of that brilliant world ahead of him is the student able to rework himself in the way we want him to.

What means have we, then, to lift that edge of the shroud for the student? As I have said, I thought—as many think—that, finding myself in that world to which I am to introduce the students, I could easily introduce them to it. I taught reading and writing, I explained natural phenomena, I told them—as it says in ABC books—that the fruits of learning are sweet, but the students did not believe me and remained aloof. I tried to read the Bible to them, and I completely captured them. The edge of the curtain had been lifted, and they surrendered themselves to me unconditionally. They fell in love with the book, with learning, and with me. All I had now to do was to guide them forward.

After the Old Testament I told them the New Testament, and they loved studying and me more and more. Then I told them about world history, Russian history, and natural history when we were through with the

Bible; they listened to everything, believed everything, and begged to go on and on. New perspectives of thought, knowledge, and poetry opened up to them. Perhaps this was accidental. It may be that in some other school the same results could be achieved with much different methods. Maybe—but this accident has been repeated in so many different contexts, in school and in the family, that I must assume that this phenomenon is anything but accidental.

There is no book like the Bible to open up a new world to the student or to make ignorant folk love knowledge. I speak even of those who do not look upon the Bible as a revelation. At least, there is no work that I know of that so unites all the aspects of human thought in such a compressed poetic form. All questions of natural phenomena are explained by this book; all the primitive relations of different races and cultures, of families, states, and religions are for the first time consciously recognized in this book. Generalized ideas—wisdom, in a childishly simple form—for the first time cast their spell on the student's mind. The lyricism of David's psalms acts not only upon the minds of grown students, but on everybody who for the first time learns from this book the whole charm of the epos in its inimitable simplicity and strength. Who has not wept over the story of Joseph meeting with his brothers? Who has not retold with a sinking heart the story of Samson bound and shorn of his hair, as he, taking vengeance on his enemies, himself perishes under the ruins of the fallen palace, and a hundred other impressions on which we have been brought up as on our mothers' milk?

Let those who deny the educational value of the Bible, who say that the Bible has outlived its usefulness, invent such a book, such stories, which explain the phenomena of Nature or phenomena from universal history—or phenomena from the imagination. If this new book is as readily received as the Biblical accounts, then we will admit that the Bible has outlived its usefulness.

Pedagogy serves as a verification of many, many of life's phenomena, and of social and abstract questions.

Materialism will then only have the right to announce itself a victor when the bible of materialism shall be written, and the children are educated by that bible. Owen's attempt cannot be regarded as a proof of such a possibility, just as the growth of a lemon-tree in a Moscow hothouse is not a proof that trees can grow without the open sky and the sun.

I repeat my conviction, which perhaps comes from one-sided experience. Without the Bible the development of a child or adult is unthinkable in our society, just as it was unthinkable in Greek society without Homer. The Bible is the book that the children should read first. The Bible, both as to its contents and to its form, ought to serve as the model for all manuals and readers for children. An idiomatic translation of the Bible would be the best popular book. The appearance of such a translation in our time would be a watershed in the history of the Russian nation.

Now on to our instruction in sacred history. All the short sacred histories in the Russian language I consider a double crime: against holiness and against poetry. All these reworkings, in the effort to make the study of sacred history easier, only make it more difficult. The Bible is read for pleasure, at home, in casual ease. These abridged versions are learned by heart with the aid of a pointer. Not only are these short stories dull and incomprehensible, they also spoil students' ability to understand the poetry of the Bible. I have observed more than once that bad, unintelligible language impairs student receptiveness of the inner meaning of the Bible. Students remember difficult words that occur in the Bible (such as *lad, abyss, flouted*) along with the incidents; these words pique the students' attention due to their novelty, and they serve, as it were, as guideposts in their stories.

Very frequently a student speaks only in order to make use of a pretty phrase for which he or she has taken a liking, and then in the simple act of imbibing a word, the content escapes. I have also observed that students from other schools always feel much little of the charm of the Biblical stories, which due to the necessity of memorizing and by the rude methods of their former teachers has been destroyed for them. These students have even spoiled the younger students and their brothers, because their retellings cannot help but reflect certain trite methods found in the abridged sacred histories. Such trite stories have, by means of these harmful pamphlets, found their way to the people, and frequently the students bring with them from home peculiar legends about the creation of the world, about Adam, and about Joseph the Beautiful. Such students as these already cannot experience what the fresh students do when the latter listen to the Bible, and with trepidation catch each word and think that now, at last, all the wisdom of the world will be revealed to them.

I have always taught sacred history from the Bible, and I regard any other instruction as injurious.

We teach the New Testament similarly, by reading the Gospels and then having the students write down the stories in notebooks afterwards. They don't understand the New Testament as well as the Old, and we need to go back over things more often.*

History and Geography

Having finished the Old Testament, I naturally thought of teaching history and geography, both because these subjects are taught in all children's schools and I myself learned them, and because the history of the Jews of the Old Testament seemed to me naturally to lead the children to the questions of where, when, and under what conditions certain events took place: What is Egypt? What is a Pharaoh and an Assyrian king? and so forth.

As is always done, I began history with antiquity. But neither Mommsen, nor Duncker, nor all my own efforts, were able to make the history interesting for the students. They were completely uninterested in Sesostris, the Egyptian pyramids, and the Phoenicians. I had hoped that questions such as who the nations were that lived side by side with the Jews, and where the Jews lived and travelled, would interest them. But the students had no need for this information. The kings, the Pharaohs, the Egyptians, and the Palestinians, figures from sometime and somewhere, do not in the least satisfy them. The Jews were their heroes, and all the others were outsiders—superfluous peoples. I did not succeed in making heroes out of the Egyptians and Phoenicians for lack of material. I don't suppose anyone can make heroes out of them; the history of the Egyptians, it seems to me, is probably better researched than that of the Jews, but the Jews did not hand the Bible down to us. No matter how many details we may know about how pyramids were built, what the social standing of the various castes was vis-à-vis one another—*what good is all that to us?*—that is, to the children? In those histories there is no Abraham, Isaac, Jacob, Joseph, or Samson. There were a few things that they remembered and liked in ancient history—such as Semiramis, and so forth—but they retained those things only incidentally, not because these

---

* Tolstoy goes on to quote two retellings of the Last Supper from student notebooks (See Weiner, pp. 313–315).

passages explained anything, but because they were fantastical, and thus aesthetically satisfying . But such passages were rare; the rest was dull, pointless, and I was compelled to abandon the study of world history.

I was confronted with the same failure in geography as in history. I sometimes tell them whatever occurs to me from Greek, English, or Swiss history, without making any connections, simply as an instructive and artistic fable.

After world history, I had to experiment with our own native history, and so I began that cheerless Russian history, which we know so well as neither artistic nor instructive, in its many retellings from Ishimova to Vodovozov. I began with it twice: the first time before having finished the whole Bible, and the second time after finishing it. Before reading the Bible, the students absolutely refused to remember the lives of the Igors and Olegs. The same thing is repeating itself now with the younger students. Those who have not yet learned to make sense of what is told them from the Bible, and to recast the stories in their own words, will listen to Ruissian history five times and remember nothing about Rurik and Yaroslav.

The oldest students now remember Russian history and take notes, but nowhere near so well as they did with stories from the Bible, and they frequently ask to have passages repeated. We read them passages from Vodovozov and from Pogodin's *Norman Period*. One of the teachers somehow got carried, and, not heeding attention to my advice, did not skip over the feudal period of medieval Russia, and landed in the hopeless, nonsensical tangle of the Mstislavs, Bryachislavs, and Boleslavs. I once came into class just as they were to recite. It is hard to describe what ensued. For a long time all were silent. Finally, those who the teacher had called upon began to speak, some more boldly and with a better display of memory. All their mental powers were directed toward recalling the "funny" names, and who had done what was a matter of secondary importance.

"So he—What's his name? Barikav..." one boy began, "went to, what do you call it?"

"Muslav, Lev Nikolaevich?" a girl asked me, trying to help the boy out.

"Mstislav," I say.

"*And put him to rout,*" another student says proudly.

"Hold on, there was a river there. . . ."

"And his son collected an army and smashed *it to rout*, what do you call him?"

"I don't get it at all," says a girl with a memory like an elephant.

"It's so funny," says Semka.

"What is it, anyway, Mislav or Chislav? The devil knows what it is good for."

"Don't bother me if you don't know any better than I do!"

"You're so smart! You're awfully clever."

"What are you pushing me for?"

Those with the best memories tried once more and managed to get some things right if they received some help. But before this everything was so horrible, and it was such a shame to see these children (they were like hens who get sand thrown to them instead of feed, and they suddenly become perplexed, begin to cackle, are all in a flutter, and all set to pick at one another) that the teacher and I decided never to make same mistake again. We passed beyond the appanage period and continued with later Russian history. Here is something from the notebooks of the older students:

From the notebook of student V— R—

Our ancestors were called the Slavs. They had neither tsars nor princes. They were divided into clans, attacked each other, and went to war. One time the Normans fell upon the Slavs, and they conquered them, and levied a tribute. Then they said: "Why are we living thus? Let us choose a prince, that he may rule over us." They chose Rurik, with his two brothers Sineuis and Truvor. Rurik settled in Ladoga, Sineus in Izborsk with the Krivichians, Truvor at the Byelozero. When those brothers died, Rurik took their places.

Then two of them went to Greece—Askold and Dir. They stopped in Kiev and said: "Who is ruling here?" The Kievans said: "There were three here: Ki, Shchek, and Khoriv. Now they are dead." Askold and Dir said: "All right, we shall rule over you." The people agreed to it and began to pay tribute.

Then Rurik ordered cities and fortresses to be built, and he sent out the boyars to collect the tribute and bring it to him. Then Rurik made up his mind to go to war against Constantinople with two hundred boats. When he rode up to that city, the emperor was not there. The Greeks sent for him. The people prayed to God all the time. Then the archpriest brought out the garment of the Virgin Mother and dipped it in the water, and there rose a terrible storm, and all the boats of Rurik were scattered. Very few of them were saved. Then Rurik went home and died there. He left one son, Igor.

When Igor was small, Oleg took his place. He wanted to conquer Kiev; he took Igor with him and travelled straight down the Dnieper. On his way he conquered the cities of Lybich and Smolensk. When they reached Kiev, Oleg sent his messengers to Askold and Dir to say that merchants had come to see them, and he hid half of his army in boats, and half he left behind. When Askold and Dir came out with a small militia, Oleg's army jumped out from underneath the boats and rushed against them. Then Oleg lifted up Igor and said: "You are no princes and not of a princely race, but here is the prince." Then Oleg ordered them to be killed and conquered Kiev. Oleg remained there, made that city a capital, and christened it the mother of all Russian cities. Then he ordered cities and fortresses to be built, and sent the boyars to collect tribute, and they brought it to him. Then he went to wage war with the neighboring tribes, and he conquered many of them. He did not want to wage war with peaceful men, but with brave men. Then he got ready to go against Greece, and he went straight down the Dnieper. When he had travelled the length of the Dnieper, he went across the Black Sea. When he reached Greece, his army leaped upon the shore and began to burn and pillage everything. Oleg said to the Greeks: "Pay us a tribute—a grivna* for each boat." They were glad and began to pay them the tribute. Oleg collected three hundred puds† and went home again.

From the notebook of student V— M—‡:

When Oleg died, Igor, the son of Rurik, took his place. Igor wanted to get married. One time he went off with his armed guard—he had to sail across the Dnieper. Suddenly he saw a girl was sailing in a boat. When she reached the shore, Igor said: "Let me come aboard." She let him on board. Then Igor married her. Igor wanted to distinguish himself. So he collected an army and went to war, straight down the Dnieper—not to the right or to the left. From the Dnieper he went to the Black Sea, from the Black Sea to the Caspian Sea. Igor sent messengers to the kagan [local ruler] to let him pass through his lands: when Igor returned from war, he would give the kagan half his booty. The kagan let him through. When they came near the city, Igor ordered the people to come out on the shore so his army could burn and cut down everything and take prisoners. When they were through with their work, they began to rest. When they had rested, they went home with great joy. They came up to the city of the kagan—Igor gave the kagan what he had promised. The people heard that Igor was coming from the war, so they began to ask the kagan to allow them to avenge themselves on Igor, because Igor had spilled the blood of their relatives. The kagan ordered them not to,

---

* *Grivna*: a unit of currency.
† *Puds* (poods): a unit of weight.
‡ *V. M.*: Presumably Vassily Morozov ("Fedka").

but the people did not obey him and began to wage war. There was a mighty battle. The Russians were overcome, and everything was taken away from them which they had conquered.

There is no vital interest in this, as the reader may see from the extracts quoted. Russian history went better than world history, only because the students were accustomed to assimilating and writing down what was told to them—and also because the question "What is this to me?" is less applicable here. For them, the Russian people were easy to make heroes of, just as the Jewish nation has been: the Jews were heroic because they are God's favorite nation, and because children found their history pleasing aesthetically; the Russians were heroic not on aesthetic grounds, but because a national feeling comes through them. But the lessons were in fact dry, cold, and tedious. Unfortunately, the history itself very seldom gives occasion for the national sentiment to triumph.

Yesterday I left my own class to drop in on the history class. I wanted to find out the cause of the animation I could hear from the other classroom. It was the battle at Kulikovo.* All were agitated. The students were all aflutter.

"Now that's history! Great! . . ."

"Listen, Lev Nikolaevich, how he scared away the Tartars!"

"Let me tell you about it!"

"No, let me!" cried several children. "How the blood flowed in a stream!"

Nearly all were able to relate the story of the battle, and all were ecstatic. But if we are to satisfy only our nationalistic feelings, what will there be left of the whole history? The years 1612† and 1812, and that is all. You cannot go through the whole of history by responding to the national feeling. I understand that it is possible to utilize the historical tradition in order to satisfy and to develop children's artistic interest, but that will not be history. To teach history, we first need to develop the historical sentiment in children. How is that to be done?

I have often had occasion to hear that the teaching of history ought to begin not from the beginning but from the end—that is, not with

---

* *The Battle at Kulikovo*: Dmitry, the Muscovite prince, defeated the Mongols at Kulikovo in 1380. Kulikovo was major turning point in Russain history.

† *1612*: A Russian army liberated Moscow from Polish occupation in the year 1612, at the very end of historical period called the "Time of Troubles."

ancient but with modern history. This idea, in essence, is absolutely correct. How can we pique a child's interest in the beginning of the Russian state when he or she does not know what the Russian state—or a state in general—is? Anyone who has had anything to do with children ought to know that every Russian child is firmly convinced that the whole world is just like the Russia he or she lives in. The same is true for a French or for a German child. Why are children—and even childishly naive grownups—always surprised to hear that German children speak German? The interest in history generally makes its appearance after the interest in art. It is interesting for us to know the history of the founding of Rome because we know that Rome flourished later—the childhood of a man whom we recognize as great is interesting in much the same way. The juxtaposition of Rome's might with an insignificance of the itinerant hordes is for us the essence of history. We watch the evolution of Rome, having already in our imagination a picture of twhat the Roman Empire attained. We are interested in the foundations of Muscovy, because we know what the Russian Empire is. By my own observations and experience, the appearance of the first germ of the historic interest is the result of the knowledge of contemporaneous history, and frequently the result of a participation in it—an interest in politics, political opinions, debates, reading the newspaper—and therefore the idea of beginning history with the present must naturally present itself to every thinking teacher.

I made these experiments in the summer; I then wrote them down, and shall give one of them here.

First lesson in history

My intention was to explain in the first lesson how Russia differed from other countries: what its borders were, the characteristics of its governmental structure, who was ruling Russia now, and how and when the Emperor ascended the throne.

TEACHER: Where do we live, in what country?

A STUDENT: In Yasnaya Polyana.

ANOTHER STUDENT: In the field.*

TEACHER: No, in what country is Yasnaya Polyana, and the province of Tula?

---

* The name Yasnaya Polyana means "clear field" (actually, a small field or glade).

STUDENT: Tula is seventeen versts from us. Where is Tula province? A province is a province and that is all there is to it.

TEACHER: No. Tula is the capital of the Tula province, but a province and a town are two different things. Well, what is the earth?

STUDENT *(who had read in geography before)*: The earth is round like a ball.

By asking questions about what country a German—whom the students all knew—had previously lived, and where they would get to if they were to travel continuously in one direction, the students arrived at the answer that they lived in Russia. Some, however, answered the second question by saying that we would get nowhere. Others said that we would get to the end of the world.

TEACHER: *(repeating the student's answer)*. You said that we would come to some other countries. . . . Where will Russia end and other countries begin?

STUDENT: Where the Germans are.

TEACHER: So, if you meet Gustav Ivanovich and Karl Fedorovich* in Tula, you will say that there are Germans, and a new country begins there?

STUDENT: No, the Germans have to be continuous.

TEACHER: No, there are places in Russia where there are many, many Germans. Ivan Formich is from one of them, and yet those lands are still Russia. Why is it so?

(Silence)

TEACHER: Because they obey the same laws the Russians obey.

STUDENT: One law? How so? The Germans don't come to our church and they eat meat on fast-days.

TEACHER: Not that law, but they obey our Tsar.

STUDENT *(skeptical Semka)*: That's funny! Why do they have a different law, and yet obey the Tsar?

The teacher feels the need of explaining what a law is, so he asks what is meant by "obeying a law, being under one law."

FEMALE STUDENT *(an independent-minded manorial girl answers hurriedly and timidly)*: To accept the law means "to get married."

---

* No doubt members of Russia's sizeable population of ethnic Germans.

The students look inquisitively at the teacher. The teacher begins to explain that the law consists in putting a man in jail and punishing him for stealing or killing.

THE SKEPTIC SEMKA: And the Germans don't have such a law?

TEACHER: There are many other laws, laws that apply to the gentry, the peasants, the merchants, and the clergy (the word *clergy* perplexes them).

THE SKEPTIC SEMKA: And the Germans don't have them?

TEACHER: In some countries there are such laws, in others not. We have a Russian Tsar, and in the German lands there is a German Tsar.

This answer satisfies all the students, even skeptical Semka.

The teacher, seeing the necessity of giving a quick explanation of the various social classes, asks the students what classes of society they know. The students begin to itemize them: the gentry, the peasants, the priests, the soldiers.

"Any more?" the teacher asks.

"The manorial servants, the merchants, the samovar-makers."

The teacher asks them to describe the different classes.

STUDENTS: The peasants plough, the manorial servants serve their masters, the merchants trade, the soldiers serve, the samovar-makers make samovars, the priests say mass, and the gentry do nothing.

The teacher explains the real distinctions of the classes, and in vain tries to explain why soldiers are needed when there is no war on—to protect the state against attack—and the role of the gentry in government service. The teacher tries to explain to them in what way Russia differs geographically from the other countries, by saying that the whole earth is divided into different states. The Russians, the French, the Germans, divided up the whole earth and said to one another: "This is mine, and that is yours," and so Russia, like the other countries, came to have borders.

TEACHER: Do you understand what borders are? Explain them to me. Anyone. . . .

STUDENT *(bright boy)*: Beyond Turkin Heights there is a border (this is a stone post standing on the road between Tula and Yasnaya Polyana that indicates where Tula County begins).

All the students were satisfied with this definition.

The teacher sees a need to point out more examples of boundaries in familiar, local contexts. He draws a plan of two rooms and shows the boundary which separates them; he shows them a map of the village, and the students recognize certain boundaries in it. The teacher explains— that is, he thinks that he explains—that Yasnaya Polyana has *its* borders, and Russia has *its* borders.

He flatters himself with his belief that all have understood him, but when he asks them how to find out how far it is from Yasnaya Polyana to the border of Russia, the students answer without the slightest hesitation that this is easy: you just measure the distance with a yardstick.

TEACHER: In which direction?

STUDENT: Just take it straight from here to the border and write down how much it is.

We go back to the drawings, plans, and maps. The need for a concept of scale, entirely lacking, becomes clear. The teacher proposes drawing a map of our village with all the streets on it. We begin drawing on the blackboard, but the whole village does not get on it because the scale is too large. We begin anew on a small scale, this time on a slate. The concepts of scale, plan, and boundary, are getting clearer. The teacher repeats all that has been said and asks what Russia is and where it ends.

STUDENT: The country in which we live and in which Germans and Tartars live.

ANOTHER STUDENT: The country which is under the Russian Tsar.

TEACHER: But where are its borders?

FEMALE STUDENT: Where the infidel Germans begin.

TEACHER: The Germans are not infidels. The Germans, too, believe in Jesus Christ. (Entrée for an explanation of religions and creeds.)

STUDENT (*with zeal, apparently happy to have recalled something*): In Russia there are laws that he who kills is put in jail, and there are all kinds of people—clergy-people, soldiers, gentry.

SEMKA: Who feeds the soldiers?

TEACHER: The Tsar. That's why money is taken from everybody, for the soldiers serve for all.

The teacher explains what the Crown is, and manages to make them repeat some way or other what boundaries are.

The lesson lasts about two hours. The teacher is convinced that the students have retained a great deal of what has been said, and continues his succeeding lessons in the same vein. He comes to the realization only much later that his methods were wrong and that all his whole approach was complete nonsense.

I had involuntarily fallen into the common pitfall of the Socratic method, which in the German *Anschauungsunterricht** has reached the highest degree of monstrosity. I did not give the students any new ideas in these lessons, all the time thinking that this was exactly what I was giving them, and it was only due to my moral influence that I made the children give the answer I wanted. *Russia* and *Russian* remained the same unconscious tokens of something hazy and indefinite, words that belonged to them and to "us." *Law* remained the same incomprehensible word it had been before. I made these experiments about six months ago and at first I was exceedingly well satisfied and proud of them. Those whom I spoke to called my work uncommonly good and interesting. But after three weeks, during which time I was unable to work in the school, I tried to continue what I had begun, and I found that what I had done before was nonsense and self-deception. Not one student was able to tell me what a border is, what Russia is, what a law is, and what the boundaries of Krapivensk County are. Everything they had learned they had since forgotten—yet all the while they knew it all in their own fashion. I was convinced of the error of my ways; but what I didn't know was whether my mistake consisted in faulty teaching methods or in my basic conception. Perhaps there is no possibility—before children reach a certain stage of development, and before the aid of newspapers and travel— of awakening in the child an interest in history and geography. Maybe that method will be found (I am still endeavoring to find it) that will make it possible. What I do know, however, is that such a method will in no way be connected with what is called history and geography—that is, in learning from books, which fails to rouse, and kills, these interests.

I have also made other experiments—with teaching modern history— and they have been very successful. I told the students the history of the Crimean campaign, about the reign of Emperor Nicholas, and the year 1812. All this I told almost in a fairy-tale tone, for the most part historically inaccurate, and grouping the events around one central historical figure. My greatest success, as could be expected, was with the story of the war against Napoleon.

---

* *Anschauungsunterricht*: literally, "visual education."

This class has remained a memorable event in our life. I shall never forget it. I had long promised the children that I would tell them history from the present backwards, while another teacher would begin from the beginning, and we would finally meet somewhere in the middle. My evening scholars had left me, and I came into Russian history class. The class was discussing Svyatoslav. The students were bored. On a tall bench sat, as always, three peasant girls in a row, their heads tied with kerchiefs. One was asleep. Mishka gave me a shove: "Look at our cuckoos sitting there—one is asleep." And they were exactly like cuckoos!

"You had better tell us from the end," someone said, and all stood up.

I sat down and began to talk. As always, about two minutes went by, two minutes of hubbub, groaning, and crowding around. Some children clambered under the table, some on the table, some under the benches, others on their neighbors' shoulders and knees. Then there was silence. (I hope to place this story with the publishing house, "Little Books," so I am not going to relate everything here.) I began with Alexander I, told them of the French Revolution, of Napoleon's successes, of his seizure of power, and of the war that ended in the peace of Tilsit. As soon as we got to Russia, one could hear sounds and words of lively interest on all sides.

"Well, is he going to conquer us too?"

"Alexander will give it to him, most likely!" said someone who knew about Alexander. But I had to disappoint them—the time had not yet come for that—and they felt insulted when they heard that there was talk of making the Tsar's sister a bride for Napoleon, and that Alexander had spoken with him on the bridge, as with an equal.

"You just wait!" exclaimed Petka, with a threatening gesture.

"Come on, come on. Tell us!"

When Alexander did not submit to him—that is, when Alexander declared war—all expressed approval. When Napoleon came against us with twelve nations, and incited the Germans and Poland, they were mortified.

A German, a friend of mine, was standing in the room.

"Ah, you were against us, too," said Petka (the best storyteller).

"Keep quiet!" cried the others.

The retreat of our army tormented the listeners, and from on all sides came the question: why? Curses were heaped on Kutuzov and Barclay.

"Your Kutuzov is no good!"

"You just wait," said another.

"Well, did he surrender?" asked a third.

When we reached the battle at Borodino, and when in the end I was obliged to say that we did not gain a victory, I was sorry for them—it was evident that I had given them all a terrible blow.

"Though our side did not win, theirs didn't either!"

When Napoleon came to Moscow and was waiting for the keys and for lines of Muscovites with caps in hand, there was a rumbling from the consciousness of the students, who knew they could not be vanquished. The burning of Moscow was, naturally, approved by all. Then came the victory—the retreat.

"When Napoleon left Moscow, Kutuzov chased after him and went to fight him," I said.

"He stopped him in his tracks!" Fedka corrected me.

Fedka, red in the face, was sitting opposite me, bending his thin, dirty fingers in excitement. (This is his habit.) The moment he said that, the whole room groaned in ecstasy of pride. A little fellow in the back row was being crushed, but nobody noticed.

"That's better! Take the keys now!" and so on.

I continued with our pursuit of the French. It pained the children to hear that someone was too late at the Berezina and that we let the French get away. Petka even groaned with pain.

"I should have shot him to death for being late."

By that time we even pitied the frozen Frenchmen a little. Then, when we crossed the border, and the Germans—who had been against us—joined forces with us, someone remembered the German standing in the room.

"How is that? First you are against us, and when your side is losing, you come on our side!"—and suddenly all stood up and started shouting at the German, so that the noise could be heard in the street. When they quieted down, I continued telling them how we followed Napoleon to Paris, placed the real king on the throne, celebrated our victory, and feasted. But the recollection of the Crimean War spoiled the whole business.

"Just wait," said Petka, shaking his fist, "let me grow up and I will show them! If we had a second chance at the Shevardino redoubt and at Mount Malakhov, we would certainly have won them back!"

It was late when I finished. Usually the children are asleep by that time. No one was, even the eyes of our three little cuckoos were burning.

As I was standing up, to my great astonishment Taraska crawled out from underneath my chair, and gave me a look that was at once lively and seriously.

"How did you get down under there?"

"He has been there from the very beginning" someone said.

There was no need to ask him whether he had understood—it was clear from his face.

"Well, are you going to tell the story now?" I asked.

"Me?" Taraska thought awhile. "I will tell the whole thing. I'll tell it at home."

"Me too."

"And me."

"Are we finished?"

"Yes."

The students all flew down the stairs, some promising to give it to the Frenchmen, others reproaching the German, still others repeating how Kutuzov had made Napolean "stop in his tracks."

"*Sie haben ganz Russisch erzählt* [Spoken like a true Russian]," the German who had been so severely reprimanded said to me in the evening. "You ought to hear how they tell the story in our country! *Sie haben nichts gesagt von deutschen Freiheitskampfen* [You said nothing about the German wars of liberation]."

I fully agreed with him that my narrative was not history, but a fanciful tale for rousing national sentiment.

Consequently, as a study of history, this attempt was even less successful than the first.

I used the same approach in teaching geography . I began with physical geography. I remember the first lesson. I began it, and immediately lost my way. It turned out—as I never would have suspected—that I did not know what I wanted my ten-year-old peasant students to know. I could explain day and night to them, but was completely at a loss when explaining summer and winter. Feeling ashamed by my ignorance, I studied up on the matter. I asked many of my acquaintances, educated people, and nobody—with exception of those who had recently been in school or were teachers—was able to give me a satisfactory explanation without a globe. I ask all my readers to verify this. I believe that only one out of a hundred people knows the reason we have seasons, although all the children learn it. Having studied it up, I tried again and, with the help of a candle and a globe, it seemed to me that I gave the students an excellent idea of why we have summer and winter. The students listened to me with great attention and interest. (It gave them especial pleasure to know that their fathers could not accept this explanation of the seasons, and that they could provoke their fathers with their newfound wisdom.)

At the end of my demonstration, the skeptic Semka, the quickest of all the students, stopped me with this question: "How is it that the earth is moving and our house is all the time in the same spot? It should move to a new place."

I saw that my explanations were a thousand versts ahead of the most intelligent student; what must the slower students have thought?

I retraced my steps to show all the proofs of the sphericity of the earth—voyages around the earth, how in the distance we see the mast of a ship before the deck is seen, and so forth. Consoling myself with the thought that this time they must have understood, I made them write out what they had learned. All wrote: "First proof—the earth is like a ball. Second proof. . . ." They had forgotten the third proof, and had to ask me. It was quite apparent that the main thing for them was to remember the "proofs." Not once, or ten times, but a hundred times I returned to these explanations, always without success. On an exam students all would have answered questions satisfactorily; but I felt that they did not understand. Recalling that I myself did not understand the problem before the age of thirty, I gladly excused them for not understanding. As I had done in my childhood, they accepted the notion that the earth was round on faith, though they had not understood a thing. It was far easier for me to understand—as my nanny impressed upon me as young boy—that earth and sky meet at the end of the world, and that where they meet, women are washing clothes, storing their laundry paddles in the sky. Our students had long ago been convinced of—and still persist in—notions that are diametrically opposed to those I am trying to instill in them. It will take a long time to break down the notions they hold dear—and their world-views, which have yet to be challenged by anything—before they will be able to understand. The laws of physics and mechanics will be the first to shatter their long-held conceptions. But they—like me and everyone else—had physical geography before studying physics.

In the teaching of geography, as in all other subjects, the most common, most serious, and most harmful error is haste. We are so happy that we know the earth is round and moves around the sun that we rush to inform the student of this fact. But what is really worth knowing is not that the earth is round, but how people discovered this was so. Very frequently, children are told that the sun is so many billions of versts from the earth, but that is neither surprising nor interesting to the child. What the child wants to know is how that was discovered. Anyone wanting to discuss these matters with children should tell them about parallaxes. This is quite feasible. The only reason why I dwelt so long on the roundness of the earth is because the situation of the earth is important to the whole of geography. Out of a thousand educated people—teachers and students aside—only one will possess a sound knowledge of why there is summer and winter, and where Guadeloupe is. Out of a thousand children, not one understands in his or her childhood the explanations of the sphericity of the earth. Not one believes that Guadeloupe is a real place, and yet all children are persistently taught both things very early on.

After physical geography I began covering the parts of the globe and their various characteristics, but from our discussion the only thing the students retained was the fun of vying to shout: "Asia, Africa, Australia." If I asked them out of the blue, "In what part of the world is France?" (having told them a minute before that England and France were in Europe), somebody would say that France was in Africa. Whenever I began geography with them, I always imagined I saw the question "Why?" in each of their minds, and in every sound of their voices. And there was no answer to that sad question, "Why?"

Just as in history the simple thought cropped up with the end, so in geography the idea naturally occurred to us to begin with the schoolroom, and with the village of Yasnaya Polyana. I had seen such experiments in Germany, and so I myself, discouraged by the failure of the usual geography, switched to descriptions of rooms, houses, and villages. As the students learn to draw plans and maps, such exercises are hardly useless, but it is not interesting for them to learn whose land lies beyond our village, because they all know that there is the village of Teliatinki. And knowing what lies beyond Teliatinki does not interest them, because there, no doubt, another village just like Teliatinki, and Teliatinki with its fields is absolutely uninteresting.

I tried to give them geographical landmarks such as Moscow and Kiev, but they found these so abstract that they had to learn them by heart. I tried drawing maps, and the maps interested them and proved to be good aids for their memories. But again the same question arose: Why? Why did they need to memorize these things? I also tried telling them about the polar and equatorial regions—they listened with pleasure and could talk about what they had heard, but they were able only to remember that which was not of a geographical nature in my stories. The main trouble was that drawing plans of the village was only drawing plans, and not geography. Drawing maps was only drawing maps, and not geography. And the stories about animals, forests, icebergs, and cities were fairy tales, and not geography. For them, the geography was only learning something by heart. All the books—Grube, Biernadsky—failed to interest them.

One little book gave the students some real geography. The students read this book with greater enjoyment than all the other books, and in my opinion is the best exemplar of what should be done to prepare children for studying geography and to stir up their interest in the subject. That book is *Parley* (1837). We used this book mainly as a prompt for the teacher, who uses it to tell students about various countries and cities. The children recite, but rarely retain the names of places on a map, which refer to particular events—it is mainly the events that they remember. This class, however, belongs more properly in the category of conversation, which we will speak of when the time is right. In spite of all the artfulness with which the study of unnecessary names is masked in this book, in spite of all our care, the children have figured out our designs to inveigle them by pretty stories, and have acquired a positive distaste for this class.

I finally came to the conclusion that in history class there is not only no need to study the dull Russian history, but also that Cyrus, Alexander the Great, Caesar, and Luther are not necessary to a child's development. All these persons and events do interest students, but their interest is not due their importance in history, but to the artistic quality of their lives and to the artistic treatments of historians—and even more so, to popular tradition.

The story of Romulus and Remus is interesting not because these brothers were the founders of the mightiest empire in the world, but because it is entertaining, funny, and lovely to hear about how they were fed by the she-wolf and so forth. The story of the Gracchi is interesting because it is as artistic, just as is the history of Gregory VII and the ruined emperor, and it is possible to grab students' attention with it. But the story of the migration of the nations will be dull and aimless because it is not artistic, just as the story of the art of printing is not interesting, no matter how much we may try to impress the students with the idea that it forms an epoch in history and that Gutenberg was a great man. Tell them well how striking matches were invented, and they will never agree with you that the inventor of matches was a lesser man than Gutenberg. In short, in a child—and in students in general, who have only just begun to live—there does not yet exist an interest in history, not to mention in universal humanity. There is only the artistic interest. It is said that after the exposition of all the material, it is possible to give students an artistic interpretation of all the periods of history—I do not see this. Macaulay and Thiers are just as inappropriate as Tacitus and Xenophon.

To make history popular, artistic window-dressing is hardly what is needed. The historical phenomena have to be personified, just as tradition and sometimes life itself personifies great thinkers and historians. Children like history only when its contents are artistic. Children have no historical interest, nor can they ever have; consequently there can be no such thing as history for children. History only sometimes serves as material for an artistic development, so as long as the historical interest is not developed, there can be no history. Bertet and Kaydanov, after all, remain the only manuals. There is an old anecdote that the history of the Medans is dark and fabulously mythological. As far as children are concerned nothing more can be made out of history; they simply lack the historical interest. Efforts to make history and geography artistic and interesting— Grube's biographical sketches, Biernadsky—satisfy neither the artistic nor historical demands. They lack historical accuracy, and skew the details to impossible dimensions.

The same is true with geography. When Mitrofanushka* was being persuaded to study geography, his mother said: "What is the use of teaching him all kinds of countries? His coachman will know how to take him where he needs to go." There has never been a stronger argument against geography, and all the learned men of the world are unable to make any reply to this ironclad argument. I am quite serious. What use was there in my studying about city of Barcelona and its river if, having lived thirty-three years, I have never once needed this information? Save for the development of my mental powers, the most picturesque description of Barcelona and its inhabitants has given me nothing, so far as I can see.

---

* *Mitrofanushka*: a character in Fon-Vizin's comedy, *The Minor*.

What use is there in Semka and Fedka knowing about the Mariinsk canal and other waterways if, as we can suppose, they will never get there. But if Semka should go there, it will make no difference whether he has studied it or not, for in real life he will find out all he needs to know about this waterway. I am quite unable to see how, for the development of his mental powers, the knowledge that hemp goes down the Volga will help him, or that tar comes up that river, that there is a harbor by the name of Dubovka, that a certain subterranean stratum goes to a certain place, that the Samoyeds travel on reindeer, and so forth. I have a whole world of information about mathematics and the natural sciences, about language and poetry, which time is too short to relate; the number of questions that surround me is endless. When a student demands an answer to one of these infinite questions of life, I must answer, before drawing pictures of the polar ice, of the tropical countries, of the mountains of Australia, and of the rivers of America.

In history and geography, experience tells us one and the same thing, and everywhere confirms our thoughts. Everywhere the teaching of history and of geography proceeds badly. For examinations, students memorize the names of mountains, cities and rivers, kings and emperors. The only possible textbooks then, are those by Arsenev and Obodovsky, Kaydanov, Smaragdov, and Bertet, and everywhere one hears complaints about the instruction in this subject, and all seek something new they cannot find.

It is amusing to hear everyone recognize that demands of geography are incompatible with the spirit of the students throughout the world, and consequently they invent a thousand clever means (such as Sidov's method) to make the children remember certain words. But the simple idea—that geography is entirely unnecessary, that there is no need of knowing these words—never enters anybody's mind. All attempts at combining geography with geology, zoology, botany, ethnography, and who knows what else—as well as history with biography—remain pipe dreams that result in such worthless books such as those by Grube, which are useful neither to young children, older ones, teachers, nor the public at large. Indeed, if the compilers of these seemingly new geography and history textbooks only knew what it is they're after, and if they themselves were to spend some time actually teaching, they would soon be convinced of the impossibility of their undertaking.

In the first place, geography combined with the natural sciences and ethnography would constitute such an extensive science that a whole life would not be sufficient for its study, and it would be even drier for a child to study than geography. Second, it is unlikely that in another thousand years there will be enough material for any manual to be written on the subject. Teaching the geography of Krapivensk district, I will be required to give students detailed information about the flora and the fauna and the geological structure of the earth at the North Pole, and details about the inhabitants and the commerce of the Kingdom of Bavaria, because I shall be in possession of this information. But I will be at a loss to say anything about the Byelev and Efremov districts, because I will have no material on them. But the children and common sense demand of me a certain harmoniousness and uniformity in my teaching. There is nothing left for me to do, then, except to teach geography from Obodovsky's textbook, or not to teach geography at all.

Just as the historical interest must be first aroused for history, so we must evoke the geographical interest for the study of geography. But the geographical interest, from my observations and experiments, is roused either by the study of the natural sciences or by travel—in ninety-nine out of a hundred cases, by travel. Just as the reading of newspapers—and especially biographies—and a sympathy with the political life of the nation generally serve as the first step in the study of history, so travel serves as the first step in the study of geography. Both are now exceedingly accessible to everyone nowadays, therefore we should have no fear renouncing the old superstitions about teaching history and geography. Contemporary life is so instructive in this regard that geographical and historical knowledge is really as necessary for our general development as it seems to be; life will always fill the void of what students fail to learn in geography or history class.

Indeed, if we can renounce the old superstitions, it will not appear so terrible to us that people can grow up without having learned as children who Yaroslav was or Otho was, and that there is such a place as Estremadura, et cetera. Haven't we stopped teaching astrology, rhetoric, and poetics? We are in the process of giving up the study of Latin, and the human race hasn't grown any more stupid. New sciences are born, and in our time the natural sciences are becoming popular; the old sciences need to drop off when they have outlived their usefulness—not the sciences, but those areas of the sciences that the birth of new sciences have made obsolete.

To rouse students' interest about knowing how the human race lives, has lived, evolved, and developed in various countries—and to rouse interest for the discovery of those laws by which humanity eternally moves—is one thing. To rouse interest in the comprehension of the laws of the phenomena of nature on the whole globe and the dispersal of the human race over it—is something different. Maybe rousing such interest is useful, but in order to attain this goal neither Ségur nor Thiers nor Obodovsky nor Grube will add anything. I know two elements necessary to achieving this goal: the artistic feeling of poetry and that of patriotism. But in order to develop both, we have to write the requisite textbooks. So long as there are none, we must seek or waste our time and energy in vain, tormenting the younger generation by making students learn history and geography simply because we have learned them. *Before university, I not only see no need for the study of history and geography, but even a great harm in it.* Beyond that, I am unsure.

The Arts

In giving an account for the months of November and December at the Yasnaya Polyana school, there now stand before me two subjects of an entirely different character. These are drawing and singing—the arts.

If I were to begin from the view that I did not know what should be taught and why this, I would have to ask myself: Will studying art be useful for peasant children, who must pass their lives worrying about their daily bread? What good is it to them? Ninety-nine out of every hundred will answer in the negative. Nor can one answer otherwise. The moment such a question is asked, common sense demands the following answer: A peasant child cannot become an artist—he will have to till the soil. If the peasant is to have any artistic aspirations, then he will not have the strength for the relentless, backbreaking work he must do, without which society as we know it would be unthinkable. When I say "he," I mean the child of the masses. Of course, this is insipid, but I rejoice at its stupidity. But wait, let us examine the causes. There is another great stupidity. This same child of the masses, every child of the masses, has just such a right—or shall I say a greater right—to enjoy art than we—the children of the happy class, who are not burdened by relentless work, but surrounded by all the comforts of life—have.

To deprive peasant children of the right to enjoy art is to deprive me, the teacher, of the right to introduce those children to the province of higher pleasures, toward which his being strives with all the powers of his soul. This is the greater stupidity of which I speak. How can we bring harmony between these two stupidities? This is not lyricism—for which I was reproached in the description of the walk which I gave in the first issue of *Yasnaya Polyana*—this is logic. Every harmonization is impossible, but is only a self-deception. I shall be told—and I have been—that if drawing is needed in a popular school, it should only be drawing from nature: that is, technical drawing, drawings of ploughs, machines, and buildings. Freehand drawing is merely an auxiliary art to mechanical drawing. This common view of drawing is also held by our drawing teacher at the Yasnaya Polyana school. But it was his experience with teaching drawing this way that convinced us of the falseness and injustice of this program of technical drawing. The majority of the pupils, after four months of careful, exclusively technical drawing—which excluded all human figures, animals, and landscapes—ended with student enthusiasm cooling off considerably in respect to the drawing of technical objects. At the same time, the students developed to such an appreciation and need for drawing that they carried around secret sketchbooks, in which they drew people and horses with all four legs coming out of one spot.

The same was true of music. The typical music curriculum in the popular schools does not include singing beyond that in church choirs. The same thing takes place here: the children either suffer through the dull and painful memorizing of certain sounds—which they produce as if they were so many throats taking the place of organ pipes—or they learn an appreciation for the artistic, which finds its satisfaction in the balalaika and the accordion and frequently in some unsophisticated song the teacher does not recognize as music. It is one of the two: either art in general is harmful and unnecessary—which is not at all so strange as it first appears—or every individual, regardless of class and occupation, has a right to art and a right to devote himself to it, on the grounds that art does not tolerate mediocrity.

The stupidity is not in this, but in posing such a question *as a question*. Have the children of the masses a right to art? Asking this is like asking whether the children of the masses have a right to eat beef—it is like asking if they have the right to satisfy their human needs. The question should be: Is the beef any good that we are offering to—or keeping from—the masses? When I offer the masses certain knowledge that we possess, and when I notice it has an evil effect on them, I do not conclude that the masses are bad because they have not received this knowledge in the right way, or that the masses have not yet developed sufficiently to receive this knowledge and make use of it as we do, but that the knowledge itself is not good, not normal, and that with the aid of the masses we must work out a new knowledge that will be more in accord with us, society, and the masses. I conclude only that this knowledge and the arts live among us and do not seem harmful, but cannot live among the masses, and seem harmful to them only because this knowledge and the arts are not things the masses generally need. I am also convinced that we have them only because we are spoiled, in the same way someone acclimated to the foul air of a factory or tavern can sit there for five hours and suffer no ill effects, while that same air would kill a newcomer.

I shall be told: "Who said that the knowledge and the arts of our cultivated society are false? How can you conclude from the fact that the masses do not accept them, that the knowledge and the arts are false?" All such questions have a simple reply: Because there are thousands of us, and there are millions of them.

I continue the comparison with the well-known physiological fact. A man comes from the fresh air into a cramped, smoke-filled room, the air of which has been exhausted by breathing. His vital functions are still vigorous, for his organism has through breathing been fed by a large quantity of oxygen from the pure air. By force of habit he begins to breathe deeply of the impure air; the harmful gases get into his blood stream to the blood in great quantities—and his organism is weakened (frequently causing fainting and sometimes death). Meanwhile, hundreds of people continue to breathe and live in the foul air because their functions have become less vigorous, or to put it another way, they are weaker and live less.

I will be told that both classes of people are alive. Who is to say whose life is more normal and better? When a man comes out from the foul atmosphere into the fresh air he frequently faints, and vice versa. The answer is simple: not only the physiologist but any commonsensical person will ask himself or herself where the majority people live: In the fresh air or in fetid prisons? (The latter.) The physiologist will make observations on the sum total of the functions of both and will say that the functions are more vigorous and the level of nutrition higher in the individual who lives in the fresh air.

The same relation exists between the arts in so-called "educated society" and the aspirations of the art of the people: I am speaking of painting, sculpture, music, and poetry. Ivanov's painting will arouse in the people nothing but admiration for his technical mastery, but it will not evoke any poetical or religious feelings—these are already evoked by the popular broadside of John of Novgorod and the devil in the jugs.*

Likewise, Venus de Milo will rouse only a legitimate feelings of distaste for the woman's nakedness and shamelessness. Beethoven's Late Quartets will appear only as disagreeable sounds, interesting perhaps because one plays the pipes and the other a fiddle. The best works of our poetry—the lyrics of Pushkin—will seem like only a collection of words, and its meaning despicable nonsense.

Introduce a peasant child to this world—you can do that and are doing it all the time with the hierarchy of the educational institutions, academies, and art classes. That child will feel, and feel sincerely the beauty of Ivanov's painting, of the Venus de Milo, of Beethoven's quartets, and of Pushkin's lyric poems. But entering into this world, this child will no longer be breathing with full lungs—the fresh air, whenever he has to go into it, will affect him painfully and adversely.

As with the case of breathing, common sense and physiology will have the same reply. With the arts, the same common sense and pedagogy (not the pedagogy that writes curricula, but the one that endeavors to study the universal paths of education and law) will reply that if an individual does not live in the world of art our educated classes enjoy, then that individual has a richer life. In other words, that the need for art, and the satisfaction that it gives are fuller and more legitimate in the masses than with us. Common sense will say that because it sees a happy majority living outside the educated class' *milieu*. The pedagogue will observe the mental functions of people living in our circles, then those outside of our

---

* *Author's note*: We beg the reader to direct his attention to this monstrous picture, which is remarkable on account of the strength of the religious and poetic feelings expressed in it, and which bears the same relation to modern Russian painting that the painting of Fra Angelico has to the painting of the followers of Michelangelo.

circles; he will observe what happens when people are introduced into the contaminated air—that is, when we expose the younger generations to art. On the basis of sophistry and the natural loathing fresh natures feel when introduced into an artificial atmosphere—and on the basis of their limited mental functions—the pedagogue will likewise conclude the people's artistic needs and aspirations are more legitimate than those of a spoiled minority, the so-called "educated class."

I have made these observations in respect to the two branches of art with which I am the more intimately acquainted and which I formerly loved passionately: music and poetry. It's terrible to say, but I came to the conclusion that everything we had been doing in music and poetry had been following a false, exclusionary path, one devoid of meaning and of a real future, which paled in comparison to the aspirations and even the actual artistic works we find among the people. I became convinced that a lyric poem, for example, "I remember the magic moment . . ." and musical works such as Beethoven's last symphony, were not as unconditionally and universally fine as the song "Steward Vanka" and the tune of "Down the Mother Volga"; that Pushkin and Beethoven please us not because there is any absolute beauty in them, but because we are just as spoiled as Pushkin and Beethoven were, and because Pushkin and Beethoven both flatter our monstrous appetites and our weaknesses. How common it is to hear the trite paradox that to comprehend what is beautiful a certain amount of training is necessary! Who said this? How has it been proved? It is only an excuse, an easy out from a hopeless situation into which we have been brought by poor and false direction, by our art's belonging exclusively to one class. Why are the beauty of the sun, the beauty of the human face, the beauty of the sounds of a popular song, and the beauty of an act of love and self-renunciation accessible to all, and why do they require no preparation?

I know that for the majority everything I have said here will appear as the merest prattle, the privileged exercises of a loose tongue, but pedagogy—free pedagogy—explains many questions by means of experiment, and by means of an endless repetition of one and the same phenomenon it transfers the questions from the field of dreams and reflections into the territory of propositions based on facts. I have for years vainly endeavored to convey to students the beauties of Pushkin's poetry and of our whole literature. The same is being done by countless teachers—and not just in Russia. If these teachers observe the results of their efforts, and if they care to be candid, they will all confess that the chief result of their efforts to develop the poetical feeling has been to kill it, that the most poetical natures among the students have shown the greatest loathing for their explanations. I had struggled for years, I tell you, without positive results—and all I had to do was accidentally to open Rybnikov's collection, and the students' needs for poetry found full satisfaction, a satisfaction that—when you calmly and unbiasedly compared to it to what I felt with the best works of Pushkin—I could not help finding legitimate.

The same happened to me in respect to music, of which I shall have to speak now.

I shall try and make a résumé of all said above. When the question is asked whether the fine arts are necessary for the masses, pedagogues generally become timid and confused (Plato was the only one who boldly answered in the negative). They say that they are necessary, but with certain limitations: that it endangers the social structure to give everybody the opportunity to become artists. They say that certain arts can exist only in certain classes of society. They say that the arts must have their own special servants who are devoted to but one art form. They say that the highly gifted natures must have the opportunity to extricate themselves from the masses in order to devote themselves exclusively to the service of art. This is the greatest concession that pedagogy makes to each individual: to make of himself what he pleases. All the cares of the pedagogues in respect to the arts are focused on these concerns.

I regard all this as unjust. I assume that the need for enjoying art and practicing art are inherent in each human personality, no matter to what race or *milieu* he or she belongs, and that this *necessity* has its rights, and should be satisfied. Taking this assumption as an axiom, I say that if obstacles and disparities arise for a given person in the enjoyment of art and its reproduction, the cause lies not in the dissemination or concentration of art among many or among few, but in the character and direction of the art itself. We must cast doubts on the art itself in such cases, in order not to foist anything false upon the younger generation, and also in order to give that younger generation a chance to create something new, both in form and in content.

I now present our drawing teacher's report for the months of November and December. His method of instruction, it seems to me, is a convenient and enjoyable way for students to overcome the technical difficulties of drawing. His method does not, however, touch upon the question of the art itself, because the teacher, when beginning the class, decided beforehand that it was useless for peasant children to become artists.

Drawing

When nine months ago I took up teaching drawing, I had no definite plan either for how to approach the instruction or how to teach the students. I had neither drawings nor models, with the exception of a few illustrated albums, which, however, I did not make use of during my course of instruction. I limited myself to simple aids, such as one may find in any village school. A painted wooden board, chalk, slates, and little square sticks of various lengths—which we used for object lessons in teaching mathematics. These we all the materials we had for our class, but this did not prevent us from copying everything that fell into our hands. Not one of the students had studied drawing before; they came to me with only their ability to pass judgment, and they were granted full liberty to express themselves whenever and however they wished. We thus hoped to discover what their needs were and then to form a definite plan for the class. For the first lesson I formed a square out of four sticks to see whether the students would, without any previous instruction, be able to draw the square. Only a few of the students drew some very irregular squares, by expressing the solid sticks forming the square by means of straight lines. I was quite satisfied with this. For the weaker students, I drew with chalk a square on the blackboard. Then we composed a cross in the same manner, and we drew it.

An unconscious, innate feeling generally made the children discover a fairly correct correlation of the lines, although they drew the lines quite poorly. I did not deem it necessary to try to achieve a regularity in the straight lines in every figure in order not to torment them in vain, and demanded only that the figure be copied. At first I intended to give the students a conception of the relation of lines from their length and direction, rather than to trouble myself with their ability to make the lines themselves neat and regular.

A child will learn right away to comprehend the relation between a long and a short line, the difference between a right angle and parallel lines, and soon learns passably to draw a straight line.

Little by little we began to draw the corners of these square little sticks, and then we composed various figures out of them.

The students paid no attention whatsoever to the slight thickness of these sticks—the third dimension—and all the time we drew only the front view of the objects.

The difficulty of clearly presenting—with our insufficient material— the position and correlation of the figures compelled me now and then to draw figures on the board. I frequently united the drawing from nature with the drawing of models, giving them certain objects to draw. If the students were unable to draw a certain object, I drew it myself on the board.

The drawing of figures from the board took place in the following manner: I first drew a horizontal or vertical line, divided it by points into different pads, and the students copied that line. Then I drew another or several other lines—perpendicular or slanting to the first line—and divided into units of the same size. Then we connected the points of division of these lines by straight lines or arcs, and thus formed a certain symmetrical figure, which as it grew was copied step by step by the students. I thought that this would be advantageous; in the first place, because one student learned objectively the whole process of the formation of the figure; and second, because through this drawing on the board that student had understood the correlation of lines much better than through the process of copying and drawing. The possibility of copying directly was lost in the process, so the figure itself—as an object from nature—had to be copied on a diminished scale.

It is nearly always useless to show students a large, completely rendered picture or figure, because the beginners will be positively confused, just as though they would be by an object from nature. But the evolution of the figure before their very eyes has a great significance. The students in this case see the skeleton of the drawing on which the whole body is later formed. I constantly called on the students to critique the lines and their relations as I had drawn them. I frequently drew the lines wrong on purpose in order to get an idea how they could judge the correlation and regularity of the lines. When I drew the next figure, I asked the children where some line ought to be added in their opinion, and I even called on the students individually, asking for suggestions.

In this manner I not only aroused a greater interest in the students, but also encouraged a free participation in the formation and development of the figure; in this way we avoided the question, "Why?" which every child naturally asks himself or herself when copying from an original.

Their greater or lesser understanding and their greater or lesser interest in drawing had the main influence on the progress of the class and the method we used. I frequently abandoned what I had purposely prepared for the lesson, simply because it struck the students as foreign or dull.

So far, I had given them symmetrical figures to draw because they are the easiest and most straightforward. Then, for experiment's sake, I asked the best students to compose and draw figures on the board. Although nearly all drew in the same way, it was nevertheless interesting to watch the growing rivalries, the judgment they passed made about one another's work, and the peculiar structures of their figures. Many of these drawings were peculiarly in harmony with students' personalities.

In each child there is a tendency to be independent. It is harmful to destroy this independence in any class, and this independence especially finds its expression in dissatisfaction with the copying of models. With the method described above, this independence was not only not killed, but developed and strengthened.

If a pupil does not learn to create by himself or herself, he or she will always imitate and copy in life, because there are few who, having learned to copy, are able to make an independent application of what they've learned.

By always keeping to natural forms in drawing, and by frequently changing the objects—for example, from leaves of a characteristic form to flowers, dishes, and objects frequently used in life, and instruments— I tried to keep out routine and mannerism from our drawing.

I approached the explanation of shades and shadows with the greatest caution, because the beginner easily destroys the sharpness and regularity of figures by shading them too much, and thus gets used to a disorderly and infinite daubing.

In this manner I soon got more than thirty students in a few months to learn quite thoroughly the correlation of lines in various figures and objects, and to render these figures in even, sharp lines. The mechanical art of line-drawing soon evolved as if of its own accord. The greatest difficulty I faced was to teach the children to keep their sketchbooks and drawings clean. The convenience in erasing what has been drawn on a slate greatly increased my problems in this regard. By giving the best, most talented students sketchbooks, I achieved a greater cleanliness in the drawings themselves; for the greater difficulty in rubbing out compels them to be more careful and tidy with the material on which they are drawing. In a short time the best students reached such a clean and true handling of the pencil that they could cleanly and regularly draw not only straight-lined figures but also the most fantastic compositions of curved lines.

I made some of the students oversee the figures of the others when they were through with their own—and playing the teacher greatly encouraged the students, for they were at once able to apply what they had just learned.

Recently I have been working with the oldest students, trying to get them to draw objects in different positions and in perspective, without clinging exclusively to the well-known method of Dupuis.

Singing

Last summer we were coming back from swimming. We were all in a good mood. A peasant boy, the same one who had been tempted by the manorial boy to steal books, a stocky boy with protruding cheekbones all covered with freckles and bandy legs that turned inward—who had all the aspect of a sturdy, grown-up peasant man and a strong, intelligent, and talented nature—ran ahead and seated himself in a cart that was driving in front of us. He took up the reins, set his cap at a jaunty angle, spit off the side of the cart, and started a long, drawn-out peasant song, and he sang with such feeling, such pauses, and such emotion! The boys laughed.

"Semka, Semka! What a good singer he is!"

Semka was quite serious.

"Don't interrupt my song," he said in a peculiar, feignedly hoarse voice between songs, and proceeded to sing another song, just as seriously and as evenly. Two of the more musical boys sat down in the cart with him, and joined in singing with him, and carried the refrain. One of them harmonized with Semka at an octave or sixth, the other boy at a third, and it was all charming. Then other boys joined them, and they began to sing "As Under Such an Apple-Tree." They made noise, but there was not much music.

That evening the singing really began. After eight months, we could sing "The Angel Lamented" and two hymns, numbers four and seven;

the whole common mass; and short songs for chorus. The best students (there are only two) write down the tunes of the songs that they know, and almost read music. But before this what they sang was not anywhere close to as good as the song they sang returning from the swimming. I say this with no ulterior motive, not in order to prove anything—I simply state a fact. Now I am going to tell how singing class proceeded, with which I am comparatively satisfied.

At the first lesson I divided all up into three voices and we sang the following chords:

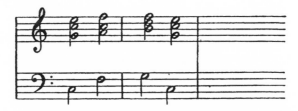

We quickly succeeded with this. Each student sang what he or she wanted. One would try soprano, and then switch to tenor, then from tenor to alto, so that the best students learned the whole chord *do-mi-sol*, and some of them even all three chords. They pronounced the notes as in French. One sang *mi-fa-fa-mi*, another *do-do-re-do*, and so forth.

"I say, that's fine, Lev Nikolaevich," they said. "It even makes something shake in the ear. Let's do some more!" We sang these chords at school, in the yard, in the garden, and on the way home, late into the night, and we could not tear ourselves away from this pastime, nor get enough of our success.

On the following day we tried the whole scale, and the more talented went through it all, while the poorer ones could hardly get as far as the third. I wrote the notes on a staff in the alto clef, the most symmetrical of clefs, and gave them the French names. The next five or six lessons proceeded in the high spirits; we also succeeded in getting new minor keys and the passages to the majors—"*Kyrie eleison*," "Glory be to the Father and Son," and a song for three voices with piano accompaniment. One half of the lesson was taken up with that, the other half with singing scales and exercises that the students invented themselves—*do-mi-re-fa-mi-sol*, *do-re-re-mi-mi-fa*, *do-mi-re-do-re-fa-mi-re*, and so forth.

I soon noticed that the notes on the staff were not clear to them, and I found it necessary to use figures instead. Besides, for the explanation of intervals and the variation of the tonic scale, the figures present a great convenience. After six lessons some of them could sing the intervals in order if I asked them to, by employing some imaginary scale. They were particularly fond of exercises in fourths—*do-fa-re-sol* and so forth, up and down. *Fa* (the lower dominant) particularly struck them with its characteristic force.

"What a whopper of a *fa*!" said Semka. "It just cuts like a knife."

The unmusical students soon dropped out, while with the musical ones the class lasted as much as three or four hours. I tried using the accepted method to give them an idea of how time and measure work in music, but the matter proved so difficult that I was compelled to separate time from tune and, writing down the sounds without the measure, to analyze the sounds only. Then, having written down the time—that is, the measure without the sounds—I had them analyze beats by tapping their fingers. Only then did we combine the two processes.

After a few lessons, when I tried to render myself an account of what I had been doing, I came to the conclusion that my method was almost the same as Chevet's method, which I had seen in practice at Paris—a method which I had not adopted sooner simply because it was a method. All those who teach singing cannot be urged enough to read Chevet's book, on whose cover it says in large letters "*Repoussé l'unanimité*" [Unanimously rejected]. The book is now sold in tens of thousands of copies throughout Europe. I saw in Paris striking examples of success with that method when taught by Chevet himself: an audience of from five to six hundred men and women, sometimes of between forty and fifty years of age, were singing in absolute harmony and *à livre ouvert* [sight reading]—whatever the teacher gave them to sing. In Chevet's method there are many rules, exercises, and prescribed methods that have no significance whatsoever, of which he, like every intelligent teacher, will invent by the hundred on the battlefield—that is, during class. There is there a very comical—though very convenient—method of keeping time without the sounds. For example, at four fourths Chevet has the student sing *ta-fa-te-fe*, at three fourths *ta-te-ti*, and at eight eighths *ta-fa-te-fe-te-re-li-ri*. All this is interesting as one means for teaching music. It is interesting as the history of a certain school of music, but these rules are not absolute and cannot form a method. But in Chevet there are ideas remarkable for their simplicity, three of which form the essence of his method. 1) An old idea of expressing the musical signs by means of figures, first introduced by Jean Jacques Rousseau in his *Dictionnaire de musique*. Whatever opponents of this method of writing may say, any teacher of singing can try this experiment, and he or she will always discover the great advantage of figures over the staff, both for reading and writing. I taught about ten lessons using the staff, and only once experimented with figures, telling students that the two systems were the same, and now they always ask me to write the figures for them and always use figures themselves. 2) A remarkable idea, belonging exclusively to Chevet, consists in teaching the sounds independently of measure, and vice versa. After using this method only once, everybody will see that it can make what appears to be an insurmountable difficulty seem so easy they can only marvel at how such a simple thought had not occurred to anyone before. How many torments would be saved the unfortunate children who sing in the high-church choirs if those in charge only tried this simple thing—making each chorister, without singing, tap out with a little stick or a finger the phrase he or she is to sing: four times for whole note, once for a quarter note or two eighth notes, and so forth. Then have them sing the same phrase without counting time. Then have them sing the measure, putting it all together. For example, the following:

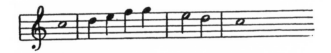

The student first will sing, without counting time, *do-re-mi-fa-sol-mi-re-do*; then, not singing but tapping out the note of the first measure, he or she will go *one, two, three, four*; then, on the first note of the third measure he or she will tap twice and go *one, two*, and for the second note of the third measure, *three, four*, and so forth. Then he or she will sing while beating time, while the other students read aloud.

This is my method, which, like Chevet's, cannot be prescribed. It is convenient, but there may be discovered more convenient methods still. The main thing is to separate the study of beats—of musical time—from sound. There may be an endless number of ways to accomplish this.

3) Finally, Chevet's third great idea consists in popularizing music and its study. His teaching method fully realizes this aim. And this is not only Chevet's wish and my assumption, but an actual fact. I saw in Paris hundreds of laborers with callused hands, sitting on benches, underneath which lay the tools with which they were returning from their shops. They were singing from sheet music, comprehending and enjoying the laws of music. As I looked at these laborers, I could easily imagine Russian peasants in their stead; if Chevet but spoke Russian, they would sing in just the same way, and would understand just as easily everything he was saying about the common rules and laws of music. We hope to have an occasion to say more about Chevet, especially about the importance of popularized music—singing, in particular—as a means of bringing back a decaying art.

I will now return to my description of our progress at the Yasnaya Polyana school. After six lessons the goats were separated from the sheep. There were left only those students with musical natures—the music lovers—and we made it through the minor scales and the explanation of intervals. The only difficulty they encountered was distinguishing the small second from the large second. The students called *fa* "Big Boy"— *do* they called "crybaby"—and so I did not have to teach them: they themselves had a feeling for the note into which the small second resolved itself, and so they had a feeling for the second itself. We had no trouble figuring out that the major scale consisted of a sequence of two large, one small, three large, and one small seconds. Then we sang "Glory be to God" in the minor scale, and by ear made it to the top of the scale—which turned out to be minor. We then figured out that this scale consisted of one large, one small, two large, one small, one very large, and one small second. Then I showed them that it was possible to sing and write a scale beginning with any sound, that when it does not come to large or small second, when necessary we may place a sharp or flat. For convenience's sake, I drew for them a chromatic scale:

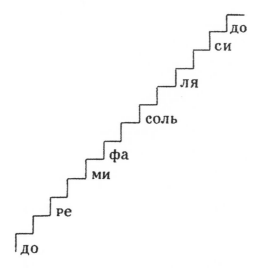

Along this staircase I made them write all the possible major and minor scales, beginning with any they chose. These exercises amused them very much, and the progress was so striking that two of them frequently passed their time between classes by writing out the tunes of songs they knew. These students are continually humming the tunes of various songs they can't name, and they hum them sweetly and tenderly. Above all, they now second [sing harmony] much better and cannot bear when all together they sing out of tune.

We had hardly more than twelve lessons during the winter. Our instruction was spoiled by ambition. The parents, we, the teachers, and the students themselves, wanted to surprise the whole village: by singing in church. We began to rehearse the mass and hymns by Bortnyansky. It seemed like the children were having a good time, but in fact the opposite was true. Although the desire to be in the choir sustained them, and they loved music, and we teachers made a special effort with this class, making it more compulsory than the rest, I often felt sorry for them as I watched some tiny Kiryushka in torn puttees* as he lost his register ("Secretly fo-o-o-oorming") and was requested to repeat a phrase ten

---

* Cloth leg wrappings worn by the peasantry.

times over. In the end, this got the boy so upset that he beat out the music with his fingers, insisting that he had been singing correctly all along.

Once we got to the church and enjoyed success, the enthusiasm was enormous, but the singing suffered from it. The lessons grew tedious for the students, and they gradually dropped out, and only at Easter time that was it possible, with great effort, to assemble a choir. Our singers began to resemble those in high-church choirs, who frequently sing well, but are skilled enough that they lose love for singing, and who know absolutely nothing about the notes, though they think they do know how to read music. I have frequently seen those with this kind of musical experience decide to study themselves, knowing nothing about notes, but they are quite helpless the moment they try to sing something that has not been drummed into their ears.

From my brief experience with teaching music, I am convinced:

1) That the method of writing the sounds down in figures is the most effective and convenient.

2) That teaching measure independently of sound is the best method.

3) That in order for musical instruction to take hold and for students to enjoy music class, it is necessary from the very start to teach the art—and not the skill—of singing and playing. Young ladies may be made to play Burgmüller's exercises, but with the children of the people it is better not to teach at all than to teach mechanically.

4) That there is nothing more harmful in musical instruction—or what is termed music—than choir performances as exams, school performances, and church performances.

5) That our goal in teaching music to the people should be to avail them of a knowledge of the common laws of music, but by no means to transmit to them any false tastes that have developed in us.

Tolstoy in 1900

Tolstoy's Other Writings on Education: Selected Excerpts

The following are excerpts selected from Tolstoy's writings on education which do not appear in full in the present volume. Most of the articles quoted below appeared in Yasnaya Polyana, Tolstoy's journal.—Editor

From "On Popular Education"

In July 1860, after the first year of teaching at his peasant school, Tolstoy left Russia for the last time in his life and went to France, Germany, Switzerland, and England to study those countries' pedagogical methods. Except for his meeting with Berthold Auerbach, a German educator and novelist with sympathetic, commonsensical views on education, Tolstoy was left disappointed. In each nation's public schooling, he saw coercion and incompetence on the part of the administrators and teachers. His fundamental objection was that public schools gave the expressed needs or desires of the students and parents no respect or consideration in determining curriculum. Tolstoy attacked schools for presuming the very thing he declared impossible—knowing beforehand what it is students need to learn.

"On Popular Education" was the first article in the first issue of Yasnaya Polyana.

Children everywhere have been sent to school by force, while parents are compelled to send their children to school by the severity of law, or by cunning—or the parents are offered tempting incentives to send their children to school. The masses everywhere, on the other hand, study of their own accord and regard education as good.

How is this? The need of education lies in every man; the people love and seek education as they love and seek air for breathing; government and society burn with the desire to educate the masses, and yet notwithstanding all the force of cunning and the persistence of governments and societies, the masses constantly express their dissatisfaction with the education that is offered to them, and submit only to force, little by little.

As with every conflict, so also here. It is necessary to solve the question: What is more lawful, the resistance or the action itself? Must resistance be broken, or the action be changed?

*   *   *   *

It was an easy matter for teachers in medieval schools to know what they ought to teach, so long as there was only one method and so long as all learning was based on the Bible, the books of St. Augustine, and Aristotle.

*   *   *   *

One frequently hears or reads the statement that domestic conditions, the rudeness of the parents, the field labor, the village games, and so forth, are the chief impediments to schooling. It may be that they really interfere with schooling as pedagogues understand it; but it is time to acknowledge that these conditions are the chief foundation of all education, and that they are far from being inimical or detrimental to schooling, but are in fact its prime and chief movers. A child could never learn to distinguish the lines that form the distinctive letters or numbers, nor could he or she acquire the ability to express his or her thoughts, if it were not for these domestic conditions. It seems strange that this coarse domestic life—which should have been able to teach the child such difficult things—should all of a sudden become unfit to instruct that child in such easy things as reading and writing, or should ever impede such instruction. The best proof of this is found in the comparison of a peasant boy who has never had any instruction with a gentleman's son who has been for five years under the care of a tutor: the superiority of mind and knowledge is always on the side of the peasant boy.

More than that. The interest in knowing anything whatsoever and the questions that it is the school's problem to answer are created only by these domestic conditions. Every curriculum ought to be a response to questions posed by life, whereas school not only does not come up with questions, but does not even answer those posed by life. School eternally answers the same questions posed by humankind several centuries ago rather than those questions springing from the intellect of the child—the educator is not interested by these. These are questions such as: How was the world created? Who was the first person? What happened 2,000 years ago? What kind of a country is Asia? What is the shape of the Earth? How do you multiply hundreds by thousands? What will happen after death? and so forth.

*   *   *   *

Schools are established not as places where it is convenient for the children to study, but where teachers may teach in comfort. Conversation, motion, and merriment are all necessary if children are to study. But these three things are not convenient for the teacher, and so in schools—which are built according to the same plans as prisons—questions, conversation, and motion are prohibited.

Instead of acknowledging that, in order to act successfully on a certain object, it is necessary to study it (in education this object is the free child), educators want to teach just as they know how, as they think best, and if they fail they want to change not the manner of their teaching, but the child's nature itself. From this conception have sprung and even now spring such systems (e.g., Pestalozzi[1]) as would allow one to *mechaniser l'instruction**—that eternal tendency of pedagogy to arrange matters in such a way that, no matter who the teacher and student may be, the method should remain one and the same.

It is enough to look at an individual child at home, in the street, or at school. Now you see a vivacious, curious child, with a smile in his eyes and on his lips, seeking instruction in everything as he would seek pleasure, clearly and frequently strongly expressing his thoughts in his own words. Next you see a worn-out, retiring being, with an expression of fatigue, terror, and ennui, mouthing strange words in a strange language—a being whose soul has retreated, like a snail, into its house. One need only look at these two conditions to decide which is more advantageous to the child's development.

That strange psychological condition that I will call the scholastic condition of the soul—which all of us, unfortunately, know far too well—consists in that all the higher faculties—imagination, creativity, inventiveness—give way to other, semianimal faculties: pronouncing sounds independently from concepts; counting numbers in succession, *1, 2, 3, 4, 5;* perceiving words without allowing imagination to substitute images

---

* *mechaniser l'instruction*: systematize, or mechanize, teaching.

for these sounds. In short, we have developed a faculty for crushing all higher faculties, so that the only faculties that can evolve are those that coincide with the scholastic condition of fear, and of straining memory and attention.

Children are anomalies in school if they do not fall into the rut of this semianimal condition. The moment the child has reached the state of having lost all independence and originality, the moment there appear in that child various symptoms of disease—hypocrisy, aimless lying, dullness, and so forth—he or she is no longer an anomaly. The child has fallen into the rut, and the teacher begins to be satisfied with him or her. Then occur the following by no means accidental and frequently repeated phenomena: that the dullest child becomes the best student, and the most intelligent the worst. It seems to me that this fact is sufficiently significant to make people think and try to explain it. It seems to me that one such fact serves as palpable proof of the fallacy underlying compulsory education.

*   *   *   *

All agree that schools are imperfect. (For my part, I am convinced that they are harmful.) All admit that many—very many—improvements must be made. All agree that these improvements must be based on a greater comfort for the students. All agree that these comforts may be recognized only by studying the needs of children of school age in general, and by studying the needs of each class of students in particular.

Now, what has been done towards the study of this difficult and complex subject? For several centuries each school has been based on the pattern of the one before it, and in each of these schools the peremptory condition is discipline—forbidding children to speak, ask questions, choose this or that course of study. In short, all measures are taken to deprive the teacher of all possibility of deducing the students' needs.

The compulsory structure of the school excludes the possibility of all progress. And yet when we consider how many centuries have passed in answering the children's questions—questions it did not occur to them to ask—and how far the present generations have departed from that ancient form of culture with which they are inoculated, it becomes incomprehensible to us how it is that these schools still exist. School, so it would appear to us, ought to be an implement of education and at the same time an experiment involving the young generation, constantly giving new results. Only when experiment is the foundation of school—only when every school will be, so to speak, a pedagogical laboratory—will school not fall behind universal progress, and will experiment be able to lay firm foundations for the science of education.

*   *   *   *

I could write whole books about the ignorance that I witnessed in the schools of France, Switzerland, and Germany. Anyone who cares about education should study schools not from the reports of public examinations, but from extended visits and conversations with teachers and pupils in the schools and outside the schools. In Marseilles I also visited a lay school, and another, a monastic school for grown-ups. Out of 250,000 inhabitants, less than one thousand—of these only two hundred men— attend these schools. The instruction is the same: the mechanics of reading, which are acquired in a year or in longer time; bookkeeping without the knowledge of arithmetic; religious instruction; and so forth. After the lay school, I saw the daily instruction offered in the churches; I saw the *salles d'asile**, in which four-year-old children hearing a whistle blow were made to march around the benches like soldiers. At a given command they lifted and folded their hands, and with quivering and strange voices sang hymns praising God and their benefactors. This convinced me that the educational institutions of the city of Marseilles were exceedingly bad.

If by some miracle, a person should see all these establishments— without having seen the people in the streets, in their shops, in the cafés, in their homes—what opinion would he or she form of a nation that was educated in such a manner? That person would certainly conclude that this nation was ignorant, rude, hypocritical, full of prejudices, and almost wild. But it is enough to interact with people, to chat with the average person on the street, to be convinced that the French nation is, on the contrary, almost what it regards itself to be: intelligent, clever, affable, free from prejudice, and quite civilized. Look at a city workman of about thirty years of age: he will write a letter, not with the mistakes that are made at school, and often without mistakes; he has an idea of politics, and consequently of modern history and geography; he knows something about history from novels; he has some knowledge of the natural sciences. He frequently draws and applies mathematical formulae to his trade. Where did he acquire all that?

---

* *salles d'asile*: "infant" school.

I involuntarily found an answer to this question in Marseilles, when after visiting the schools, I began to stroll down the streets, to frequent the dram-shops, *cafés chantants*, museums, workshops, quays, and book-stalls. The very boy who told me that Henry IV had been killed by Julius Caesar knew very well the history of the *Three Musketeers* and of *Monte Cristo*. I found twenty-eight illustrated editions of these [two books] in Marseilles, costing from five to ten centimes. To a population of 250,000 they sell 30,000 of them—consequently, if we suppose that ten people read or listen to one copy, we find that everyone knows their history. In addition there are the museum, the public libraries, the theaters. Then there are the cafés—two large *cafés chantants*, where each may enter for fifty centimes' worth of food or drink, and where there are daily as many as 25,000 people—and this is not counting the smaller cafés, which hold as many more—in each of these cafés they produce little comedies and skits, and recite verses. Taking the lowest calculation, we get one-fifth of the population—one-fifth who get their daily oral instruction just as the Greeks and Romans were instructed in their amphitheaters.

Whether this education is good or bad is another matter; but here it is, this unconscious education that is so much more powerful than the one by compulsion. Here is the unconscious school that has undermined the compulsory school and has made the latter's substance dwindle down to almost nothing. The only thing left is a despotic form, one almost without content. I say "almost without content" because I exclude the mere mechanical ability of putting letters together and writing down words—the only knowledge that can be taken away after five or six years' study. Here it must be remarked that even the mere mechanical art of reading and writing is frequently acquired outside of school in a much shorter period, and that frequently the students do not take this ability with them when they leave the school—or it is lost, finding no application in life. Where school attendance is made compulsory by law, there is no need to teach a second generation to read, write, and figure, because the parents, we should think, would be able to do that at home, and the children would learn much more easily that way than in school.

What I saw in Marseilles takes place in all the other countries: every-where the greater part of one's education is acquired not at school but in life. Where life is instructive—in London, Paris, and generally in all large cities—the masses are educated; where life is not instructive, in the coun-try, the people are uneducated, in spite of the fact that the schools are the same in both. The knowledge acquired in the country is lost. The direction and spirit of the popular education, both in the cities and in the villages, is absolutely independent from, and generally contrary to, the spirit that it is intended to instill in the schools. Education goes on quite independently of the schools.

* * * *

So the less educated people want to be better educated, and the educated class wants to educate the masses, but the masses submit to education only under constraint. We have looked in philosophy, experience, and history for those principles that would give the educating class the right to do this, but we have found none. On the contrary, we are now convinced that human thought is constantly striving to find ways to free people from constraint in matters of education.

* * * *

Let us cease regarding the people's resistance to our education as a hostile element of pedagogy. On the contrary, let us see in it an expression of the people's will which alone should guide our activities. Let us finally profess that law that so painfully tells us—both from the history of pedagogy and from the whole history of education—that for the educators to know what is good and what is bad, those being educated must have the full power to express their dissatisfaction, or at least to bypass education that instinctively does not satisfy them—that the criterion of pedagogy is liberty in the first place.

We have chosen this latter path in our pedagogical activity.

The conviction that we not only *do not know*—but that we *cannot know*—what the education of the people is to consist of is what forms the basis of our activities. We believe that not only does there not exist a science of education—pedagogy—but that the first foundation of it has not yet been laid; that the definition of pedagogy and of its aims in a philosophical sense is impossible, useless, and injurious.

We do not know what education is to be like, and we do not acknowledge the whole philosophy of pedagogy, because we do not acknowledge the possibility of a man's knowing what it is he ought to know. Education and culture present themselves to us as the historical facts of one set of people acting upon another; therefore, the only problem of the science of education in our opinion is the discovery of the laws that govern the actions of one set of people upon another. We not only do not recognize in our generation the knowledge—nor even the right of a knowledge—of what is necessary for man's perfection, we are also convinced that if humanity were possessed of that knowledge, it would not be in its power to transmit—or not transmit—such knowledge. . . .

A mother teaches her child to speak only so that they may understand each other. She instinctively tries to come down to the child's view of things, to his language, yet the law of educational progress does not permit her to descend down to the child, but compels the child to rise to her knowledge. The same relation exists between the author and the reader, the same between the school and the pupils, the same between the state and society—the people. The activity of the person who educates has one and the same purpose. The problems of educational science are only the study of the conditions under which a confluence of these two tendencies for one common end takes place, and the recognition of those conditions that impede this confluence.

Thus on the one hand, the science of education becomes easier to us in that it no longer poses questions such as: What is the final aim of education, and for what must we prepare the younger generation? and so forth. It is immeasurably more difficult than this. We are compelled to study all the conditions that have aided in the confluence of the tendencies in the educator and in the student. We must define what that freedom is: the absence of that which impedes the confluence of both the tendencies and that alone serves as our criterion of the whole science of education. We must move step by step, from an endless number of facts to the solution of the questions of the science of education.

We know that our arguments will not convince many. We know that our fundamental convictions that the only method of education is experiment and its only criterion is freedom will sound to some like trite nonsense, to some an indistinct abstraction, to others again a visionary dream. We should not have dared to violate the quiet of the theoretical pedagogues and to express these convictions, which run contrary to all experience, if we had to confine ourselves to the reflections of this article. But we sense our ability to prove, step by step and fact by fact, the applicability and legality of our "wild" convictions, and to this end alone do we devote the publication of the periodical *Yasnaya Polyana*.

From "On Methods of Teaching the Rudiments"

Much of this article details methods specific to Russian-language sounds and alphabet combinations; the main thrust, however, is that new teaching methods are harmful when they renounce the old, since all methods need to be employable, depending on the student. Again, Tolstoy asserts, teaching is not an exclusive but an inclusive art: "Experience has convinced us that there is no single good or bad method; that the failure of a given method consists in the exclusive adherence to one method, and that the best method is the absence of all method—or, to put it another way, the knowledge and use of all methods and the invention of new ones according to the difficulties encountered."²

To print good books for the masses! How simple and easy it looks, just like all great ideas. There is just one difficulty: there are no good books for the people, not only in our country, but not even in Europe.³

* * * *

The rudiments—a conception which exists not only in our country, but in all Europe—are acknowledged to be the curriculum of the popular elementary school. *Lesen und schrieben, lire et écrire, reading and writing.* What are these rudiments, and what do they have in common with the first steps in education? The rudiments are the art of composing words out of certain signs, and of representing words with these signs. What is there in common between the rudiments and education? The rudiments are a definite skill (*Fertigkeit*); education is a knowledge of facts and their correlations. Is this skill of composing words essential for a person to take the first step in education, and is there no other road? We do not see this at all; we very frequently perceive the diametrically opposite—if, when speaking of education, we shall understand "education" not simply as something relating to school, but something necessary to life.

With people at a low level of education we notice that the knowledge or ignorance of reading and writing in no way changes the degree of their education. We see people who are well acquainted with all the facts necessary for farming, and with a large number of interrelations of these facts, who can neither read nor write. We see excellent military commanders, excellent merchants, managers, superintendents, master mechanics, artisans, contractors, and people simply educated by life, who possess a great store of information and make sound decisions based on that information, but who can neither read nor write. On the other hand, we see those who can read and write, and who on account of that skill have acquired no new information. Anyone who seriously undertakes to examine the education of the people—not only in Russia, but also in Europe—will involuntarily come to the conclusion that education is acquired by the people quite independently of the knowledge of reading and writing.

*   *   *   *

If only the question were put like this: Is primary education useful to the people or not? No one could answer it in the negative. But if we ask: Is it useful or not to teach the people to read when they have no books for reading? I hope that every unbiased man will answer: "I do not know, just as I do not know whether it would be useful to teach the whole nation to play the violin or to make boots."

*   *   *   *

Experience has convinced us that there is no singularly bad or good methods; that the failure of a given method consists in exclusive adherence to that method, and that the best method is the absence of all method—or, to put it another way, the knowledge and use of all methods and the invention of new ones according to difficulties encountered.

We have divided methods into three categories, although this division is not essential. We only did so for the sake of clarity; properly speaking, there are no methods, and each one includes all the rest. Everybody who has taught someone else to read has made use of, if unconsciously, all the existing methods and of all those that may ever exist. The invention of a new method is only the consciousness of that new angle from which the student may be reached and by which he or she may understand, and therefore any new method does not exclude the old. This new method is not only no better than the old, but may even be worse, because in the majority of cases the essential method is divined in the beginning. In most cases the invention of the new method was considered the annihilation of the old, although in reality the old method remained the essential one. By consciously refuting the old methods with newly invented methods, we only complicate matters, actually falling behind those who consciously use the old—and unconsciously the new and the future methods.

* * * *

Leaving out the fact that I know hundreds of cases of the rapid acquisition of the art of reading by the old method *buki-az—ba**, and hundreds of cases of very slow acquisition by the new methods, I only affirm that the old method has this advantage over the new: it includes all the new methods, even if unconsciously. Meanwhile the new excludes the old, and moreover, the old method has a further advantage: it is free, while the new method is compulsory. "What, free?" they will ask me, when with the old method, spelling was hammered into the students with rods, and with the new, the children are addressed as "you"† and politely asked to understand?

It is right here that the child suffers the worst and most injurious violence: when he or she is asked to understand in precisely the same manner that the teacher understands it.

* * * *

Here Tolstoy finds a deficiency of his own "methods"—when they are employed by rote and not combined with the skills and experience of the teacher.

I will relate a few cases near at hand. This autumn, a teacher who had studied in the Yasnaya Polyana school opened a school in a village where out of forty pupils one-half had been learning by *azes* and syllabication methods. One-third of the students could read. After two weeks, the peasants expressed their universal dissatisfaction with the school. Their main grievances were that the teacher taught *a, be* [the German way] and not *az, buki* [the Russian way]; that he taught fairy tales, not prayers; and that there was no order at school. Upon meeting the teacher I informed him of the peasants' views. The teacher, a man with a university training, explained to me with a contemptuous smile that he taught *a, be* instead of *az, buki* in order to facilitate spelling; that they read fairy tales because they are more in keeping with the students' intellectual level; and that in conformity with his new method, he considered it unnecessary to punish the children, and that therefore the strict order to which the peasants

---

* *Buki-az—ba:* a widely used mnemonic system for learning the Cyrillic alphabet.
† Tolstoy means the formal form of the second person here. The informal form of *you* is always used when addressing children.

were accustomed, who had seen their children with pointers on the syllables, was unnecessary.

I visited this school two weeks later. The boys were divided into three classes, and the teacher carefully went from one class to another. Some students in the lowest class were standing at the table and memorizing certain parts of a paper chart with the letters from the alphabet. I began to ask them questions. More than one-half of them knew the letters and named them: *az, buki,* and so forth. Others knew even syllabication; one could read, but was learning for a second time, pointing with his finger and repeating *a, be, ve,* imagining that he was getting something entirely new. Still others, in the middle class, were spelling *s, ka, a—ska,* with one student asking questions and the others answering them. They had been doing this for more than two weeks, even though one day is more than enough time to learn the process of casting off the superfluous unvoiced letters. Among these students, I also found some who knew syllabication in the old fashion and who could read. Just like the others, these students were ashamed of their knowledge and recanted it, imagining that there was no salvation except in spelling *be, re, a—bra.* The third, in fine, were reading. These unfortunate ones were sitting on the floor, each holding a book right before his eyes and pretending to read, repeating aloud the two verses:

There where ends the vaulted sky,
People eat nor wheat nor rye—

Once they had finished, they began reading the same two verses again with saddened and anxious faces, now and then squinting at me, as if asking me whether they were doing well.

It is terrible and incredible to mention. Of these boys, some could read well, and others could not spell; those who could read kept themselves back from feelings of camaraderie; those who could not had for the last three weeks been repeating these two verses from the most abominable reworking of Ershov's fairy tale, which is poor as far as the masses are concerned.

I began to examine them in sacred history: nobody knew anything, because the teacher, according to the new method, did not make them memorize, but told them stories from the abbreviated religious history. I examined them in arithmetic. Nobody knew anything, although the teacher—again according to the new method—had been showing all the students numbers up to millions, all at once, without making them learn by heart. I examined them in the prayers. No one knew anything; they made errors saying the Lord's Prayer, as they had learned it at home. And all of them were excellent boys, full of life, and intelligence, and eagerness to learn! The most terrible thing about it is that it was all done according to my own method! Here were all the devices employed at my school: learning the alphabet by having students write all the letters at the same time, in chalk; the oral spelling; the first intelligible reading for the child; the oral account of history; mathematics without memorizing. At the same time, the device most familiar to the teacher—learning by rote—could be felt. The teacher was consciously avoiding rote learning, but he had mastered it, and had unconsciously applied it in the new context. He made the students memorize—not prayers, but Ershov's fairy tale, and religious history not from the book, but from his own poor, dead recitations. The same was true of mathematics and spelling. It is impossible to knock it into the head of this unfortunate teacher of university training that all the accusations of the rude peasants are a thousand times just—that a sexton teaches incomparably better than he and that if he wants to teach, he can teach reading according to the *buki-az—ba*, by making the students memorize. That way he would be of some practical benefit to his students. But this teacher with the university training had, to use his own words, *studied the method* of the Yasnaya Polyana school, which he for some reason wanted to accept as a template.

* * * *

Each individual, in order to acquire the art of reading in the shortest possible time, must be taught in a distinctly different way from any other, and therefore there must be a separate method for each. What presents an insuperable difficulty to one does not in the least keep the next one back, and vice versa. One student has a good memory, and it is easier for him to memorize the syllables than it is to comprehend the "vowellessness" of the consonants; another reflects calmly and will understand most rational sound methods; a third has good instincts, and grasps the rules of word combination by reading whole words at a time.

The best teacher is the one who can instantly recognize what is bothering a particular student. This ability in turn gives the teacher a knowledge of the greatest possible number of methods; the ability to invent new methods; and above all—rather than the blind adherence to one method—the conviction that all methods are one-sided, that the best possible method is the one that answers best all the possible difficulties incurred by the student. This is not a method, but an art and talent.

Every reading teacher must be well-grounded in the one method that has evolved with the people, and must further verify it by his own experience. The reading teacher must endeavor to find out the greatest number of methods, employing them as auxiliary means. Every teacher must endeavor to regard every imperfection in a student's comprehension not as a defect of that student, but as a defect of his or her own instruction—to develop within the ability of discovering new methods. Every teacher must know that every method invented is only a step on which he or she must stand in order to go farther. Teachers must know that if they themselves will not use a newly invented method, another will assimilate that method and will use it to go farther. Teachers must know that the business of teaching is an art: possibilities for completeness and perfection are unobtainable, while possibilities for development and perfectability are endless.

From "A Project of a General Plan for the Establishment of Popular Schools"

With characteristic impatience and occasional sarcasm, Tolstoy discusses government legislation on setting up new schools. The Tsarist government passed laws in 1862 that essentially made it illegal for any unauthorized person to set up a school. The laws also mandated, in an unrealistic and uninformed fashion, curricula and methods. "I say only that every program for the popular [public] school is absolutely impossible, and every such curriculum is only words, words, words. I can comprehend a program that defines the obligation that teachers— or the body establishing the school—take upon themselves; I can understand how one may say to the Commune and to the parents: I am the teacher; I open the school, and I undertake to teach your children this or that, and you have no right to ask of me that which I have not promised you. But to open a school and to promise that one will not teach this or that is both imprudent and absolutely impossible. And it is precisely such a negative program that the Project proposes for all of Russia and for the public primary schools."

While "A Project of a General Plan for the Establishment of Popular Schools" yields comparatively few nuggets of wisdom, it contains much information. For instance, "It must be kept in mind that by far not all the children study now, and that the girls form but one-twentieth of all the students."

In a way similar to Tolstoy's much later essays on civil disobedience—in which he publicizes his own "lawlessness" and practically insists the government take legal action against him—Tolstoy points out how he disobeyed the government's senseless laws on education: "A critic of the Project, who is unacquainted with Russian life, will note the law of 1828, according to which the opening of schools and private instruction is prohibited, and—comparing the older restrictive measures with the new Project, in which one is only asked to give information about the opening of a school—will say that in matters of public education the Project gives incomparably greater freedom than was the case before. But for us, actually living in Russia, the matter appears different.

"The law of 1828 was only a law, and it never occurred to any one to comply with it. All, both society and the executors of the law, acknowledged its impracticality, and the impossibility of carrying it out. There have existed and still exist thousands of schools established without permission, and not one superintendent or director of a high school has ever raised his hand to close these schools because they do not comply with the law of 1828. By tacit consensus, society and the executors of the law accepted the law of 1828 as nonexisting, and, in reality, in the teaching and opening of schools men were guided by the complete, time-honored liberty of action. The law passed by entirely unnoticed. I opened a school in 1849, and only in March of 1862 did I learn, upon the occasion of the promulgation of the Project, that I had no right to open such a school."

Tolstoy wryly noted: "It is very likely that I am committing a crime when I use unapproved books in my school, and that the Communes are also criminal in changing and appointing teachers without the director."

I cannot help but remark that all attempts at training teachers—both in our Pedagogical Institute, as well as in German seminaries and French and English normal schools—have so far yielded no results, and have only convinced us of the impossibility of training teachers, especially for the popular schools, just as it is impossible to train artists and poets. Teachers are educated only in proportion to the general demands of education, and with the raising of the general level of education.

* * * *

For teaching to progress successfully, teachers must have the means to form their own curricula, and full liberty in the choice of methods. It is convenient for one to teach by *buki-az—ba* method, and for another by the *be-a*, and for a third by the *b-a* method, each being his own master. For the teacher to assimilate different methods, it is not enough to recognize this and to prescribe a method to that teacher—the teacher must believe that the method is the best one, and he must love that method.

* * * *

Everybody who knows the popular schools knows how difficult and how impossible it is, by inspection or by an examination, to ascertain the degree of success and the direction of a given school. How often a conscientious teacher—with feelings of dignity, not allowing himself to show off his students—will appear in a worse light than the martinet who has been ruining his pupils for a year and who is only looking towards the final parade!

From "Education and Culture"

This article consists of Tolstoy's most aggressive argument against compulsory schooling. Tolstoy offers an alternative: The freedom to acquire "culture," which he defines as "the consequence of all those influences that life exerts on humankind." (By "culture," Tolstoy meant same as when we say, "a cultured person.")

Education is a compulsory, forcible action of one person upon another for the purpose of forming a person who will appear to us to be good. Culture, however, is the free relation of people, having as its basis the need of one person to acquire knowledge, and of the other to impart that which he or she has acquired. Instruction, *Unterricht*, is a means of both culture and education. The difference between education and culture lies only in the compulsion, which education deems itself in the right to exert. Education is culture under restraint. Culture is free.

* * * *

Education is the tendency of one man to make another just like himself. (The tendency of a poor person to take the wealth away from a rich one, the feeling of envy in an old person at the sight of fresh and vigorous youth, i.e., the feeling of envy, raised to a principle and theory.) I am convinced that the educator undertakes the education of the child with such zeal for the ulterior reason that the educator envies the child's purity. The educator desires to make the child like himself, that is, to spoil the child.

I know a usurious innkeeper who has been making money by all kinds of rascalities, and who, in response to my persuasion and flattery to have him send his fine twelve-year-old boy to my school at Yasnaya Polyana, makes his red mug bloom into a self-satisfied smile while constantly making the very same reply: "That is so, your Excellency, but it is more important for me first to instill my boy with my own spirit." And so he takes the boy around with him and boasts of the fact that his son has learned to cheat the peasants who sell his father wheat. Who does not know fathers, educated in military schools as junkers*, who deify the culture that is permeated with the spirit in which their fathers were educated? Do not professors in the universities and monks in the seminaries instill their students with their own spirit in just such a way?

I do not want to prove what I have already proved, and which is very easy to prove: that education as a premeditated molding of persons according to certain templates is *sterile, unlawful,* and *impossible.* Here I will confine myself to just one question. Education has no rights. I do not acknowledge any such rights, nor have any such rights been acknowledged—nor will they ever be—by the young generation now in school, which always and everywhere is set against compulsion in education. *How are you going to prove this?* I know nothing and assume nothing, but you acknowledge and assume a new and for us nonexistent right for one person to make of others just such people as that person pleases. Try to prove this right by any other argument than by the fact that the abuse of power has always existed. You are not the plaintiffs, we are. You are the defendants.

*　　*　　*　　*

If such an abnormal condition as the use of force in culture—education—has existed for ages, the causes of this phenomenon must be rooted in human nature. I see these causes: 1) in the family, 2) in religion, 3) in the state, and 4) in society.

---

* *Junkers*: members of the privileged, militaristic landowning class in Prussia.

The first cause is due to the fact that the parents, whoever they be, wish to make their children like themselves, or, at least, as they would like to be. This tendency is so natural that one cannot be upset about it. So long as the right of each individual to free development has not yet entered into the consciousness of all parents, nothing else can be expected. Besides, more than anybody else, parents are dependent on what will become of their children; consequently their tendency to educate their children in their own fashion may be called natural, if not just.

The second cause that produces the phenomenon of education is religion. As long as a person—Mohammedan, Jew, or Christian—believes firmly that a person who does not recognize his teaching cannot be saved, and forever loses his soul, that person cannot help wishing, even though by force, to convert and educate every child in his tenets.

I repeat: religion is the only lawful and sensible basis of education.

* * * *

Everything imaginable may be proved by experience. The reader of the psalter proves by experience that the best method for teaching reading is to make one study the psalter; the shoemaker says that the best way to learn his art is to make the boys fetch water, chop wood, and so forth for two years. In this manner you may prove anything you please. I say all this so that the defenders of the university may not tell me of the historical meaning of the mysterious cultural influence, of the common bond of the governmental and educational institutions, so that they cite me the examples of Oxford and Heidelberg, but so that they will allow me to discuss the matter according to good common sense, and that they themselves may do so.

All I know is that when I enter the university, between the ages of sixteen to eighteen, the circle of my knowledge is already defined for me—as it was in the department that I entered—and it is defined quite arbitrarily. I come to any one of the lectures prescribed for me by the department, and I am supposed not only to hear everything the professor is lecturing about, but even to commit it to memory—if not word for word, at least sentence for sentence. If I do not learn it all, the professor will not give me the necessary diploma after the final or biennial examinations. I do not speak of the abuses that are repeated a hundred times. In order to receive this diploma, I must have certain habits which the professor approves of: I must always be sitting on the first bench and taking notes; I must have a frightened or a merry look at the examination; I must share the professor's opinions; I must regularly attend his evenings at home (these are not suppositions, but the students' opinions which one may hear at any university). While listening to the professor's lecture, I may differ from his view. I may, on the basis of my readings in the subject, find that the professor's lectures are bad. Still I must listen to them—or at least memorize them.

In the universities there exists a dogma which the professors do not promulgate: this is the dogma of the professor's papal infallibility. Moreover, culture is imparted to the student by the professor precisely as all priests do it: secretly, in the cell, and with a demand for reverential respect from the uninitiated and from the students.

*   *   *   *

Why is it absolutely necessary to lecture? Why can't the students be given a good book, their own or somebody else's, one or two or ten good books?[4]

The condition of university instruction, that the professor must lecture and that his lectures must be absolutely something of his own, belongs to the dogmas of university practice, in which I do not believe and which are impossible to prove. "The oral transmission impresses the minds better, and so forth," I shall be told. This is entirely untrue. I know myself, as do many others who are not exceptions but examples of the common rule, that many people understand nothing when told orally, but comprehend well only when they quietly read a book at home. The oral transmission would mean something only if the students had the right to oppose it: if the lecture were a conversation, and not a lesson.

*   *   *   *

The whole trouble, both in the matters of university instruction and of culture in general, is caused mainly by people who do not reflect, but who submit to the ideas of the age, thus imagining it possible to serve two masters at once. . . .

These people seem to be agreeing with you in order to take possession of your thoughts, and then change and cut and lop them according to their own fashion.

*   *   *   *

No one has ever thought of establishing universities based on the needs of the people. That was impossible because the needs of the people have remained unknown. The universities were founded to answer certain needs, partly those of the government and partly those of higher society. Then, to supply the universities with students, we created a complex preparatory ladder of educational institutions that has nothing in common with the needs of the people. The government needed officials, doctors, jurists, and teachers, and the universities were founded in order to train these. Now higher society needs liberals of a certain mold, and the universities train these people. The only blunder is that the masses do not need these liberals at all.

It is generally said that the defects of the universities are due to defects in the lower institutions. I affirm the opposite: the defects of the public, especially the county schools are mainly due to the false exigencies of the universities.

*   *   *   *

Public lectures and museums are the best examples of noncompulsion in education. Universities are examples of compulsion in education. In universities, the students are confined to certain limits by a definite course, a program, a code of selected studies, by the exigencies of the examinations, and by the granting of rights based mainly on these examinations— or, more correctly, by the stripping of rights in case of noncompliance with certain prescribed conditions. . . .

Public lectures, whose number is continuously increasing in Europe and in America, on the contrary, not only do not confine one to a certain circle of knowledge, and do not demand attention under threat of punishment, but expect from the students certain sacrifices, by which they prove, in contradistinction to the first, the complete freedom of choice, on the basis of which they are created. That is what I mean by interference and noninterference of school in education.

If I am told that such noninterference, which is possible for the higher institutions and for adults, is not possible for the lower schools and for minors because we have no examples for it in the shape of public lectures for children and so forth, my answer will be that if we are not going to understand the word *school* in the narrowest sense but accept it with the definition above, we find in the lower stages of knowledge and in younger people many influences of liberal culture—or noncompulsion in education—corresponding to those in higher institutions and to public lectures. Such is the acquisition of the art of reading from a friend or brother; such are popular children's games (whose cultural value we intend to discuss in a special article[5]); such are public performances of all kinds; such are pictures and books; such are fairy tales and songs; such is work; and, finally, such are the experiments of the school at Yasnaya Polyana.

* * * *

What then must school be if it cannot interfere in matters of education? Education is, as said above, the conscious action of a person (the teacher) who passes down culture to others. How is that person to act in order not to transgress the limits of culture, that is, of freedom?

I reply: the school must have one aim—the transmission of information, of knowledge, without attempting to pass over into the moral territory of convictions, beliefs, and character. The goal is to be like science, but *not* the results of science upon human personality. The school must not try to foresee the consequences produced by science, but in transmitting it, must leave full freedom for its application. The school must not regard any one science, nor a whole code of sciences, as necessary, but must transmit that information which it possesses, leaving the students the right to acquire it, or not.

The structure and program of a school must be based not on theoretical speculations, not on the beliefs in the necessity of this or that science, but on what is immediately possible—that is, the knowledge of the teachers.

I will explain by example.

I want to establish an institution of learning. I form a program of study that is based on my theoretical conceptions, and on the basis of this curriculum look about for teachers, but I propose to all who apply that they lecture on or teach such subjects as they know best. Of course, my former experience will guide me in the selection of these lessons: we shall try not to offer subjects that nobody wants to listen to—in a Russian village we will not teach Spanish, astrology, or geography, just as a merchant will not open shops of surgical instruments or of crinolines in such a village.

We may foresee a demand for what we offer, but the final judge will only be experience. We do not think we have the right to open a single shop in which we are to sell tar on the condition that to every ten pounds of tar each customer must buy a pound of ginger, or of pomade for one's hair. We do not trouble ourselves about the use to which our wares will be put by the customers, believing that they know what they want, and that it is enough for us to find out their needs and to satisfy them.

It is quite possible that we will get one teacher of zoology, one teacher of medieval history, one of religion, and one of the art of printing. If these teachers know how to make their lessons interesting, these lessons will be useful in spite of their seeming incompatibility and accidentalness. I do not believe in the possibility of a theoretically established, harmonious code of sciences, but that every science, being the subject of free instruction, harmonizes with all the others into one code of knowledge for each person.

I shall be told that in such an accidentally formed curriculum there may enter useless, even harmful sciences into the course, and that many sciences are out of bounds because the students would not be sufficiently prepared for them.

To this I will reply that, in the first place, if that is so, there are no harmful and no useless sciences for anybody, and that we have as an assurance of that the common sense and the needs of the students, who, since instruction is free, will not admit useless and harmful sciences. In the second place, prepared students are desirable only to a poor teacher: for a good teacher it is easier to begin algebra or analytical geometry with a student who does not know arithmetic than with a student who knows it poorly, just as it is easier to lecture on medieval history to students who have not studied ancient history. I do not believe that a university professor who lectures on differential and integral calculus or on the history of the Russian civil law cannot teach arithmetic or Russian history in a primary school—I do not believe that he could be a good professor. I see no use and no merit in good instruction in one part of a subject—and actually no possibility of having it this way. Above all, I am convinced that the supply will always correspond to the demand, and that at each stage of learning a subject there will be found a sufficient number of both students and teachers.

But how, I shall be told, can a person who teaches culture help but wish to produce a certain educational influence by means of his or her teaching? This tendency is most natural; it is a natural exigency in the transmission of knowledge from one who offers culture to one who receives it. This tendency only imparts strength to teachers to occupy themselves with their subjects—it gives them that degree of enthusiasm which is necessary to them. It is impossible to deny this tendency, and it has never occurred to me to deny it; its existence all the more cogently proves to me the necessity of freedom in the matter of instruction.

The man who loves and teaches history cannot be prohibited from endeavoring to impart to his students the concepts of history he himself possesses, which he regards as useful and absolutely necessary for a person's development; a teacher must be allowed to follow that method in the study of mathematics or natural science that he or she considers best. The teacher's foreknowledge of educational methods encourages him or her. The thing is that the educational element of any subject should not be imparted by compulsion. I cannot direct the reader's attention carefully enough to this fact.

The educational element—let us say, in mathematics or in history—then is only imparted to the students when the teacher is passionately fond of his or her subject and if that teacher knows it well. Only if these things are present does the teacher's love communicate itself to the students and does it have an educational influence upon them. In the contrary case—that is, when it has been decided somewhere that such and such a subject has an educational value, and the teacher is instructed to teach, and the students to listen—the teaching accomplishes the very opposite results: the teaching not only does not educate scientifically, and also makes the subject loathsome.

It has been said that science has in itself an educational element (*erziehliges Element*); this is true and untrue, and in this very statement lies the fundamental error of the existing paradoxical view of education. Science is science and has nothing in itself. The educational element lies in the teaching of the sciences, in the teacher's love for his science, and in the love with which it is imparted—in the teacher's relation to his students. *If you wish to educate the student by science, love your science and know it, and the students will love both you and the science, and you will educate them; but if you yourself do not love it, the science will have no educational influence, no matter how much you may compel them to learn it.* Here again there is one measuring stick and one salvation: that exact same freedom for the students to listen or not to listen to the teacher, to imbibe or not to imbibe the teacher's educational influence. In other words, it must be up to the students to decide whether the teacher knows and loves his or her subject.

Well then, what would school be if education were noncompulsory?

The answer is that education would be a comprehensive, highly varied conscious activity directed by one person on another for the purpose of transmitting knowledge, without compelling the student by direct force. Or, to put it a little differently, education is our effort to avail students— in a highly diplomatic manner—of that which we want that student to know. Such a school perhaps would not be a school as we understand it— with benches, blackboards, a teacher's or professor's platform—it may be a panorama, a theater, a library, a museum, a conversation. The code of the sciences, the curriculum, will probably be different everywhere. (I know only my experiment: the school at Yasnaya Polyana, with its subdivision of subjects which I have described, in the course of half a year completely changed, partly at the request of the students and their parents, partly on account of the insufficient knowledge of my teachers.)

"What are we to do then? Will there really be no county schools, no gymnasia, no chairs of the history of Roman law? What will become of humanity?"

There certainly will be none if the pupils do not need them and you are not able to make them good.

"But children do not always know what they need; children are mistaken," and so forth.

I will not enter into this discussion. This discussion would lead us to the question: Is human nature right before the tribunal of man? and so forth. I do not know that it is, and do not take that stand. All I say is that if we can know what to teach, you must not prevent me from teaching Russian children—by use of force—French, medieval genealogy, and the art of stealing. I can prove everything as you do.

"So there will be no gymnasia [high schools] and no Latin? Then, what am I going to do?"

Don't be afraid! There will be Latin and rhetoric, and they will exist another hundred years, simply because the medicine is bought, so we must drink it (as a patient said). I doubt whether the idea I have expressed—perhaps indistinctly, awkwardly, and inconclusively—will become common currency in another hundred years; it is not likely that within a hundred years those ready-made institutions—schools, gymnasia, universities—will become extinct, and that within that time there will grow up freely formed institutions, having as their basis the freedom of the learning generation.

From "Progress and the Definition of Education"

Here Tolstoy attacks the "historical view," concluding that "progress" means the equalization of the relationship between teacher and student.

We are endeavoring to find the common law that has guided human activity in education, and which therefore could be a criterion for the correct human activity in education. The historical view answers all our questions by saying only that Rousseau and Luther were the products of their time. We are searching for the eternal principle that found its expression in Rousseau and Luther. We are told about the cases in which the common law of education found its expression, and how to identify these expressions, how to classify them according to various categories.

We are told that *the criterion is that one must teach in conformity with the demands of the time,* and we are told that that is very simple. I understand teaching according to the dogmas of the Christian or of the Mohammedan religion, but teaching according to the demands of the time is something of which I fail to comprehend a single word. What are these demands? Who will determine them? Where will they be expressed? It may be very amusing to discuss up and down the historical conditions that compelled Rousseau to express himself in the particular form that he did, but it is impossible to discover those historical conditions in which a future Rousseau will express himself. I can understand why Rousseau should have written polemics about the artificiality of life. But I positively fail to see why Rousseau appeared, and why he discovered great truths. I have no business with Rousseau and his surroundings; I am interested only in the thoughts he expressed, and I can verify and comprehend his thoughts only by thinking, and not by reflecting on his place in history.

It was my problem to express and determine the criterion in pedagogy, whereas the historical view, not following me on this path, replies to me that Rousseau and Luther were in their place (as if they might be in somebody else's place), and that there are different schools (as though we did not know that), and that each carries a kernel to that mysterious historical heap. The historical view can breed many pleasant conversations when there is nothing else to do, and can explain what everybody knows; but it is not able to say a word on which to build reality. If it does utter something, it is a cliché; for instance, one must teach according to the demands of the time.

Tell us, what are these demands in Syzran, in Geneva, along the Syr-Darya? Where can we find the expression of these demands and of the demand of time—of what time? When it comes to talking about what is historical, I will say that the historical moment is only in the present. One person assumes the demands of the year 1825 for the demands of the present; another person knows what the demands will be in August 1892; a third person regards the demands of the Middle Ages as our present demands. I repeat that if the phrase *to teach according to the demands of the time*—not one word of which has any meaning for us—is written with due reflection, we ask you: point those demands out to us. We say frankly, with all our heart, that we should like to know those demands, for we do not know them.

* * * *

Love can exist only with freedom. In all the schools founded on the convictions of the school at Yasnaya Polyana the same phenomenon has been repeated: the teacher fell in love with his school. I am sure that the same teacher, with all the idealization possible, could not fall in love with a school where the children sit on benches, walk to the ringing of bells, and are whipped on Saturdays.

* * * *

The only instruction that has been regarded as good everywhere and in all ages takes place when the pupil becomes completely equal to the teacher—and the more this occurs, the better the school is, and the less so the worse. Precisely the same phenomenon may be observed in literature. We regard the best books as those in which the author or educator transmits *all his or her knowledge* to the reader or the learner.

Thus, by considering the phenomena of education as the mutual activity of educator and learner, we see that this activity—from both sides—has as its basis one and the same thing: the human tendency toward equalized knowledge.

From "On Popular Education" (1874)

Tolstoy published this article in a popular magazine called Notes of the Fatherland. *By this time Tolstoy had become famous for* War and Peace, *and perhaps
for this reason "On Popular Education" received more contemporary interest
than anything he had published in* Yasnaya Polyana. *For the only time in his
published articles on education, he acknowledges his own special talent for teaching, which he modestly but wonderfully describes as "a certain pedagogical tact."*

In order to elucidate what I consider the unquestionable foundations of
every pedagogical activity, I am compelled to repeat myself: that is, to
repeat what I said fifteen years ago in the pedagogical journal, *Yasnaya
Polyana*, which I then published. This repetition will not be tedious for the
pedagogues of the new school, because what I wrote then is not exactly
forgotten, but has never been considered by the pedagogues—and yet I
still think that just what I expressed at that time might have placed pedagogy on a firm theoretical foundation.

* * * *

Because, as I said, I took up the matter of popular education without preconceived notions—or because I took up the business without prescrib-
ing laws from a distance about how I ought to teach, but became a
schoolmaster in a village popular school in the backwoods—I could not
reject the idea that there must of necessity exist a criterion by means of
which this question could be solved: What to teach and how to teach it?
Should I teach the Psalter by heart, or the classification of the organisms?
Should I teach according to the sound alphabet translated from the German, or from the prayer-book? In my efforts to solve this question I was
aided by a certain pedagogical tact with which I am gifted, and especially
by my close and impassioned relation to the problem.

When I entered at once into the closest direct relations with those
forty tiny peasants that formed my school (I call them "tiny peasants"
because I found in them the same characteristics of perspicacity, the same
immense stores of information from practical life—of jocularity, simplicity, and loathing for everything false—which distinguish the Russian peasant), when I saw that susceptibility, the students' readiness to acquire the
information that they needed, I felt at once that the antiquated church
method of instruction had outlived its usefulness and was not good for

them. I began to experiment with other proposed methods of instruction. But because compulsion in education, both by my conviction and by my character, are repulsive to me, I did not exercise any pressure, and the moment I noticed that something was not readily received, I did not compel my students and looked for something else. From these experiments it appeared to me—and to those teachers who taught with me at Yasnaya Polyana and in other schools based on this same principle of freedom— that nearly everything which the pedagogical world wrote about schools was separated by an immeasurable abyss from reality, and that many of the proposed methods—such as object lessons, the natural sciences, the sound method, and others—elicited contempt and ridicule, and were not accepted by the students. We began to look for those subjects and those methods that the students readily took up, and achieved the core of what forms my method of instruction.

But this method stood in a line with all other methods, and the question of why it was better than the rest remained as unsolved as before. Consequently, the question of what the criterion was to be, what to teach and how to teach, received an even greater meaning for me; only by solving it could I convince myself that what I taught was neither harmful nor useless. This question both then and now has appeared to me as a cornerstone of all pedagogy, and to the solution of this question I devoted the publication of *Yasnaya Polyana*. In several articles (I do not renounce anything I then said), I tried to put forth the question in all its significance and to solve it as much as I could. At that time I found no sympathy in any pedagogical journals, not even any contradiction, but rather the most complete indifference to my question. There were some attacks on certain details and trifles, but the question itself evidently did not interest anyone. I was young then, and that indifference grieved me. I did not understand that with my question, "How do you know what to teach and how to teach?" I was like a man who, let us say, in a gathering of Turkish pashas discussing the question in what manner they may collect the greatest revenue from the people, proposes to them the following: "Gentlemen, in order to know how much revenue to collect from each, we must first analyze the question on what your right to exact that revenue is based." Obviously all the pashas would continue their discussion of the measures of extortion, and would reply only with silence to his irrelevant question. But the question cannot be circumvented. Fifteen years ago no attention was paid to it, and the pedagogues of every school, convinced that everybody else was talking to the wind and that they were right, most calmly prescribed their laws, basing their principles on philosophies of a very doubtful character, which they used as a substratum for their tiny little theories.

And yet this question is not quite so difficult if we only renounce completely all preconceived notions. I have tried to elucidate and solve this question, and, without repeating those proofs—which readers may look up in this article—I will put forth the results to which I was led. "The only criterion of pedagogy is freedom, the only method—experience." After fifteen years I have not changed my opinion one hair's breadth.

*   *   *   *

In the popular school, the right to determine what the children will learn—no matter from what standpoint we consider the question—belongs just as much to the masses—that is, either to the students themselves, or to the parents who send the children to school—and so the answer to the question "What the children are to be taught in a popular school?" can come only from the masses. But perhaps we will say that we, as highly cultured people, must not submit to the demands of the rude masses and that we must teach the masses what to wish. Many think this way, but to this I have only one answer: give us a firm, incontrovertible foundation why you have chosen this or that. Show me a society in which two diametrically opposed views on education do not exist among the cultured people—where it is not eternally repeated that if education falls into the hands of the clergy, the masses are educated in one sense, and if education falls into the hands of the progressives, the people are educated in another sense. Show me a state of society where that does not exist, and I will agree with you. So long as that does not exist, there is no criterion except the freedom of the learner.

*   *   *   *

The masses, everywhere and always, regard the natural sciences as useless trifles. The science curriculum is remarkable not only for its unanimity and firm definiteness, but in my opinion also for the breadth of its demands and the correctness of its view. The masses admit two spheres of knowledge, the most exact and the least subject to vacillation from a diversity of views—the languages and mathematics; everything else they regard as trifles. I think that the masses are quite correct. In the first place, for them there can be no half-information, no falseness, in this knowledge—that they cannot bear. Second, the scope of those two areas of knowledge is immense. Russian and Church Slavonic grammar on the one hand, and calculation on the other (that is, the knowledge of one living and one dead language, each with its etymological and syntactical forms and its literature, and arithmetic, the foundation of all mathematics) are the cornerstones of study in language and mathematics. Unfortunately, only a select few of the cultured class possess this rarefied knowledge. In the third place, the masses are right, because by this program they will be taught in the primary school only what will open to them the more advanced paths of knowledge, for it is evident that the thorough knowledge of two languages and their forms—and, in addition to them, knowledge of arithmetic—completely opens the paths to an independent acquisition of all other knowledge. The masses, as though sensing a false relation to them when they are offered incoherent scraps of all kinds of information, shrink back from this lie, saying: "I need know but this much—the church language and my own and the laws of the numbers, but that other knowledge I will take myself if I want it."

* * * *

Education and instruction are generally considered in the abstract: that is, by asking the question, "What is the best and easiest manner for achieving a certain act of instruction in a certain subject (whether to one child or a mass of children)?" This approach is quite faulty. All education and instruction can be viewed only as a certain relationship of two persons or of two groups of persons having as their goal education or instruction.

* * * *

Consequently, the questions of how to teach and what is the best method are the same question as: What is the best relation between teacher and student?

Nobody, I suppose, will deny that the best relation between teacher and student is that of naturalness, and that the contrary relation is that of compulsion. If so, the measure of all methods is to be found in the greater or lesser naturalness of relations and, therefore, in the lesser or greater compulsion in instruction. The less the children are compelled to learn, the better is the method; the more—the worse. I am glad that I do not have to prove this evident truth. Everybody is agreed that just as in hygiene the use of any food, medicine, or exercise that provokes loathing or pain cannot be useful, so also in instruction can there be no necessity of compelling children to learn anything that is tiresome and repulsive to them. Furthermore, if necessity demands that children be compelled, it only proves the imperfection of the method. Anyone who has taught children has no doubt observed that the less the teacher himself knows the subject he or she teaches and the less that teacher likes it, the more will the teacher have to have recourse to severity and compulsion. Conversely, the more the teacher knows and loves his or her subject, the more natural and easy will that teacher's teaching be. All the pedagogues at our school opposed to me agree with the idea that for successful instruction what is desirable is not compulsion, but the rousing of the student's interest. The only difference between us is that the notion that teaching must rouse the child's interest is with them lost in a mass of other conflicting notions about "development," the value of which they are convinced by, and in which they exercise compulsion. Whereas I consider the rousing of the student's interest the easiest thing possible, and therefore I consider non-compulsion and naturalness of instruction as the fundamental—and singular—measure of good and bad instruction.

* * * *

In my pedagogical articles I have given theoretical reasons why I find that only freedom of choice on the learners' part—as to what they are to be taught and how—can form the foundation for any instruction. In practice I have always applied these rules in the schools under my guidance, at first on a large scale, and later in narrower limits, and the results have always been very good, both for the teachers and the students, and also for the evolution of new methods. This I assert boldly, for hundreds of visitors have come to the Yasnaya Polyana school and know all about it.

The consequences of this relationship with the students were the following for our teachers at the Yasnaya Polyana school: they did not only consider the method they knew best, but tried to discover other methods; they became acquainted with other teachers in order to learn those teachers' methods, and tested new methods; and, first and foremost, our teachers were learning something new all the time. My teachers never permitted themselves to think that in cases of failure it was the students' fault—their laziness, playfulness, dullness, deafness, stammering—but were firmly convinced that they alone were to blame, and the teachers tried to find a remedy for every failure of a student or of all the students. The result for the students was that they learned readily, always begged the teachers to give them evening classes in the winter, and were absolutely free in the school—which, in my conviction and experience, is the chief condition for successful progress in instruction. Between teachers and students relations were always friendly and natural—which makes it possible for teachers to know their pupils well. If, from a first, external impression of the school, we were to determine the difference between a church school, a German school, and my own school, it would be this: in a church school you hear the peculiar, unnatural, monotonous shouting of all the students and now and then the stern cries of the teacher; in the German school you hear only the teacher's voice and now and then the timid voices of the students; in mine you hear the loud voices of the teachers and the students, almost simultaneously.

From Talks with Tolstoy *by A. B. Goldenweizer. (translated by S. S. Koteliansky and Virginia Woolf)*

Goldenweizer was a famous pianist who knew and visited with Tolstoy in the last dozen years of Tolstoy's life. This fine book catches some of the sharp, surprising, often jocular remarks by Tolstoy that Chekhov worried would be lost to posterity for lack of a Russian Boswell.

The best educational institution that I know is the Kensington Museum in London. There is a large public library where many people work, and they have professors of various special subjects. Everyone who works, if he has a question to ask, gives notice of it, and, when several such questions have accumulated, the professor issues a notice to say that he will lecture on such and such subjects, and those who wish may come and hear him. Such an arrangement is most in keeping with the true object of teaching—to answer the questions which arise in the minds of the students. But in every other institution, lectures which are of no use to the students are read by professors who are for the most part entirely without gift.

Notes

1. Johann Heinrich Pestalozzi (1746–1827) was an influential Swiss educator whose progressive ideas on popular education resulted, Tolstoy believed, in a closed system.

2. A dozen years later, Tolstoy returned to the topic of teaching reading: "During the whole of 1874 Tolstoy made strenuous efforts to get his system of education generally adopted. On 15th January, overcoming his dislike of speaking in public, he addressed the Moscow Society of Literacy on the best way to teach children to read. . . . The German *Lautiermethode* had been adopted by Russian pedagogues in a way Tolstoy considered arbitrary and pedantic, and his appeal was against that method.

"The large hall in which the meeting took place was crowded. The President of the Society, Mr. Shatilov, invited Tolstoy to open the debate, but Tolstoy preferred to reply to questions and remarks other speakers might put. . . . To prove the advantage of his way of teaching reading, Tolstoy offered to give a practical demonstration in one of the schools attached to the Moscow factories. This was done, with the result that the Society of Literacy decided to start two temporary schools for the purpose of testing the rival methods during a period of seven weeks. The one school was taught by an expert in the *Lautiermethode*, while in the other school Tolstoy's method was taught by a teacher from one of the schools near Yasnaya. After seven weeks the children were examined by a committee, but the members of the committee disagreed and handed in contradictory reports. At the meeting of the Society there was again a great divergence of opinion, and Tolstoy, who considered that the test had not been made under proper conditions (most of the pupils being too young, and the constant presence of visitors having prevented the teacher from holding the children's attention), but that his method had nevertheless shown its superiority, decided to appeal to a wider public and did so by publishing a letter addressed to Shatilov [which appeared in *Notes of the Fatherland* as "On Popular Education."]." From Aylmer Maude's *The Life of Tolstoy*. Volume 1. p. 344.

3. And yet producing "good books for the masses" is what Tolstoy eventually did do with his graded *Readers* (1872–1874). These were collections for children of retellings and adaptations of folk stories as well as original stories by Tolstoy himself. In 1884, Tolstoy and his friend Vladimir Chertkov began a successful publishing venture called "The Intermediary" (*Posrednik*), which printed and distributed inexpensive editions of classic or new moral works.

4. Samuel Johnson: "People have now a-days, (said he,) got a strange opinion that every thing should be taught by lectures. Now, I cannot see that lectures can do so much good as reading the books from which the lectures are taken. I know nothing that can be best taught by lectures, except where experiments are to be shewn. You may teach chymistry by lectures.—You might teach making of shoes by lectures!" Quoted (of course) by James Boswell in *Life of Johnson* (Oxford, 1980), p. 56.

5. This editor has found no evidence of any such published article.

Using Tolstoy's Fiction to Write Imaginatively

by Bob Blaisdell

Proverbs

> As I wrote in the second issue of *Yasnaya Polyana*, I tried many different ways of giving the students themes to write on. I gave them, according to their inclinations, specific, artistic, touching, funny, epic ones—and all for naught. Here is how I unexpectedly came up with the right method.
>
> Reading Snegirev's collected proverbs has long been one of my favorite occupations—or rather, enjoyments. For each proverb I imagine faces in the crowd and individual conflicts to fit the context. Along with a number of unrealizable fantasies, I always imagine a series of pictures, or stories, written to fit the proverbs. Once, last winter, after dinner I lost myself in Snegirev's book, and came to school with it the next day. The class was studying Russian.
>
> "Well, write something on a proverb!" I said.
>
> —Leo Tolstoy, *"Are the Peasant Children to Learn to Write from Us, or Are We to Learn from the Peasant Children?"*

Following Tolstoy's example, ever since I started teaching I have used proverbs as the basis of essays and stories in freshman and remedial English and in soup kitchen writing workshops. Even though I haven't been able to find a volume of Ivan Mikailovich Snegirev's proverbs translated into English, there are abundant sources for proverbs arranged by country, culture, or topic.

Usually I announce the assignment by saying, "We're going to write on a proverb." If they don't ask, I ask, "What's a proverb?" A few of the students know the definition, and once it's stated I ask for examples and we put some on the board. Then I hand out a sheet of two dozen of my favorite proverbs—usually Russian ones. The success of the writing depends on how well I illustrate one or two proverbs.

I point to a proverb on the blackboard: "'You can lead a horse to water, but you can't make him drink.' That's a good, familiar proverb," I say. "What's it mean?"

"The horse ain't thirsty?"

"That's true! But it doesn't mean only that."

The students go stone-faced, as if I'm trying to trick them.

"Come on, most of you have heard that proverb. What do you understand by it?"

"Like when, oh, I got it," says Caroline. "This was last year, and I was trying to get my friend into the college. She couldn't because she didn't have all the paperwork garbage you got to have. There's too much paperwork, you know, but—be that as it may—you know what I did? I got it all arranged. I went to her mother, her father, her old job—I got everything, all them pieces of paper the school said she got to have. All she'd got to do then was show up here on the right day, take some placement tests, and sign on at the financial aid office. I was already in, so I led her around—I pulled her around—we got everything done. It was like my job, getting her enrolled here. And then you know what she did? She didn't come. I couldn't make her come to class, I couldn't make her get up in the morning and come to school. You see what I mean with the proverb?"

We all see. I say, "Caroline's story illustrates the proverb."

Reg asks, "You have to use the proverb in the story?"

"No, just as the title. But you can also use it in the story."

I often have to give the students this reminder: "Don't explain the *meaning* of the proverb. Show the truth—or falsity—of it. The meaning is already there in a nutshell. Your job is to describe it as a story."

In *Tolstoy in London*, Victor Lucas tells us: "Among the schools he visited was the Practising School attached to the College of St. Mark in Chelsea. . . . On 12 March 1861 Tolstoy spoke with the boys of Class 3B. He asked them each to write him an essay on what they had done that day, and on things of interest they had seen on their way to school; an essay we have all written in our time."* My point, and Lucas's (I think), is that Tolstoy's originality and gifts as a writing teacher did not depend on especially inventive forms or topics.

---

* Victor Lucas, *Tolstoy in London* (Evan Brothers, 1979), pp. 7–8.

Even though I love using proverbs, I have to remind myself not to be embarrassed to use such simple, old-fashioned topics! Tolstoy used many hackneyed themes and still prompted interesting writing.

Anna Karenina

If it's true, as Tolstoy says, that "every artistic word . . . differs from the inartistic in that it evokes an endless mass of thoughts, images, and explanations,"* there are an endless number of themes, topics, and scenarios to choose from and to be inspired to write about in *Anna Karenina*. I'll suggest three.

One semester, the first story I asked my community college composition students to read was "The Three Hermits." At the beginning of our discussion of it, a young student named David asked if the scene in which the bishop meets the three hermits didn't remind me of a scene in *War and Peace* in which Prince Andrei meets some peasants.

"What?"

He made a disappointed face and said, "You've read *War and Peace*, right?"

"Yeah."

"You remember that scene?"

"No."

"But you read it?"

"Yeah! I just can't remember."

"OK, but what do you think? Does it remind you of it?"

"It's very much like other of his stories, this scene—but, David, I think we should stick with this story, with what everyone's read. I mean, how many of you guys have read *War and Peace*?"

Two of the other twenty-five students raised their hands!

"Really?" I said.

I was impressed. I had taught for eight years in a program for upper-division literature majors, and the percentage of *those* students who had read *War and Peace* would have been about the same.

"I don't know what you all are talking about," said a student.

---

* Tolstoy, in "Are the Peasant Children to Learn to Write from Us, or Are We to Learn from the Peasant Children?"

I felt obliged, then, to say a little about what *War and Peace* is and who Tolstoy was. Something came to mind: a friend of mine had given a copy of *Anna Karenina* to a tough-skinned student of his in an inner-city Los Angeles high school (she read it, then scolded him because it made her cry).

I said, "If you like soap operas—and I know some of you like soap operas—*Anna Karenina*, another big novel he wrote, is the greatest soap opera ever written. Tolstoy came to dismiss it as one—but it's great. If anybody wants to read it, I'll give you a copy. I have some spares."

Two young women in the back of the class raised their hands.

"Yeah?" I asked, thinking they each had a question.

"I want one."

"Me too."

"Oh," I said. "OK."

When I brought in the two copies the next meeting, I decided to read aloud the first chapter while the late students trickled in. I read, then reread, the famous first sentence, "Happy families are all alike; every unhappy family is unhappy in its own way."*

"How's that sound?"

"Fine!"

"Is it true?"

"Well," said Francisca, "I don't know any happy families, so I guess every family's different—right?"

*   *   *   *

Many readers, by the end of the second paragraph of the first page, dislike wonderful Stiva Oblonsky for the chaos he has brought to his family. By the end of the chapter, nine paragraphs later, he has won at least a little (if not complete) sympathy and understanding. A few good writing exercises based on this first chapter are:

• *Write a description of someone you don't like waking up in the morning.* Writers familiar with the way Tolstoy treats characters such as Oblonsky realize the virtues of granting hitherto flat, stereotypical characters a third dimension. There is something universal (and therefore humanizing) about our solitary, waking selves—sins don't really dominate anyone's

---

* Constance Garnett's translation.

every conscious moment. When I used this exercise in a creative writing course, the immoral, simple, flat characters the students had been describing all semester suddenly gained life and energy. There was gusto and communicated pleasure in the way they ate their ham and eggs or Cheerios. My suggestion to that class that any characters, moral or immoral, are good if they're alive on the page and bad if they're not, was finally illustrated in their own work.

• *Use Tolstoy's first sentence as your own first sentence.* Then describe two happy or unhappy families. The comparisons, and their limitlessness, become obvious. The hardest thing to learn or teach about writing is what Tolstoy usually does in his—to keep it open, aware of the infinite particularity of the world.

• *Describe someone you admire and love, and then have that person do something you have always regarded as morally reprehensible (e.g., become a Republican, a liberal, a liar, a criminal, a meateater, an adulterer).* This, a bigger, harder theme, is connected with Tolstoy's relationship to his characters—in the most obvious case, to Anna. This exercise helps students to move away from programmatic characters whose every motivation is predictable.

"God Sees the Truth but Waits"

Aksenov, a good merchant with an imperfect past, is believed to have murdered and robbed another merchant. He is sent away to Siberia as punishment for the crime. After twenty-six years the real murderer turns up in the prison. Aksenov resists an overwhelming temptation to expose the real murderer, Makar Semenich, and Makar ends up confessing.

The last time I taught "God Sees the Truth but Waits," it was in back-to-back freshman English classes as an intermission in our trek through *Crime and Punishment.* A student named Jerome rephrased the somewhat puzzling proverb-title for us before we started reading: "God knows it all, but he don't act on it right away necessarily.") I read the story to the students. There was no confusion—only excited, responsive attention. However, when with the first class I reached the part where Makar Semenich unwittingly reveals that he planted the knife, I made the mistake of asking "Why does Aksenov feel sure this man had killed the merchant?" By asking this I received right and wrong answers and created confusion where none had been. An hour later, with the next class, I simply read better—tonally italicizing the passage:

> "Perhaps you heard who killed the merchant?" asked Aksenov.
>
> Makar Semenich laughed, and replied, "It must have been him in whose bag the knife was found! If someone else hid the knife there—'He's not a thief till he's caught,' as the saying is. How could anyone put a knife into your bag while it was under your head? It would surely have woke you up."*

And as I read, Yusef shouted out, "How'd he know where the bag was!"

"Because he's the thief!" declared several students.

After the story, I answered a few questions about details, and then wrote on the board "Wrongfully Accused," "Vengeance," and "Forgiveness." We would write for ten or fifteen minutes.

It was as if we were all still in the middle of an artistic experience, because, even though we were in a college freshman English class, no one asked, "A *story* about forgiveness? Or an essay?" Tolstoy had so deeply put into our minds and feelings these three themes (and others) that I decided against directing the students more specifically.

Ralph wrote about "Vengeance." His neighborhood had long been taken over by drug dealers, and a couple of years ago one of them, Ralph's friend, had met and gotten together with a new girlfriend who was visiting in the neighborhood. When the girlfriend's ex-boyfriend came to the neighborhood to try to win her back, he was beaten up. Five days after that the ex-boyfriend drove up to the corner where Ralph's friend did business, got out of the car, strode up to Ralph's friend and the girlfriend, and shot Ralph's friend dead. The murderer, vengeance complete, was never arrested (Ralph told me later that the ex-girlfriend and all the other witnesses were too scared of repercussions to ever testify) and was never seen around there again.

Angelica wrote about "Forgiveness"—how during a temporary breakup with her boyfriend (she knew it would be temporary), she became romantically involved with a longtime family friend. Guilt haunted her even before she got back together with her boyfriend; it so demoralized her that finally she confessed. Her boyfriend was shocked, but got over it and forgave her.

---

* "God Sees the Truth but Waits." In *Twenty-Three Tales* (Oxford, 1906), p. 7.

For "Wrongfully Accused," Jason Montero wrote this:

It was about ten years ago, during a hot summer. I decided to ask my mother if I could go to Spain for the summer with my grandfather. She said yes, and while I was there, back home my friend Chris, who looked a lot like me and lived only two houses away, was playing with this kid who lived across the street and Chris bit this kid and then ran home. The kid's mother decided to go to my house and my mother answered the door. The lady said, "Your son Jason bit my son on the arm." My mother was going along with it. And she said, "Did you see my son bite your son on the arm?" The woman said yes. So my mother even asked, "Did you see my son run home after he bit your son on the arm?" The lady said yes. So my mother turned around and said, "Well, my son is in Spain right now, but when he returns I'll gladly beat the shit out of him." The lady's face dropped and she turned and walked home.

"Alyosha the Pot"

Describing her reactions almost simultaneously as she read this story at home, Preeti Kumar, a first-year New York City community college student from Bombay, wrote this in her response journal:

I don't think that Alyosha went to school at all. In the story it says that he started working when he was six years old. I feel very sorry for him. Poor Alyosha was happy with his brother's old boots and his father's cap and coat. I wonder how he would feel if these were brand-new. . . . I am very upset at the way the merchant and his family treat Alyosha.

Unbelievable! What kind of father is he? He takes away all Alyosha's pay. Looks like Alyosha is a slave to his father. And look, Alyosha is afraid that his father will be annoyed because he bought the boots for himself. He is afraid as if he has committed a big crime. He has no personal life, his life belongs to his father. It's too bad.

I wonder how come the merchant's family was nice enough to give some tips to Alyosha. I guess that they didn't want him to leave the job since he works so much. It's good that Alyosha has someone to care for him, Ustinja [the cook]. I love the way Tolstoy describes the unusual experience of Alyosha's life. I love how he puts it, "a relationship that a person has with another who is in no way necessary to him." It is so true in real life when you fall in love, you love that person so much, you care about the person and you need that person so much even though that person is in no way necessary in your life. In the beginning I thought that nobody will love Alyosha since he is not good-looking, but it's very good that Ustinja loves him.

I am angry at Alyosha's father and also the merchant. What is this? Was Alyosha born to be abused by everyone? Come on, you are taking everything away from him, at least don't take his heart away. Why don't you understand he loves Ustinja? You don't love someone because you want to love that person. It just happens. Please understand this, you, Alyosha's father. If I was there with Alyosha I would do anything to fight for his right. I love Alyosha and it hurt me when he wept. It proves that this little machine has some feelings. Tolstoy shouldn't have ended this story this way. I hate sad endings. I didn't expect Alyosha to die. It really hurts my feelings that this good young man who sacrificed everything for his family has died. I love Alyosha.

Preeti's commentary does a better job than I could in describing the very short story's devastating pathos, but here is a more objective summary: Alyosha is sent to work for a merchant when his brother leaves to join the army. Though not physically robust, he is a relentless worker, and never shirks his duties or complains about the seemingly endless new ones heaped upon him. He does not begrudge his father taking his pay, leaving Alyosha only the tips. Alyosha falls in love with the cook, Ustinja, the only person who does not exploit him for his services. The merchant and father forbid their marriage, and Alyosha humbly, though tearfully, resigns himself to their decision. Soon after Alyosha suffers an accident and dies.

I like to read this story aloud with my students. Their responses are sympathetic, to a point, but by the end they are usually groaning with frustration, and remark sarcastically, "Thanks, Bob. That story really cheered me up!"

Even so, there is a good exercise that comes from this story: "The Worst Job I Ever Had."

To get us going we talk about how dutiful and eager we are when first on the job, and how the duties, given lip service by our fellow employees, are heaped upon us. And that is where our resemblance to Alyosha ends, since he goes into overdrive and never rebels, whereas we break down, shift the weight of our responsibilities onto the new guy, bitch and moan, or quit. Through students' essays and stories, I have learned the drawbacks of being the owner of a deli, a homecare attendant, a fast-food chef, a little league coach, a teacher's aide, a car parts salesman, a drug dealer, a ninety-nine-cent store clerk, a stockperson, a busboy, a crop irrigator, and a commercial photographer, among others.

"The Bear-Hunt"

"The Bear-Hunt" is a true story of an expedition in the snow and how a clever peasant named Damian leads Tolstoy on the trail. Tolstoy is eventually run over by the frightened, fat bear and nearly eaten by it.*

Though Tolstoy later renounced hunting and became a vegetarian, this very short story is the most thrilling of the several short autobiographical tales he wrote for his graded *Readers* for children in the early 1870s.

The bear is so clever he walks backward out of the forest onto the road and thus makes Tolstoy, but not Damian, believe there is a new bear in the vicinity. After having tracked the rough location of the wily bear, Damian and Tolstoy take a well-earned nap.

> Two hours later I woke up, hearing something crack.
> I had slept so soundly that I did not know where I was. I looked around me. How wonderful! I was in some sort of a hall, all glittering with white with gleaming pillars, and when I looked up I saw, through delicate white tracery, a vault, raven black and studded with colored lights. After a good look, I remembered that we were in the forest, and that what I took for a hall and pillars, were trees covered with snow and hoar frost, and the colored lights were stars twinkling between the branches.†

Fresh, first sights are wonderful. *Try using the phrase "I had slept so soundly that I did not know where I was" as the first sentence of a story or poem.*

A bear hunt is not a bullfight: there are no rules, so it's hard as we read to know what to expect. Tolstoy communicates the excitement of the hunter *and* the bear:

> Something was coming towards me like a whirlwind, snorting as it came; and I saw the snow flying up quite near me. I glanced straight before me, and there was the bear, rushing along the path through the thicket right at me, evidently beside himself with fear. He was hardly half a dozen paces off, and I could see the whole of him—his black chest and enormous head with a reddish patch. There he was, blundering straight at me, and scattering the snow about as he came. I could see by his eyes that he did not see me, but, mad with fear, was rushing blindly along; and his path led him straight at the tree under which I was standing. I raised my gun and fired. He was almost upon me now, and I saw that I had missed. My bullet had gone past him, and he did

---

* The near-death event occurred January 3, 1859.
† "The Bear-Hunt." In *Twenty-Three Tales*, pp. 47-48.

not even hear me fire, but still came headlong towards me. I lowered my gun, and fired again, almost touching his head. Crack! I had hit, but not killed him!

He raised his head, and laying his ears back, came at me, showing his teeth.

I snatched at my other gun, but almost before I had touched it, he had flown at me and, knocking me over into the snow, had passed right over me.

"Thank goodness, he has left me," thought I.

I tried to rise, but something pressed me down, and prevented my getting up. The bear's rush had carried him past me, but he had turned back, and had fallen on me with the whole weight of his body. I felt something heavy weighing me down, and something warm above my face, and I realized that he was drawing my whole face into his mouth. My nose was already in it, and I felt the heat of it, and smelt his blood. He was pressing my shoulders down with his paws so that I could not move: all I could do was to draw my head down towards my chest away from his mouth, trying to free my nose and eyes, while he tried to get his teeth into them. Then I felt that he had seized my forehead just under the hair with the teeth of his lower jaw, and the flesh below my eyes with his upper jaw, and was closing his teeth. It was as if my face were being cut with knives. I struggled to get away, while he made haste to close his jaws like a dog gnawing. I managed to twist my face away, but he began drawing it again into his mouth.

"Now," thought I, "my end has come!"*

An assignment: *Use this last sentence to write about an experience.*

Most of know what it is like momentarily not to realize that we are injured. Another related assignment comes from when the bear is driven away, and Tolstoy, though the flesh is hanging "in rags" above his eyes, tells us, "in my excitement I felt no pain." *Describe an experience in which in your excitement you "felt no pain."*

"Hadji Murad"

Several semesters ago I reread Tolstoy's introduction to *Hadji Murad*, wherein he describes how his memory of the Tartar warrior was triggered by the sight of a blossoming thistle that resisted his attempts to pick it, and I realized I had a new and useful way to assign a research paper:

> And I remembered a Caucasian episode of years ago, which I had partly seen myself, partly heard of from eye witnesses, and in part imagined.

---

* Ibid., pp. 22–23.

The episode, as it has taken shape in my memory and imagination, was as follows.*

What "follows" is the sensational novella, as great as or greater than any of his more famous short works.

"That," I told the students after reading aloud the quote, "is what we're going to do in our 'research papers.'" I added, "Tolstoy made some of this up. OK? But it's about a real thing that happened. In history, there was such a Hadji Murad. But Tolstoy doesn't know what Hadji Murad said at all those points. He doesn't know what Hadji Murad was thinking. Tolstoy doesn't know what all those Russians are thinking. But it all took place where he says it did, and the way Hadji Murad was caught, and why he tried to leave, that's all true—I think. You can't tell, anyway, or I can't, where Tolstoy was personally involved, what he made up, and where he researched it—and he researched a lot!"

This approach gives students lots of room to manuever—it allows them to write about their neighborhoods, historical moments, or family crises that they otherwise might have avoided for lack of published material on them. It can show them how much can be known about a topic, and how little, sometimes, we have to go on when we write about it, and how much our imaginations help us see real events.

"Master and Man"

This long story about the "master," Vasilli Andreevich Brekhunov, a proud, cheating merchant, and the "man," Nikita, a peasant, tells of the snowstorm that brings Vasili to the understanding that he is a lesser man than humble Nikita. Though imperfect and given to drink, Nikita is admirable and sympathetic, while Vasilli, in spite of his self-pride, habitual swindling of customers, and thoughtless condescension, is—unlike the more famous Ivan Ilych—vigorous and clever enough to be interesting. He's so smart we don't mind identifying with his everyday, calculating selfishness. However, trapped in a sled by the snow one night on his way to conduct some bit of underhanded business, unable to move on, aware of the straits in which he and Nikita are in, as a result of his own

---

* Louise and Aylmer Maude's translation. In *Great Short Works of Leo Tolstoy* (Harper and Row, 1967), p. 550.

greed, fear begins to overtake Vasilli: "Again he began bragging to him-self and feeling pleased with himself and his position, but all this was con-tinually disturbed by a stealthily approaching fear. . . ."*

Tolstoy helps us see that even a bad man has the gamut of human feel-ings, but the topic I suggest for writing is "a stealthily approaching fear," because Vasili's distractedness, even in the face of death, is so well described. We have to think about the gradual accumulation of percep-tions that lead to, for instance, fear, love, or hate.

Exercise: start a story somewhere before there is any suggestion of one of the three above-named feelings. For *love* or *hate*, the story is at the other end of the spectrum from "love or hate at first sight." For *fear*, we see that fear is not the constant state of anybody: it comes to us.

The Cossacks

A young, typically dissolute, aristocratic, self-conscious young man named Olenin leaves his friends in Moscow to travel to the Caucasus mountains, where he will serve as a "cadet," a noncommissioned, volunteer officer in the Russian army. Before Olenin arrives, Tolstoy shows us the little village of proud, independent Cossacks, the ethnic Russian frontierspeople who live in casual, constant, and customary guerilla warfare with the moun-tain-dwelling Tartars. The Russian soldiers descend on the village and lodge with the resentful Cossacks. Olenin and his servant Vanyusha rent the front house of a moderately well-off family, among whom is the strik-ingly attractive Maryanka. She is to be engaged to a Cossack brave named Lukashka.

Though *The Cossacks* is Olenin's story, the real hero is Daddy Eroshka, an old, storytelling, hard-drinking, cadging, womanizing hunter who befriends the newcomer. Eroshka is everything the awkward, Tolstoy-like Olenin is not—and is fabulous. Tolstoy presents Eroshka as sympatheti-cally and fully as any male character in his fiction.

Of course Olenin falls in love with Maryanka. He fights that feeling, then romantically imagines a Cossack life for himself. Meanwhile, the village life exists, separately and without Olenin—Tolstoy continually reminding us that the world does not revolve around his alter-ego.

---

* *Master and Man.* In *Great Short Works of Leo Tolstoy*, p. 486.

The Cossacks is one of the greatest novels rarely read. It contains, among hundreds or thousands of exciting details, an idea (in Olenin's thoughts) that describes Tolstoy's unsurpassable artistic sense of distinct, individual characters: ". . . Above me, flying in among the leaves which to them seem enormous islands, mosquitoes hang in the air and buzz: one, two, three, four, a hundred, a thousand, a million mosquitoes, and all of them buzz something or other and each one of them is separate from all else and is just such a separate Dmitri Olenin as I am myself."*

Writing ideas:

See Chapter 1: "Setting off on a long trip"—its satisfactions, the memories it triggers, its anticipations.

See Chapter 2: Show a young man or woman insisting to himself or herself and to others that there is no such thing as love. Then look at chapter 42 ("He loved Maryanka more than ever, and knew he could never be loved by her"), and describe that person's lovesick agony.

See Chapter 3: Olenin prepares himself for the grand sighting of the Caucasus mountains. Describe a poor first impression of something or someone you had heard so many good things about; then describe the amazed second impression.

In chapter 20, Olenin and his dog, out hunting, are attacked by mosquitoes:

> He was about to go home, but remembering that other people managed to endure such pain he resolved to bear it and gave himself up to be devoured. And strange to say, by noontime the feeling became actually pleasant. He even felt that without this mosquito-filled atmosphere around him, and that mosquito-paste mingled with perspiration which his hand smeared over his face, and that unceasing irritation all over his body, the forest would lose for him some of its character and charm.†

A good writing exercise is to describe an intensely unpleasant environment you got used to and then even valued in itself.

Tolstoy ends the novel with Olenin, full of regretful, sentimental feelings, leaving the village. The heartwarming good-bye is undercut by Olenin's and our realization that his beloved Maryanka and Eroshka will live on, as before, just fine without him:

---

* *The Cossacks.* In *Great Short Works of Leo Tolstoy*, p. 164.
† Ibid., p. 163.

Olenin turned round. Daddy Eroshka was talking to Maryanka, evidently about his own affairs, and neither the old man nor the girl looked at Olenin.*

"A Prisoner in the Caucasus"

This is a short, exciting, life-and-death adventure, accessible to anyone, written for the graded *Readers*. It's about Zhilin, a Russian officer serving in the Caucasus, much in the way a U.S. Cavalry officer in the nineteenth century might have served on the Great Plains to "pacify" the Native Americans. Zhilin has to leave the service to return home to his dying mother, who wishes to see him married. But instead, almost immediately he is captured by the native Tartars and made a prisoner in their village. Zhilin befriends a young Tartar girl by making her dolls of clay, and she brings him food. Zhilin and a fellow officer attempt an escape, but are caught and returned to the village and imprisoned in a deep, dank hole. The Tartars mean to kill him this time, but again the girl helps him, and he escapes, barely making it back to the fort. The other officer is eventually ransomed.

The story suggests several writing assignments, among them "In a New Place." On Zhilin's first days in the Tartar village he seems to notice everything: the people's clothing, ways of talking, appearances.

Another writing topic comes practically in the form of a proverb. Zhilin adamantly refuses to request from home a ransom larger than 500 rubles, which angers the Tartars, but he thinks to himself: "The more one fears them, the worse it will be."†

When a Tartar is killed, Zhilin has an opportunity to observe the village's funeral customs. The assignment: Describe a funeral you attended that was different from the funerals in your own culture.

The first escape attempt is terribly exciting. "A Desperate Attempt" is an assignment that speaks for itself.

As Zhilin and his comrade sneak through the woods, they hear sounds that stop when they stop and resume when they resume. To their relief they discover it's a stag! It's possible to use Zhilin's comment, "We were afraid of him, and he is afraid of us,"‡ as the basis for a story.

---

* Ibid., p. 243.
† "A Prisoner in the Caucasus." In *Twenty-Three Tales*, p. 20.
‡ Ibid., p. 34.

Zhilin's comrade whines and moans the entire first escape attempt, and his foolhardiness leads to their being detected. Even so, Zhilin reflects, "What am I to do with him? It won't do to desert a comrade." That realization is another possible topic.

Finally, Zhilin, exhilarated by his successful escape, tells the story of his capture and remarks, "That's the way I went home and got married! . . . No, it seems plain that fate was against it!"* The assignment: "Fate was against it."

"The Three Hermits"

The three old hermits, living out their humble lives on a remote island, are visited by a worldly bishop who presumes to teach them how to pray. The hermits humbly and stumblingly learn the Lord's Prayer from the patient bishop. But when the bishop has departed on a ship, they forget the words and glide over the water to chase him down for more teaching. The bishop, hitherto confident in his superior understanding of prayer, realizes after seeing the old men walk on water that he has nothing to teach them but much to learn.

Tolstoy is making fun of rote learning, and underscores that point with the epigraph from the Gospel of Matthew: "And in praying use not vain repetitions, as the Gentiles do: for they think that they shall be heard for their much speaking. Be not therefore like unto them: for your Father knoweth what things ye have need of, before ye ask Him."†

We all have experiences of rote learning, but a good and healthy exercise is to write about an experience in which we learned something without being taught. This is an excellent theme for students of all ages.

"What Men Live By"

Don't be put off by the six biblical epigraphs. Skip them if you like, and return to them once you've finished reading the story. Tolstoy often affixes epigraphs to his work, and students—once they understand the epigraphs' relevance—enjoy putting their own reading to such use.

---

* Ibid., p. 43.
† "The Three Hermits." In *Twenty-Three Tales*, p. 193.

In this story, an angel named Michael (though we and the shoemaker's family with whom he lives don't know he is an angel until the end of the story) is punished by God, and sent to live as a man among men until he learns the three truths set out for him by God. The family life and the shoemaker's discovery of Michael are described beautifully. The last few pages explain the story and the truths Michael has learned, but there is something too precise and mathematical in them compared to the loveliness of the unfolding story.

Writing exercises from this story include "A Stranger in Our Home." This topic can help remind us of the suddenly fascinating and important everyday details and routines of our home, because now they are being interrupted. There is another place at the table, a new voice in the air, there are new items and smells in the bathroom, and sleeping accommodations are rearranged.

Quotes also provide themes, for example, "My Conscience Smote Me."

> So the shoemaker hurried on, leaving the shrine behind him—when suddenly his conscience smote him and he stopped in the road.*

Even those students who have never heard *smote* will like the word. Tolstoy is so precise and simple in his descriptions of these wavering feelings that, after pointing them out to my students, I find it difficult to elucidate further, beyond defining vocabulary. If the students seem hesitant, I offer an example of my own, perhaps about my having walked past a panhandler, and, in spite of feeling touched by his plea, suppressing my impulse to give him some change and walking on. Instead of feeling justified, my conscience, smiting me, returns me to that panhandler or prompts my gift to the next.

The Death of Ivan Ilych

Although I feel that this well-known novella impedes some readers from discovering other, better fiction by Tolstoy, it's accessible to teachers and students through numerous anthologies. And though at times shamelessly heavy-handed ("Ivan Ilych's life had been most simple and most ordinary

---

* "What Men Live By." In *Twenty-Three Tales*, p. 58.

and therefore most terrible"*), it is also sometimes affecting and haunting ("For three whole days, during which time did not exist for him, he struggled in that black sack into which he was being thrust by an invisible, resistless force"†).

The very first pages, where Ivan Ilych's friends and colleagues read of his death and say the proper things but think selfish ones, offer a good point of discussion and a good model for a writing assignment: i.e., thoughts improper to speak aloud on the reception of bad news.

Ivan Ilych's skillful work routine and his deliberate killing of feeling while at work, could lead to a topic on jobs. "For instance," I explain, "describe your friend or your relative on the job and acting all official, and suddenly seeing you. What happens to her face? What happens to her tone of voice? If someone interrupts and needs her official attention, does she switch back into her role or keep acting like her private friendly self?"

I sometimes like to give students "fill-in-the-blank" sentences to generate stories and essays, such as: *"He acknowledged that whatever disagreeable incident happened in his life, the pleasure that beamed like a ray of light above everything else was to. . . ."‡*

"Was to do what?" asks Yusef.

"Was to . . . you're supposed to supply your own answer. What do you do to make yourself feel better after getting yelled at by your boss?"

"Sex!" calls out Diana.

"No!" laughs Yusef. "Not when I'm mad at my boss. Not when I'm feeling humiliated. No. It's more like . . . my music. Certain music. That's the only surefire one. Other stuff works, but music always works. The right music."

"Okay, go with that. Describe the last time you suffered . . . a 'disagreeable incident,' and all the misery you felt, and then how you got yourself to the music. This is what Ivan Ilych does."

Another exercise: reread the next three paragraphs and answer the question that follows the excerpt.

> In the depth of his heart he knew he was dying, but not only was he not accustomed to the thought, he simply did not and could not grasp it.

---

* *The Death of Ivan Ilyich.* In *Great Short Works of Leo Tolstoy,* p. 255.
† Ibid., p. 301
‡ Ibid, p. 268.

The syllogism he had learnt from Kiezewetter's Logic: "Caius was a man, men are mortal, therefore Caius is mortal," had always seemed to him correct as applied to Caius, but certainly not as applied to himself. That Caius—man in the abstract—was mortal, was perfectly correct, but he was not Caius, not an abstract man, but a creature quite, quite separate from all others. He had been little Vanya, with a mamma and a papa, with Mitya and Volodya, with the boys, a coachman, and a nurse, afterwards with Katenka and with all the joys, griefs, and delights of childhood, boyhood, and youth. What did Caius know of the smell of that striped leather ball Vanya had been so fond of? Had Caius kissed his mother's hand like that, and did the silk of her dress rustle so for Caius? Had he rioted like that at school when the pastry was bad? Had Caius been in love like that? Could Caius preside at a session as he did? "Caius really was mortal, and it was right for him to die; but for me, little Vanya, Ivan Ilych, with all my thoughts and emotions, it's altogether a different matter. It cannot be that I ought to die. That would be too terrible."

Such was his feeling.*

If you knew you were dying within the next few months, weeks, days, how would you think back over your life?

Another exercise: I ask, "Can you imagine this?" And I read:

His mental sufferings were due to the fact that that night, as he looked at Gerasim's sleepy, good-natured face with its prominent cheekbones, the question suddenly occurred to him: "What if my whole life has really been wrong?"†

"This is something like 'a revelation.' What if you suddenly found out—this is fairly common—you were adopted?"

"Or your girlfriend's cheating on you!" says Calvin.

"Or your *boy*friend!" says Jennifer.

"Right. Ivan Ilych is having that kind of revelation—a world-turning-upside-down one."

"How Much Land Does a Man Need?"

Just as Chaucer can turn a simple joke and punch line into a vital, real story, so does Tolstoy with this folk legend.

---

* Ibid., p. 280.
† Ibid., p. 280.

Try having the students answer the question of the title, either in writing or discussion, before they start reading. Having almost always committed to the "wrong" answer, we then have to write ourselves out of a hole afterward—which I find to be a good exercise.

The hero is an ambitious peasant named Pahom who seeks more and more land, never content with the good fortune he has. He goes to the land of the Bashkirs on the Russian steppes, where, he discovers, he can buy for a thousand rubles as much land as he can walk in a day. He is not a bad man, but he exemplifies our greed. Having been too ambitious, he hastily returns at sunset and falls dead.

> The Bashkirs clicked their tongues to show their pity.
>
> His servant picked up the spade and dug a grave long enough for Pahom to lie in, and buried him in it. Six feet from his head to his heels was all he needed.*

Exercise: write down a short joke you've told or heard. Then write it with characters, "real" people in a "real" situation.

Other obvious themes include "Tempting Fate": "If I had plenty of land, I shouldn't fear the Devil himself!"†

"What does that mean, 'tempting fate'?" I ask. We talk about how if we mock someone with a disability, we're tempting fate to bring that disability on ourselves. If we say we're superior to human vulnerabilities (love, dependence, anger), we're sure to have that arrogance punished. We admit that we enjoy seeing a tempter of fate receive his due punishment.

Another theme is "Discontent." What does discontent do to us? What is it? Tolstoy says Pahom "might have gone on living contentedly." We discuss how discontent has to do with our restlessness, our wanting just a little more than we have.

"Where Love Is, There God Is Also"

Martin the shoemaker, having lost his wife, raises his son, who also dies. He loses faith in God until a stranger leads him to read the New Testament. This reading becomes Martin's comfort and pastime after work every evening. One night he dreams or sees Jesus, who says he'll come to

---

* "How Much Land Does a Man Need?" In *Twenty-Three Tales*, p. 226.
† Ibid., p. 208.

visit Martin the next day. In the morning Martin wakes up, proceeds with his work, but continually half-expects to see Jesus. Instead, glancing out his basement shop window, he finds the means to help one person after another. That night Jesus and all the people Martin helped come to visit him, and Jesus reminds him that to help people is to help Jesus.

Many of us in public education, myself included, might be inclined to avoid a story that focuses on Christ, but that would be a shame, because "Where Love Is" is marvelous in many ways, and has not alienated any of my hundreds of students of all religious persuasions (including atheism).

Martin's involvement with his reading describes the reading experiences I most value:

> When Avdyeich read these words, there was joy in his heart. He took off his glasses, put them on the book, leaned his arms on the table, and fell to musing. And he began to apply these words to his life.*

If you read this story aloud with your students, as I do with mine, there will likely be an unusual and profoundly satisfying atmosphere in the classroom. Even so, religion seems to me a private affair, or at least one of those private affairs that I lack the wit for discussing, and I find myself directing the discussion toward reading. I write on the board, "A Reading Experience," and we write.

Some students will write about reading the Bible or the Koran or even Tom Clancy, and some will write about reading a Dear John letter. But forever after, when I talk about their reading journals, I can tell them, "Whenever you 'fall to musing,' start writing about that very part. Tell me what it is you're musing about."[1]

Childhood

It's easy to see why this novel, written and published when Tolstoy was in his early twenties, made his contemporaries sit up and take notice.† There are unbelievably striking impressionistic moments that are rivalled in world literature only by Tolstoy himself:

---

* "Where Love Is, There God Is Also." In *The Collected Works of Count Tolstoy* (Dana Estes & Co., 1904).
† I deal in this essay only with the first of the three (originally separately published) sequential volumes.

By the bare roots of the oak under which I was sitting, the dry grey earth, the dead oak-leaves, the acorns, the dry bare twigs, the yellowish-green moss, and the green grass-blades that sprouted here and there, teemed with swarms of ants. One after another they hurried along paths they had made, some of them loaded, others not. I took up a twig and barred their way. It was a sight to see how, despising the danger, some crawled under the twig, others over it, and some, especially those carrying loads, seemed quite bewildered and did not know what to do: they stopped, looked for a way round, or turned back, or came up the twig to my hand and, I think, intended to crawl up the sleeve of my jacket. My attention was diverted from these interesting observations by a butterfly with yellow wings that fluttered very enticingly before me. As soon as it had drawn my attention it flew a couple of paces from me, circled a few times round an almost withered white clover-flower, and alighted on it. I do not know whether it felt the warmth of the sun or was drinking juice from that flower, but it evidently felt very well satisfied. It now and then moved its wings and pressed close to the flower, and at last it became quite motionless. I rested my head on both hands and watched the butterfly with pleasure.*

Describe yourself or your fictional character watching something "with pleasure."

Childhood is relatively plotless but can be a model for writing first-person stories about one's past in short, vivid thematic chapters (see "The Kind of Man My Father Was"; "Something Akin to First Love"):

Another exercise I like to give my students is this: describe someone from your past through "the tears of the imagination":

So many past memories arise when one tries to recall the features of a beloved being that one sees those features dimly through the memories as if through tears. They are the tears of the imagination.†

Though *Childhood* is Tolstoy's first published work, it shares much with his later fiction in its simple and profound observations of feeling. Nikolai's "shyness" is at once a topic in itself and a revelation of the hero-narrator's character:

Those who have experience of shyness know that this feeling increases in direct proportion to its duration, and that one's resolution diminishes in the same ratio: that is to say, the longer that condition lasts the more insuperable it becomes and the less resolution remains.‡

---

* *Childhood, Boyhood, and Youth* (Oxford), pp. 34-35.
† Ibid, p. 13.
‡ Ibid, p. 66.

Later, in a chapter called "Before the Mazurka":

> The sufferings of shy people arise from their uncertainty as to what opinion has been formed about them. As soon as that opinion is clearly expressed (be it what it may), the suffering ceases.*

Describe a scene in which you or somebody you know has been shy. Trace the development of the shyness: its decrease, increase, indissolubleness, or disappearance.

In the novel's preface, the first-time author offers a writing tip for all of us:

> One may sing in two ways: from the throat or from the chest. Is it not true that a voice from the throat is much more flexible than one from the chest, but then, on the other hand, it does not act on your soul? A chest voice, on the contrary, even if coarser touches you to the quick. As for me, if even in the most trivial air I hear a note taken from the depths of the chest, tears involuntarily come into my eyes. It is the same in literature: one may write from the head or from the heart. When you write from the head the words arrange themselves obediently and fluently on paper; but when you write from the heart, so many thoughts crowd into your mind, so many images into your imagination, so many memories into your heart, that the expressions become inexact, inadequate, intractable, and rough.
>
> It may be a mistake, but I always checked myself when I began to write from my head, and tried to write only from my heart.†

War and Peace

When you think of this novel you won't likely first think of the old prince, Nicholas Andreevich Bolkonsky, and "the regular routine of life in the old prince's household" (Book One, Chapter 22):

> He used to say that there are only two sources of human vice—idleness and superstition, and only two virtues—activity and intelligence. He himself undertook his daughter's education, and to develop these two cardinal virtues in her gave her lessons in algebra and geometry till she was twenty, and arranged her life so that her whole time was occupied. He was himself always occupied: writing his memoirs, solving problems in higher mathematics, turning snuffboxes on a lathe, working in the garden, or superintending the building that was always going on at his estate. As regularity is a prime condition facilitating activity, regularity in his household was carried to the high-

---

* Ibid, p. 91.
† Ibid, p. 5.

est point of exactitude. He always came to table under precisely the same conditions, and not only at the same hour but at the same minute. With those about him, from his daughter to his serfs, the prince was sharp and invariably exacting, so that without being a hardhearted man he inspired such fear and respect as few hardhearted men would have aroused.*

Other people's routines are fascinating and, we sometimes think, laughable. The order of their lives seems, to us, so unnecessary, but to themselves so vital. Tolstoy, however, begrudgingly admires and even identifies with the prince in this description.

Describe a loved one's daily, fastidious, necessary routines. (Why a loved one's? Because with them our mocking or our incomprehension will be counterbalanced by our understanding or at least awareness of the rest of their lives. We know they are more than their routines.)

As a teacher, the old prince seems at first glance to share very little with his creator:

> "Well, madam," he began, stooping over the book close to his daughter and placing an arm on the back of the chair on which she sat, so that she felt herself surrounded on all sides by the acrid scent of old age and tobacco, which she had known so long. "Now, madam, these triangles are equal; please note that the angle ABC. . . ."
>
> The princess looked in a scared way at her father's eyes glittering close to her; the red patches on her face came and went, and it was plain that she understood nothing and was so frightened that her fear would prevent her understanding any of her father's further explanations, however clear they might be. Whether it was the teacher's fault or the pupil's, this same thing happened every day: the princess' eyes grew dim, she could not see and could not hear anything, but was only conscious of her stern father's withered face close to her, of his breath and the smell of him, and could think only of how to get away quickly to her own room to make out the problem in peace. The old man was beside himself: moved the chair on which he was sitting noisily backward and forward, made efforts to control himself and not become vehement, but almost always did become vehement, scolded, and sometimes flung the exercise book away.
>
> The princess gave a wrong answer.
>
> "Well now, isn't she a fool!" shouted the prince, pushing the book aside and turning sharply away; but rising immediately, he paced up and down, lightly touched his daughter's hair and sat down again. He drew up his chair, and continued to explain.

---

* *War and Peace.* Translated by Rosemary Edmunds, pp. 99–100.

"This won't do, Princess; it won't do," said he, when Princess Mary, having taken and closed the exercise book with the next day's lesson, was about to leave: "Mathematics are most important, madam! I don't want to have you like our silly ladies. Get used to it and you'll like it," and he patted her cheek. "It will drive all the nonsense out of your head."*

The great teacher and novelist depicts, perhaps as well as can be done, the agony we suffer with a bad or incompatible tutor. What is it that the prince doesn't understand about teaching? Or does he not understand his student, his own daughter? (Within a year or two of completing *War and Peace*, Tolstoy began teaching his own children mathematics, and would, on occasion, blow his top at their incomprehension. Did Tolstoy know, in describing the old prince, that he was describing his own impending impatience in teaching his children?[2])

Why, as a teacher, do I read about the prince and poor Mary and realize all too well the panicked, dumbfounded reaction of some of my students in one-to-one teaching? There is often such an emotional charge (for good and bad) between student and teacher that it's understandable why such short-circuiting occurs when we're in direct, immediate contact. And of course parents who are teachers sometimes have little professional patience left when teaching their own children (as was true for Tolstoy, for instance).

Describe a bad scene between you and your teacher (or you and your student), where he lost his temper, became obviously impatient, or you suddenly became stupid (or vice versa). As a variation or complication in writing such a narrative, if you were the suffering student take the point of view of the teacher; if you were the irate teacher take the point of view of the student. Use dialogue as much as possible.

Resurrection

If you're unfamiliar with *Resurrection* because you skipped it in favor of *War and Peace* and/or *Anna Karenina*, you'll probably find it's of a different order from the earlier great novels. There are a lot of closed doors here; Tolstoy has contracted the universe. There is less art and more willpower. Even so, there are great moments and long stretches of luxurious, precise, never-failing description and narration.

---

* Ibid., p. 101–102.

Tolstoy continually makes fiction writing look effortless and simple:

Nekhlyudov descended the steps from the porch and, using patches of frozen snow as stepping-stones, made his way across the puddles to the window of the maids' room. His heart beat so fiercely in his breast that he could hear it; his breath now stopped, now burst out in a heavy gasp. In the maids' room a small lamp was burning. Katusha sat alone by the table, looking thought-fully in front of her. Nekhlyudov watched her for a long time without mov-ing, wanting to see what she would do, believing herself unobserved. For a minute or two she sat quite still; then she lifted her eyes, smiled and shook her head as if chiding herself, and, changing her position, abruptly placed both her hands on the table and fell to gazing before her.

He stood and looked at her, involuntarily listening to the beating of his own heart and the strange noises from the river. There on the river, in the mist, a slow and tireless labor was going on, and he could hear sounds as of something wheezing, cracking, showering down, and thin bits of ice tinkling like glass. [Part 1, Chapter 17]*

It was a dark, rainy, windy night in autumn. The rain now splashed down in warm, heavy drops, now stopped again. In the field they could not see the path beneath their feet but in the wood it was black as pitch, and Katusha, though she knew the way, lost it in the woods and reached the lit-tle station where the train stopped for three minutes, not ahead of time, as she had hoped, but after the second bell. Hurrying on to the platform, Katusha saw him at once at the window of a first-class carriage. This carriage had a particularly bright light. Two officers without their tunics were sitting opposite each other on the velvet seats, playing cards. On the small table near the window two stout dripping candles were burning. In close-fitting breeches and a white shirt he sat on the arm of a seat, leaning against the back and laughing at something. As soon as she saw him she tapped at the carriage window with her benumbed hand. But at that very instant the last bell rang and the train, after a backward jerk, slowly began to move, and then one after another the carriages jolted forward. One of the players rose with the cards in his hand and looked out. She tapped again and pressed her face to the window. At that moment the carriage where she was standing gave a jerk and began to move. She went with it, looking through the window. [Part I, Chap-ter 37]†

Using these passages as models, describe someone observing a loved one, when the latter does not know he or she is being watched.[3]

---

* *Resurrection*. Translated by Rosemary Edmunds, p. 90.
† *Ibid.*, p. 175.

Is the hardest thing in writing fiction bringing characters to life? This next exercise is inspired by Tolstoy's survey of the fifteen inhabitants of the heroine Maslova's cell. See Part I, Chapter 30.

In three and a half pages Tolstoy suggests, in quick, simple, striking detail, fifteen real people—not types. Movies and books often try to create these immediate characterizations, but the people are nearly always stereotypes and caricatures. What Tolstoy shows here is what he shows throughout his fiction—that nobody is background: each woman could be the center of her own novel. He describes the women and children from the observable outside and from within their skin; he also tells us what our first obvious question would be: Why is she in jail?

> It was still quite light, and only two of the women were lying on their plank-beds: one, an imbecile arrested for having no identity papers, who spent most of the time asleep with her head wrapped in her prison cloak; and the other, a consumptive serving a sentence for theft. She was not asleep but lay with wide-open eyes, the prison-cloak folded under her head, trying to keep back the phlegm that filled and tickled her throat, so as not to cough. . . . †

In Part II, Chapter 13, Nekhlyudov visits Maslova in prison; he reassures her he will marry her—though she has emphatically stated she does not want to marry him. She will not in fact ever marry him, but his dedication to his promises impresses and pleases her. She is happy, but she won't let herself show that to her seducer, the man who precipitated her downfall:

> She lifted her head, and her black squinting eyes rested on him and looked beyond him, and her whole face shone with happiness. But the words she spoke were not at all what her eyes were saying.
> "It's no use you talking like that," she said.
> "I'm saying it so that you should know."
> "We've gone over it all, and there's no more to be said," she replied, with difficulty restraining a smile.
> There was a sudden noise in the ward, and the sound of a child crying.
> "I think they're calling me," she said, looking round anxiously.
> "Well, good-bye, then," he said.
> She pretended not to see his outstretched hand and without taking it turned away, trying to hide the elation she felt, and walked swiftly back along the strip of matting down the passage.†

---

* Ibid., p. 147.
† Ibid., p. 318.

Here is one writing idea: describe someone who is happy but won't allow herself to show it.

Notes

1. Avoid the unvirtuously bowdlerized version of this story in William J. Bennett's *The Book of Virtues for Young People: A Treasury of Great Stories*. I recommend Leo Wiener's translation of this story, if only for the important phrase, "fell to musing." Ronald Wilks and Louise and Aylmer Maude translate it as "pondered." The story of this story is little known, and not mentioned by A. N. Wilson in his introduction to the Penguin collection that includes it, *How Much Land Does a Man Need and Other Stories*, translated by Ronald Wilks. Tolstoy freely adapted a story by a French pastor named Ruben Saillens, "Le Père Martin," not knowing where the story originated. A friend had given Tolstoy a copy of a journal, *Russian Worker*, where the story, unattributed to anyone, appeared. Encouraged to adapt the story, Tolstoy did so. Believing the story came from the English, Tolstoy tagged on a parenthetical subtitle, "Adapted from the English," but that tag was not reproduced by the printer on the published work. (See Tolstoy's apologetic letter, in French, to the outraged Saillens in Tolstoy's *Letters*, pp. 438-439.)

2 "Tolstoy proved to be a poor teacher when he came to instruct his own son Sergei. They were both nervous; the father was upset by his son's slowness, and the son made such an effort, strained himself to such an extent, and was so afraid of not satisfying his father, that he in the end was slow-witted." Alexandra Tolstaya. *Tolstoy: A Life of My Father*, p. 197.

3. These two passages happen to be unusually Thomas Hardy-like. (Coincidentally, Hardy was mistakenly but understandably led to believe that Tolstoy had read *Tess of the d'Urbervilles*, and modelled *Resurrection* after it.)

Chronology

by Bob Blaisdell

1828 *September 9*. Leo Nikolayevich Tolstoy born at Yasnaya Polyana as the fourth of four brothers; elder brother to Maria.

1830 *September 7*. Mother dies.

1837. Moves with family to Moscow. Father dies.

1841. Moves with aunt to Kazan.

1844–47. Attends Kazan University, first studying for a degree in Oriental languages.

1845. Switches course of study to law.

1847. Leaves school without degree.

1849. Passes two exams in Criminal Law at St. Petersburg University. Leaves before taking the next two that would give him a degree.

1849. Sets up short-lived peasant school at Yasnaya Polyana.

1851. Begins writing *Childhood*.

1857. On European "Grand Tour," conceives a "very important idea": to set up a school for peasant children.

1859. Sets up school for peasant children on his estate, Yasnaya Polyana.

1860–1861. Leaves Russia in July with sister Maria for Western Europe, where their brother Nikolai is dying of tuberculosis. Leo Tolstoy, deeply immersed in the practical problems of teaching, has many questions about pedagogy and hopes to find solutions in the advanced cities of Europe. Nikolai dies in October. Tolstoy continues his tour, impressed by the "cultural" education of the urban populations of Europe, and is disappointed by European school systems. In March, 1861, meets with Alexander Herzen, Russian exile, in London. Tours London schools on permission from Matthew Arnold. Serfs are emancipated in Russia. On April 21, meets his pedagogical hero Berthold Auerbach in Berlin.

1861 *April.* Returns from Europe and applies for permission to publish a journal on education.

1861 *June:* Begins work as county arbiter. By following spring sets up fourteen new schools in the district of Tula.

1862 *February.* First issue of *Yasnaya Polyana* appears, with the article, "The School at Yasnaya Polyana."

1862 *May.* Exhausted by duties as county arbiter and teaching,and fearing the tuberculosis that recently killed his brother, Tolstoy leaves to recuperate on the steppes with a servant and two students.

1862 *July 18.* Tsarist secret police search his house and property for anti-government materials and a printing press. Nothing incriminating is found, but when Tolstoy learns of raid, is so angry he considers leaving Russia forever.

1862 *October 5.* Tolstoy marries Sonya Behrs.

1862 *October.* Tolstoy expends far less energy on his own school and the schools he set up in Tula. Most of the schools shrink in size, or close.

1863 *Winter.* Last, late issues of *Yasnaya Polyana* appear.

1869. Completes *War and Peace.* Begins formal education of his own children. (He and Sonya eventually have thirteen children.)

1870–1874. Writes and publishes various editions of ABC books and *Primers.*

1872 Supervises new school for peasant children in his house; his children and wife share teaching duties.

1874 *January 27.* Addresses Moscow Society of Literacy (a rare public speaking appearance) on teaching reading; subsequent public contest of his method versus German method yields indecisive results.

1874 *September.* Publishes "On Popular Education."

1874–1876, Tries to establish teachers' college for peasants.

1877. Finishes *Anna Karenina.*

1885. Founds the publishing company called The Intermediary (*Posrednik*), to print "good books for the masses."

1890. Helps teach in daughters' school for peasant children. Within a few months the school is closed down by the government

1898. Finishes *What Is Art?*

1907. Teaches small, informal classes to children, using Bible stories and moral lessons. 850 schoolchildren from Tula come to visit him on his estate.

1909. Addresses a group of school teachers on "The Chief Problems of the Teacher" and suggests they focus on moral lessons rather than on the required curricula. Writes a new "On Education."

1910. Dies on November 20.

Bibliography

by Bob Blaisdell

Selected Works by Leo Tolstoy

Anna Karenina. There are numerous inexpensive editions of *Anna Karenina*, one of the greatest novels ever written. Perhaps the best edition is the translation by Louise and Aylmer Maude, which is also available in paperback from Oxford University Press and from various electronic libraries on the Internet, e.g., <http://ccel.wheaton.edu/Tolstoy>.

A Calendar of Wisdom. Translated by Peter Sekirin. New York: Scribner, 1997. Over the last decade of his life, Tolstoy compiled, translated, adapted, and arranged by subject thousands of quotations from the sages of world religion and literature; he offered as well his own remarks and explications. These are not like the witty folk proverbs Tolstoy so enjoyed as a younger man, but weighty nuggets intended to be digested slowly.

Childhood, Boyhood, and Youth. These are three consecutive novellas, detailing the life of a boy something like Tolstoy in character. There is a Penguin edition, as well as good excerpts in *The Portable Tolstoy* (also published by Penguin).

Collected Works of Count Tolstoy. Translated by Leo Wiener. Boston: Dana Estes & Co., 1904. See Volume 4 for the *Yasnaya Polyana* articles; Volume 23 for the 1874 "On Popular Education" and the "Notes on Education and Instruction"; Volume 12 for selections from Tolstoy's *Readers*.

Fables and Fairy Tales. Translated by Ann Dunnigan. New York: New American Library, 1962. Most of the tiny tales in this small paperback volume come from Tolstoy's *Readers* (the graded readers, or primers, for children) of the 1870s. Out of print.

Great Short Works. Translated by Louise and Aylmer Maude. New York: Harper and Row, 1967. This inexpensive edition features the outstanding *Cossacks* and *Hadji Murad*, as well as *Master and Man*, the very short "Alyosha the Pot," *Family Happiness, The Death of Ivan Ilych*, and the anti-lust novellas, *The Devil, The Kreutzer Sonata*, and *Father Sergius*.

How Much Land Does a Man Need? and Other Stories. Translated by Ronald Wilks with an introduction by A. N. Wilson. London: Penguin, 1993. The other stories are "The Woodfelling," "Two Hussars," "Where Love Is, God Is," "What Men Live By," "Neglect a Spark and the House Burns Down," "The Two Old Men," "The Raid," and "A Prisoner of the Caucasus." Five of the nine tales are first-rate.

The Kreutzer Sonata and Other Short Stories. Edited by Stanley Appelbaum. New York: Dover, 1993. This is a good buy, if only for two stories—"How Much Land Does a Man Need?" and *The Death of Ivan Ilych*, both translated by Louise and Aylmer Maude. The translation of *The Kreutzer Sonata* is by an unnamed translator from a bowdlerized edition and should be avoided.

The Portable Tolstoy. Selected and edited by John Bayley. Translated by Louise and Aylmer Maude. London: Penguin, 1978. If you're going to order one book of Tolstoy's and it's not *Anna Karenina*, this is the one. Bayley's introduction is very good. The chronologically arranged sections include fiction ("God Sees the Truth but Waits," *The Kreutzer Sonata*, and *Master and Man*, plus selections from *Childhood, Boyhood, and Youth* and *The Cossacks*), a complete play (*The Power of Darkness*), *A Confession*, and literary criticism (including selections from *What Is Art?*).

Recollections & Essays. Translated by Aylmer Maude. London: Oxford University Press, 1937. The "Recollections" are a neat, incomplete compendium of notes and reminiscences compiled for Tolstoy's biographers. Among the eighteen essays (written between 1890 and 1910) is "Shakespeare and the Drama," in which Tolstoy argues that Shakespeare was neither a great nor a moral artist. This essay is usually dismissed out-of-hand, but it is more invigorating, persuasive and interesting than *What Is Art?* Surprisingly dull is the late collection of twenty short plays (including one on "Education") in "The Wisdom of Children." Out of print.

Resurrection. This is the least famous and least read (and justly so) of Tolstoy's three major novels. There are a few paperback translations; Louise Maude's translation is available from electronic libraries on the Internet. Part One comes close to the power and vitality of Tolstoy's earlier fiction.

Tolstoy on Education. Translated by Leo Wiener. Chicago: University of Chicago Press, 1967. Except for the addition of an introduction by Reginald D. Archambault, this volume is a reproduction of Wiener's 1904 translation of the "Pedagogical Articles." Out of print.

Tolstoy on Education. Selected and edited by Alan Pinch and Michael Armstrong. Translated by Alan Pinch. Rutherford, N.J.: Fairleigh Dickinson University Press, 1982. The introductory essays, though informative, often sneer at Tolstoy the man, author, and teacher. "An Extract from the Reminiscences of a Teacher at Yasnaya Polyana School" by P. V. Morozov and "Extracts from the Reminiscences of a Pupil at Yasnaya Polyana School" by V. S. Morozov (a.k.a. "Fedka") are especially interesting. Out of print.

Tolstoy's Diaries. Volumes 1 and 2. Edited and translated by R. F. Christian. New York: Scribner Press, 1985. The early, private diaries are cryptic and sparse, with frequent self-castigations. The later ones seem more like miniature essays for a global audience than unguarded private reflections—though the secret diary Tolstoy kept at the end of his life reveals much about his exasperated last days with his wife.

Tolstoy's Letters: Volume 1 and 2. Selected, edited, and translated by R. F. Christian. London: Athlone Press, 1978. The letters are more intense, revealing, informative, and candid than the public-minded later diaries.

Tvorcheskie Raboty Uchenikov Tolstogo v Yasnoi Poliane. Polnoe Sobranie Sochinenii, Tom 8 (Creative Works by Tolstoy's Students at Yasnaya Polyana. Complete Collected Works, Volume 8). The standard Russian edition of Tolstoy's works (ninety volumes)—nicknamed "The Jubilee Edition" (1928–1953) —contains the complete writings from *Yasnaya Polyana*, as well as variant drafts, notes, and as-yet-to-be translated articles on education.

Tvorcheskie Raboty Uchenikov Tolstogo v Yasnoi Poliane (Creative Works by Tolstoy's Students at Yasnaya Polyana). Edited and with an introduction by Thomas G. Winner. Providence, R.I.: Brown University Press, 1974.

"The pieces in this collection, reprinted from *Yasnaya Polyana* for the first time," explains Winner, "include all the original writing by children that was published in that journal," as well as Tolstoy's "Are the Peasant Children to Learn to Write from Us, or Are We to Learn from the Peasant Children?" Many of the students' pieces are short and most have never been translated into or published in English.

Twenty-Three Tales. Translated by Louise and Aylmer Maude. London: Oxford University Press, 1906. Out of print, but available from Internet libraries (e.g., http://home.aol.com/Tolstoy28). The Maudes divide this book into seven sections; "Tales for Children" come from Tolstoy's *Readers* and include the absolutely first-rate, for-all-ages "God Sees the Truth but Waits," "A Prisoner in the Caucasus," and "The Bear-Hunt."

War and Peace. As with *Anna Karenina*, there are numerous inexpensive translations, with Maudes' translation also available from electronic libraries on the Internet.

What Is Art? This famous work is more an attack on art than an examination of its pleasures. Tolstoy answers the title question more generously and briefly in his writings on education. The hard-to-find 1930 Oxford edition by Aylmer Maude (*What Is Art? and Essays on Art*) is very good, with the "Essays on Art" being Tolstoy's excellent introductions to works by other writers; "Schoolboys and Art" is Maude's lone translation from the *Yasnaya Polyana* articles (it's the section about Tolstoy's walk in the snow with the peasant children).

The Works of Leo Tolstoy. Translated by Aylmer and Louise Maude. Oxford: Oxford University Press, 1928–1937. The first two of the twenty-one volumes are Aylmer Maude's biography of Tolstoy. Most of the volumes were translated in the first two decades of this century, and so are out of copyright and available through Internet libraries. Many of the volumes have been issued as Oxford Classics.

Works about Tolstoy

Baudouin, Charles. *Tolstoi: The Teacher.* Translated by Fred Rothwell. New York: E. P. Dutton, 1923. A series of reflections on and articles about Tolstoy's school, in the form of selections Baudouin made from various biographies.

Bayley, John. *Tolstoy and the Novel.* New York: Viking, 1967. This is a sympathetic, illuminating study by the contemporary dean of English critics.

Berlin, Isaiah. *The Hedgehog and the Fox.* New York: Touchstone, 1986. One of several brilliant insights of Berlin's "essay on Tolstoy's view of history" is this: "He is not, he is remote from being, a hedgehog; and what he sees is not the one, but, always with an ever growing minuteness, in all its teeming individuality, with an obsessive, inescapable, incorruptible, all-penetrating lucidity which maddens him, the many." Though Berlin's focus is on *War and Peace*, he also delves into Tolstoy's intellectual and artistic dilemmas.

Birukoff [Biryukov], Paul [Pavel]. *Leo Tolstoy: His Life and Work.* New York: Charles Scribner's Sons, 1906. An excellent biography, full of quotations from Tolstoy's works, letters, and recollections. This might be considered the "authorized biography," since Tolstoy provided his friend with documents, answers to queries, and notes.

Bulgakov, Valentin. *The Last Year of Leo Tolstoy.* Translated by Ann Dunnigan. Introduction by George Steiner. New York: Dial Press, 1971. Bulgakov served as Tolstoy's secretary in 1910. He took down as many of the great old man's words as he could, including: "An idea becomes close to you when you are aware of it in your soul, when in reading about it it seems to you that it had already occurred to you, that you knew it and are simply recalling it."

Crankshaw, Edward. *Tolstoy: The Making of a Novelist.* New York: Viking, 1974. This is really a book of photographs and illustrations, with a short, readable biography running through its pages.

Crosby, Ernest. *Tolstoy as a Schoolmaster.* Chicago: Hammersmark Publishing Co., no date. The copy I found at Columbia University's Butler Library, however, was inscribed: "Professor Dewey / with the compliments of the author. [Signed] Ernest H. Crosby, March 27, 1905." For the most part, Crosby's study consists of paraphrasings and quotations from French translations of Tolstoy's articles on education.

Eikhenbaum, Boris. *Tolstoi in the Sixties.* Translated by Duffield White. Ann Arbor: Ardis, 1982. Eikhenbaum, a Russian formalist critic esteemed by Isaiah Berlin for his other studies of Tolstoy, tells us: "[P. B.] Annenkov ... made the perceptive remark that Tolstoi's pedagogical work 'is neither more nor less than a new form of artistic work. . . . Tolstoi approaches the children of his well-known school with the same demands that he makes on the imagined characters of his fiction and on the surrounding world in general. Behind the teacher's desk, as behind the writer's desk, he is the same: an acute observer, and a fanatic adherent of his faith in the beauty of everything that is natural'" (p. 65).

Goldenweizer, A. B. *Talks with Tolstoy.* Translated by S. S. Koteliansky and Virginia Woolf. New York: Horizon Press, 1969. Goldenweizer was a pianist, a friend of Tolstoy in the later years. There are marvelous quotations throughout.

L. N. Tolstoi: Zhizn' i Tvochestvo. Dokumenti. Fotografii. Rukopisi. (L. N. Tolstoy: Life and Work. Documents. Photographs. Manuscripts.) M. Loginova, L. Podsvirova, N. Serebrianaya, and I. Shcherbakova. Moscow: Planeta, 1995. This is a simply gorgeous book of photographs (unfortunately available only in Russian). Unlike the washed-out or retouched-seeming prints of the Soviet era, the photos here are clear and bright.

Lucas, Victor. *Tolstoy in London.* London: Evans Brothers Limited, 1979. A short but first-rate illustrated book on the sixteen days Tolstoy spent in London during his European pedagogical tour of 1861. Lucas writes well and intelligently about Tolstoy the teacher.

Maude, Aylmer. *The Life of Tolstoy.* London: Oxford University Press, 1929. This is the best-known of the comprehensive biographies in English.

Mudrick, Marvin. "Tolstoy" in *On Culture and Literature.* New York: Horizon, 1970. "Father Knows Best" in *Books Are Not Life But Then What Is?* New York: Oxford University Press, 1979. Mudrick appreciatively communicates Tolstoy's greatness while surveying the battlegrounds where Tolstoy's art contended with his moral strivings.

Murphy, Daniel. *Tolstoy and Education.* Dublin: Irish Academic Press, 1992. "Tolstoy is seen as an educator," writes Murphy, "not only in a direct sense but also in an indirect sense." The "indirect sense" is Tolstoy presented as a moral or religious teacher through his fiction and nonfiction. In the "direct sense," Murphy is sympathetic to Tolstoy's school practices and ideals, and provides useful background details about nineteenth-century Russian popular education. He also makes intelligent comparisons between Tolstoy's ideas and those of twentieth-century educators such as John Dewey, Martin Buber, and the Ukrainian Vassily Sukhomlinsky.

Polner, Tikhon. *Tolstoy and His Wife*. Translated by Nicholas Wreden. New York: W. W. Norton, 1945. Polner was a friend of Tolstoy's, but his treatment of the marriage is sympathetic to both parties. This is the best short biography of Tolstoy in English. Out of print.

Reminiscences of Lev Tolstoy by His Contemporaries. Translated by Margaret Wettlin. Moscow: Foreign Languages Publishing House, no date. The "Reminiscences" include V. S. Morozov's "Recollections of a Pupil of the Yasnaya Polyana School," Sonya Tolstoy's notes on her husband's life, and excellent descriptive recollections by writers and artists who visited Tolstoy.

Schuyler, Eugene. "Count Leo Tolstoy Twenty Years Ago." In *Selected Essays* [by Eugene Schuyler]. New York: Scribner's Sons, 1901. Schuyler, a Yale-educated American diplomat, visited Tolstoy at Yasnaya Polyana in 1868, and discussed literature and education with him. Out of print.

Shklovsky, Viktor. *Lev Tolstoy*. Translated by Olga Shartse. Moscow: Progress Publishers, 1978. A full-length biography, more poetic, opinionated, and less "nose-to-the-grindstone" than the best standard biographies in English by Simmons and Maude.

Simmons, Ernest J. *Leo Tolstoy*. New York: Vintage Books, 1960. This is an excellent biography, less blustery than Maude's. It is out of print, but readily available in used bookstores and libraries.

Speirs, Logan. *Tolstoy and Chekhov*. London: Cambridge University Press, 1971. Speirs's fine book is well balanced and also continually and quietly perceptive; he is sympathetic to both writers.

Tolstaya, Alexandra. *Tolstoy: A Life of My Father.* Translated by Elizabeth Reynolds Hapsgood. New York: Harper and Brothers, 1953. Tolstoy's youngest daughter—his favorite—wrote this good, serious-minded biography.

Tolstoy, Ilya. *Tolstoy, My Father.* Translated by Ann Dunnigan. Chicago: Cowles Book Company, 1971. An agreeable book by Tolstoy's most troublesome son. It includes a short passage with Ilya's reminiscences of 1872's school for peasant children (pp. 17–18).

Tolstaya, Tatyana. *Tolstoy Remembered.* Translated from the French by Derek Coltman. McGraw-Hill: New York, 1977. Tolstoy's eldest daughter recollects her father in fragmentary scenes, some of them quite vivid. For instance, she remembers how her father would have the children clear their minds before mathematics lessons by doing a series of jumps.

Zuzminskaya, Tatyana A. *Tolstoy as I Knew Him: My Life at Home and at Yasnaya Polyana.* Translated by Nora Sigerist et al. New York: Macmillan, 1948. Tatyana Zuzminskaya was Tolstoy's sister-in-law, the youngest and liveliest of the Behrs sisters. Her memoirs extend only to 1868.

The gates to the Yasnaya Polyana estate

About the Editor

BOB BLAISDELL teaches writing and literature at Kingsborough Community College in Brooklyn, N.Y. He has edited *Emperor of Ice Cream and Other Poems* by Wallace Stevens (forthcoming), *North American Indian Speeches* (forthcoming), *Snake and Other Poems* by D. H. Lawrence, *The Selected Poems of Thomas Hardy*, Hardy's *"The Fiddler of the Reels" and Other Stories*, Giovanni Boccaccio's *Selected Tales*, and *The Imagists: An Anthology*, all published by Dover Books. Blaisdell has published essays in two books published by Teachers & Writers, *Classics in the Classroom: Using Great Literature to Teach Writing* and *The T&W Guide to William Carlos Williams*. *Tolstoy as Teacher* evolved from an article he published in *Teachers & Writers* magazine (Vol. 29, No. 2) titled "Tolstoy, the Writing Teacher."

About the Translator

CHRISTOPHER EDGAR is a poet, writer, translator, editor, and teacher. He studied Russian history and literature at Columbia University's W. Averill Harriman Institute and has translated works by Vladimir Mayakovsky, Velimir Khlebnikov, Nikolai Gumilev, and other Russian writers. Edgar is coeditor of *Educating the Imagination, Volumes 1 & 2*, *Classics in the Classroom: Using Great Literature to Teach Writing*, *Old Faithful: 18 Writers Present Their Favorite Writing Assignments*, and *The Nearness of You: Students and Teachers Writing On-line*, all published by Teachers & Writers. He is Publications Director of Teachers & Writers Collaborative, and is an editor of *The Hat*, a literary magazine.

OTHER T&W BOOKS YOU MIGHT ENJOY

The T&W Guide to Walt Whitman, edited by Ron Padgett. The first and only guide to teaching the work of Walt Whitman from K–college. "A lively, fun, illuminating book"—Ed Folsom, editor of *The Walt Whitman Quarterly.*

The Teachers & Writers Guide to William Carlos Williams, edited by Gary Lenhart. Seventeen practical and innovative essays on using Williams's short poems, fiction, nonfiction, and long poem *Paterson.* Contributors include Allen Ginsberg, Kenneth Koch, and Julia Alvarez.

The Teachers & Writers Handbook of Poetic Forms, edited by Ron Padgett. This T&W bestseller includes 74 entries on traditional and modern poetic forms by 19 poet-teachers. "A treasure"—*Kliatt.* "The definitions not only inform, they often provoke and inspire. A small wonder!"—*Poetry Project Newsletter.* "An entertaining reference work"—*Teaching English in the Two-Year College.* "A solid beginning reference source"—*Choice.*

Poetry Everywhere: Teaching Poetry Writing in School and in the Community by Jack Collom and Sheryl Noethe. This big and "tremendously valuable resource work for teachers" (*Kliatt*) at all levels contains 60 writing exercises, extensive commentary, and 450 examples.

Classics in the Classroom: Using Great Literature to Teach Writing, edited by Christopher Edgar and Ron Padgett. Nineteen informal essays that give ideas on how to use works by Sappho, Aristophanes, Ovid, Catullus, Rumi, Shakespeare, Basho, Shelley, Charlotte Brönte, and many others, as well as *The Epic of Gilgamesh*, the Bible, and Beowolf.

Luna, Luna: Creative Writing Ideas from Spanish, Latin American, & Latino Literature, edited by Julio Marzán. In 21 lively and practical essays, poets, fiction writers, and teachers tell how they use the work of Lorca, Neruda, Jiménez, Cisneros, and others to inspire students to write imaginatively. *Luna, Luna* "succeeds brilliantly. I highly recommend this book: it not only teaches but guides teachers on how to involve students in the act of creative writing"—*Kliatt.*

Sing the Sun Up: Creative Writing Ideas from African American Literature, edited by Lorenzo Thomas. Twenty teaching writers present new and exciting ways to motivate students to write imaginatively, inspired by African American poetry, fiction, essays, and drama. Essays in the book discuss work by James Baldwin, Gwendolyn Brooks, Zora Neale Hurston, Jean Toomer, Aimé Césaire, Countee Cullen, Lucille Clifton, Jayne Cortez, Rita Dove, and others.

Personal Fiction Writing by Meredith Sue Willis. A complete and practical guide for teachers of writing from elementary through college level. Contains more than 340 writing ideas. "A terrific resource for the classroom teacher as well as the novice writer"—*Harvard Educational Review.*

Educating the Imagination, Vols. 1 & 2, edited by Christopher Edgar and Ron Padgett. A huge selection of the best articles from 17 years of *Teachers & Writers* magazine, with ideas and assignments for writing poetry, fiction, plays, history, folklore, parodies, and much more.

Old Faithful: 18 Writers Present Their Favorite Writing Assignments, edited by Christopher Edgar and Ron Padgett. A collection of sure-fire exercises in imaginative writing for all levels, developed and tested by veteran writing teachers.

For a complete free T&W publications catalogue, contact
Teachers & Writers Collaborative
5 Union Square West, New York, NY 10003-3306
tel. (toll-free) 888-BOOKS-TW
Visit our World Wide Web site at http://www.twc.org